François Laruelle

Philosophy and Non-Philosophy

translated by Taylor Adkins | Univocal

Philosophie et non-philosophie by François Laruelle
© Pierre Mardaga, 1989

Translated by Taylor Adkins
as *Philosophy and Non-Philosophy*

First Edition
Minneapolis © 2013, Univocal Publishing

Published by Univocal
123 North 3rd Street, #202
Minneapolis, MN 55401

Thanks to John David Ebert and Ben Woodard

Designed & Printed by Jason Wagner

Distributed by the University of Minnesota Press

ISBN 9781937561123
Library of Congress Control Number 2013941851

for my daughter Marlène

TABLE OF CONTENTS

Translator's Introduction...i

Preface..1

Introduction:
New Practices and New Writings of Philosophy...................5
From "open" philosophies to "non-philosophy"......................5
Philosophy as non-philosophy's simple material....................11
From Unity-of-contraries to vision-in-One.........................14
A scientific practice of philosophy...............................16
Philosophy's change in function and
the abandonment of its traditional functions......................21
The "manipulation" of philosophical decision and its limits.....24
Non-philosophy as "human philosophy"..............................27
Practical and collective perspectives of non-philosophy..........30

Chapter I: Of vision-in-One...................................33
From the One's figures to the One's essence.......................33
Possible matrices of description of the One's essence.............37
Contingency of language:
the suspension of the unitary postulate............................45
Determination in the last instance,
specific coherence of a thought of the One........................51
The developed concept of vision-in-One............................56

Two paradigms: perception and vision-in-One...........................59
What is seen in-One or vision-in-One's noematic content.........62
How the One sees or vision-in-One's noetic content...................68
A transcendental deduction of philosophical transcendence........73
From vision-in-One to the
theory and practice of non-philosophy..75

Chapter II: Non-philosophy's theorem....................................79
Non-philosophy's first dimension:
its effectivity, or the philosophical.......…...................................79
Non-philosophy's second
dimension: its reality, or the material...82
Non-philosophy's third dimension:
its objectivity, or the possible...85
Non-philosophy's genetic code..88
The method of dualysis (the unitary and the dualitary)..............91

**Chapter III: The "non-Euclidean" mutation in
philosophy and non-philosophy's scientific foundation**.........97
The scientific or "non-philosophical" practice of philosophy.......97
The Greek constriction of thought:
the unitary or Heraclitean postulate..102
The suspension of the unitary or Heraclitean postulate.............105
Vision-in-One as generalization of
the metaphysical operation or of the Other...............................108
Vision-in-One as generalization of the transcendental
operation: the foundation of the radical opening of
philosophical decision as "non-philosophy"...............................113
Vision-in-one as equivalence of
philosophical decisions and a prioris of decision........................115
The spontaneous non-philosophical practices
of philosophy and their scientific foundation............................118
Example of the archive:
the illegalities of philosophical practice.....................................123
Science of philosophy, non-philosophy, pragmatics...................125

**Chapter IV: The procedures
of non-philosophical pragmatics**..129
The six basic procedures of non-philosophical practice.............129
List of the rules of procedures...130

Preliminary rule: on the constitution
of philosophical material in its specificity..................................133
Rule 1: on the reciprocal
description of NTU and of the material.....................................137
Rule 2: on the chaos of philosophical decisions
and the reduction of material to support functions...................139
Rules 3 and 4: on the reciprocal redescription
of the a prioris of objectivity and of the material.......................146
Rule 5: on the "signal" or "support"
function of the material and its transcendental sense.................150
Rule 6: on the non-thetic Universe
or non-thetic Reflection (of the) real..153

Chapter V: Universe-languages and
universal or non-philosophical pragmatics...........................159

Treating language as a whatever material.................................159
The concept of "universe-language"
and of "universal pragmatics"...164
The performativity of description..167
Immanent and mystical pragmatics...169
The suspension of philosophical "rationality"...........................170
Non-philosophy is not a negative henology..............................173

Chapter VI: On non-philosophy as post-deconstruction
or "non-Heideggerian" deconstruction................................177

The concept of "post-deconstruction"......................................177
How non-philosophy is distinguished from deconstruction......179
A non-linguistic pragmatics of language..................................181
The unitary presupposition of restrained deconstruction..........184
Deconstructions and the impossible
dislocation of philosophical decision......................................186
In what sense non-philosophy "generalizes" deconstruction......191
The aporias of textual deconstruction.....................................193
How to generalize restrained deconstruction...........................196
The concept of "non-Heideggerian"...199
The rigorous foundation of deconstruction as non-unitary.......201
The non-thetic Other and the
critique of Levinas and of Derrida...203

Chapter VII: The non-philosophical opening........................211
Thought's absolute opening and the "exit" out of philosophy....211
Non-philosophy's multiplicity
and the rarity of philosophical possibles.....................................219
Non-thetic fiction as an element of universe-languages.............227
Philosophical experimentation,
non-philosophy's simple material..235
Non-philosophy as philo-fiction or hyperspeculation................239
Non-philosophy's philosophical appearance..............................241
Non-philosophy produces no effect "in" philosophy.................244
The non-philosophical or human appearance of thought..........246

The Translator's Scylla and Charybdis: An Odyssey of the Non-

by Taylor Adkins

I was introduced to François Laruelle (in particular *Philosophy and Non-Philosophy*) by two provocative footnotes in Deleuze and Guattari's final book *What Is Philosophy?* I immediately obtained a copy of *Philosophie et non-philosophie* and it soon became the impetus and *raison d'être* for my humble existence as a translator. Rather than waxing nostalgic in a confessional mode that monumentalizes the past (a personal history/history of philosophy), let's turn toward the future and see if we can scramble and betray everything beforehand, for non-philosophy, in its instantiations, has already transformed and continues to mutate before our very eyes....

Philosophy and Non-Philosophy authorizes a transcendentally equivalent and indifferent usage of philosophy as its object. There are a finite number of philosophical decisions and philosophers considered in this work (Deleuze, Derrida, Heidegger, Husserl, Kant, Nietzsche ...), but the multiple allusions to their work and the non-philosophical transformations involved therein (not to mention the potential extrapolation to other philosophies ...) start to veer toward the infinite. As such, it would be impossible and perhaps pointless to try and catalog it all within the space of an introduction. In that sense, let's bracket particular philosophies and philosophy in particular (although we'll keep them in mind) so that we can cast a wholly generalized gaze on philosophy globally. But also, in order to cast a somewhat stranger gaze on "non-philosophy" itself as it is laid out in this work, let's consider some of the themes and allusions to phenomena that are not philosophical (which is not to say non-philosophical). In other words, without endeavoring to sketch a crash course in the history of philosophy, its uses and abuses, its norms and perversions, its margins and center, let's treat this introduction as a leading-into philosophy, but before it and anterior to its regime, so that we can consider the other-than-philosophical (somewhat clandestine) phenomena, materials and language that went into writing this book.

Rather than the reduction of philosophy's apparent seduction (of its effectively prudish and sometimes naive apparatus of capture), or an introduction into non-philosophy's philosophical material, into its procedures of induction and deduction …; rather than the interminable production and reproduction of commentary that places (trans-lates) the placelessness (trans-cendental equivalence) of philosophy's emplacement (trans-plantation) by the atopic real (the untranslated), what we want to carry-across here in this limited and preliminary space is a *transduction* (although this will have to be rectified) of the foreign elements at play in this work. This is partly a bad translator's joke (*traduction* in French means "translation"), but more seriously it reveals a simple truth in its evident redundancy, which is that the only "proper" translator's introduction (that which would "belong" to the work as a whole and carry the reader across *into* the One, from sufficient philosophy to the One's last-instance) is an illusion. At least in its claim to reality.

In other words, it would be possible (posit-able and positionable) to claim the rights of a proper introduction, but then, and more importantly, that would never be a 'real' introduction. This is because there is no real introduction or introduction (in)to the real: "*we are here in it, we are of it, we are it.*" This is to say that we do not have to be led anywhere: we do not have to be led out of philosophy into the real, or to suppose the real to get into philosophy. If there is an across in translation and transduction for the entrance (of the) real, then it already in-volves a uni-lation (unilaterality) that suspends the reversibility of its back-and-forth and irreversibly carries and 'turns' it "from" the One: this is the principle of trans-lation's "uni-versality," it's One-turning. Translation's "sense"—in the sense in which "sense" *means* both "meaning" and "*di*-rection"—no longer goes "across" except from the One in-the-last-instance, which indicates its uni-rectional vector. To continue this guiding thread, to push the non-etymological riffing into the rift of a fractal abyss or *mise en abyme* of describing the stakes of transforming (or uni-forming) trans-lation into a uni-lation, let's consider several variations that might lift the great "translator's burden" of bearing and carrying across of the philosophical logos:

1) translation revolves around the verbatim, the circular exchange of the word-for-word, and bears across the movement of the Same; uni-lation ensues anterior to all crossing, like a river from its source; it pre-cedes and de-rives the heroic de-cision of carrying that would claim to have crossed this Rubicon that can solely remain separated-without-separation (from the world, history, philosophical imperialism) without alienating itself in a line of demarcation. There is no taking back of the One-die that is cast, because it precedes all casting and is instead what is thrown-without-thrownness, which is not to say that it cannot be thrown-under in a subject through cloning (transcendentally), but that it cannot be thrown-onto in the manner of an ob-ject (for it remains the real uni-ject).

2) transduction, like introduction, would in fact remain restrained appearances of what could perhaps be called "uni-duction," or duction-without-intro-or-exit ... This is a perverse way of restating that we cannot be led into or out of the One-real but that we can be oriented from it. And if the One leads as guiding thread, then this means that as last-instance it serves as a real anchor ("across" the transcendental "toward" philosophy). This is why the real e-ducation, the outside to which the One leads, is a radical in-stasis whose force (of) thought knows that philosophy's knowledge knows nothing, that this knowledge does not lead to or from the One but across Being ... to being (or vice versa).

3) the version of transliteration, its twists and turns or transversality, in the sense of turning from a source-language to a target-language, i.e. the principle of sufficient translation, does not constitute uni-versality, which is the turning (into) One of phrases (words, signifiers, terms ...), the tongue's One-turn that is neither monolingual nor bilingual but indivi-dual-lingual (in the sense that language now envelops the dual without dividing the One);

4) the transposition of spacing and relation via syntax, the syn-taxis of philosophical ordering and hierarchies, is suspended in favor of a uni-tax that aligns all orderings with the One in-the-last-instance: this is an ordination that suspends equivocation by way of uni-vocality, which is neither the clamor of Being nor a hearkening to it, nor the silence that envelops them, but the One's

precedence over and foreclosure to tongues and silences, i.e. its indifference, but *for* them and not solely *to* them. In other words, uni-tax articulates the juxta-position of various philosophical decisions and philosophical languages that already envisions the suspension of their hierarchies and distributions in a chaos that renders them transcendentally equivalent or equally valid as material ('uni-valent'). Rather than the tactical and syntactical assemblages of philosophical war machines in their effective deployment, uni-tax indicates their sense (of) identity as their loss of internecine con-flict, where the One in-flicts on them the affliction that they resist the most: the science of their warmongering positions in a process that suspends the philosophical regime as such by their manifestation in-immanence.

Two observations, albeit provisional and with an irony for which only myth will suffice, can serve to gather all these suggestions here. The first is that the translator is like a transcendental Sisyphus who must ultimately give up the unicity of his burden and allow it to be swept away as the sediment to be borne by the One's irreversible de-rivation, which means that he must give up his burden-across in order to make way for the borne-without-borneness. Somewhere down the line the sediment will 'fall out' and give rise to another "oc-casion," thereby provoking the ongoing rectification that the non-philosophical pragmatics of language necessitates. This means that Sisyphus, the translator as tragic-hero, must move from the affect of the ab-surd (the senseless or without-hearing) to the affect of sol-itude, which is not solipsism in general but where the translator becomes uni-lator in his identity by way of the burden (of the) One, which reposes in itself but cannot carry itself across by means of trans-cendence.

The second observation is that the translator is perpetually concluding in a circumlocutory way, whereas the One precludes this circularity and turns everything from it. This means that the uni-lator cannot turn back toward the One and cannot revolt against it or revolve around it. This is the One's uni-versality and fore-closure, and it is the uni-lator's lot to give up the narcissistic reflection that would consist in turning back toward the One in a minimal glance backwards that would instantiate the failure of Orpheus once again. To look back and cling would not betray the One—which cannot be betrayed in its essence due to its indifference or uni-ference—but force (of) thought, which does not in its essence fall into the spectacles and fantasy-spaces of images of thought, but it can be seduced to give into the exploitation that philosophy's sufficiency and authority effectively harnesses. This gaze back, the proverbial moment of recognition, is another way of saying auto-position and auto-fetishization, the veritable philosophical crimes for which Orpheus is torn apart (de-cision) by the vengeful Maenads (who repeat the founding gesture of Dionysian ecstasy-in-de-ciding). This is a shattering of philosophy's mirror stage, of its interminable identifications and complexes, and the uni-lator neither fades into the background nor vanishes in the foreground of these fractured images, but remains right at the limit, at the mirrorless threshold, turned from the One toward the World one-time-each-time, falling there only momentarily, only occasionally and with light feet....

The One's odyssey renders the translator without home, without name, without kingdom, without paternal dynasty.... This is the death of the translator, correlative with the death of the author, and this death is the non-auto-positive freedom of the universal opening. But this death is the only life that can be formulated for the translator in a regime without sufficiency, where the lived-without-life (of) cloning becomes the only viable basis for translators-as-One(s)....

It is perhaps evident that this new regime of non-philosophy sometimes seems to lean on an analytic framework, but this is merely a semblance. "*Non-philosophy apparently resembles other contemporary attempts: from afar, it evokes a certain psychoanalysis of philosophy; a certain therapeutic critique of metaphysics; a certain deconstruction of logocentrism.*" Philosophy is already its own doctor and medicine, its own care and concern, its own midwife and assisted suicide: in a word, auto-therapeutics. Philosophy has already concluded from its self-analysis to its own cure, and this is precisely the regime of its self-belief and sufficiency. Non-philosophy suspends this self-medicated state of philosophy (auto-position), distilling (dualyzing) its "in-dox-icating" mixtures and essences, but without the effective instance of an intervention *into* philosophy as such. Even if philosophy at its limit might claim to provisionally break its own habit with the logos (there's always the high of mysticism and the sobriety of mathematics) and regulate its own addictions, non-philosophy is neither the universal vaccine for this malaise, nor a prophylactic for philosophical contamination, but the One-turnedness or Uni-versality whereby philosophy can advene as a symptomatic pretention for speaking "of" (rather than according-to) the One. Thus philosophy advenes to its non-analysis ("dualysis"), but this is not at all the same as non-philosophy inter-vening into the regime of philosophy as such, which would continue to validate its resistance and self-defense mechanisms as sufficient in themselves. This advent is not the *ousia* or *par-ousia* (second-coming) of philosophy, its salvation from its death-spiral, from its playing-dead or its self-proclaimed end, but its safeguarding in multiple, relatively autonomous futures that determines it in-the-last-instance rather than abandoning it to its narcissistic (auto-positing, sufficient, auto-fetishized) past.

This is the same thing as saying that there can be no Copernican revolution to anchor a discussion "of" non-philosophy around a supposed center, philosophical or otherwise. Not even non-philosophy (as science) can occupy the center once we see from vision-in-One:

> The Occident's true malaise [recasting of *Freud's Civilization and its Discontents*] therefore does not stem from its relation to philosophy alone, as Heidegger repeats after all the philosophers who suppose it as determining. The malaise stems from philosophy's hallucinatory relation to science, which makes us believe, for example and at best, that philosophical Decision is at the center of thought and that science is the Other that haunts its margins and peripherally inhibits it. If there is a real task of thought, it is instead in what is no longer completely a reversal and definitely not a Copernican reversal. To put science at the center—and philosophy at the periphery? Not quite, for when science is really "at the center," there is no longer center or periphery. Nothing, not even philosophy, turns around it. Science is so sufficient that it de-rives every other thought without return. Rather than being placed once again at science's point of articulation "in" the philosophical circle, rather than still analyzing the symptom, thought must be replaced in science's very essence, in the relation (to the) real that it postulates immanently and by extracting conclusions from it with regard to the philosophical Authorities.[1]

On the other hand, a mutation of non-philosophy (Lobachevskian or otherwise), in its own recurrent and heretical way, is already required not only by the solitude and strangerhood of varieties of non-philosophical style, but also by its "ordinary/unified" theory and practice of philosophy, the elaboration and articulation of which remain open and disposed to infinite rectification, reformulation, rehandling in line with the One-real. Thus it calls for a perpetual pragmatics of uni-version of terms and

---

1. François Laruelle, "Programme," *La decision philosophique 1* (1987), 23-24.

language, whose one-turning can always fall into the stratification of a centrality, a re-volution back ... to philosophy qua vicious circle. This is why the One-real in its transcendental effectuation uni-verts its descriptions *from* it rather than *around* it, for it is not the circular mid-place but the atopic 'last-instance' for philosophy and its language, and why non-philosophy's formulations themselves must be resubmitted to ongoing labors of reworking, lest they repose on their sufficiency and authority alone. Language in its recasting is turned one-time-each-time via uni-version (uni-verse-languages or One-turned-languages), which is to prohibit its philosophical conversion and eventual reversion back into the active concealing or repressing of the real as last-instance.

Last-instance implies the "root" of radicality, but in a non-phenomenological sense that generalizes its restrained roots in previous decisions, whether phenomenological explicitly (Husserl, Henry ...) or not (Blanchot ...):

> The old radical style, that of Husserl for example, is nothing but an impossible nostalgia, a dream aborted in the dream, which combines systematically with the possibility of its deconstruction due to the very fact that the root instead of being simply the non-thetic lived experience (of) the One, remains caught there in representation or transcendence.[2]

Thus for a translation to be really radical, it would be necessary to identically say and do everything in the unique and irreversible turn of phrase ... but this is the unitary dream and illusion, the aborted dream that must relinquish this notion of a translation *in* the Real. At best, it can strive to not only align itself with the One-real, but also to reveal translation's conditions of effectuation in the roots of its force (of) translation:

> It is thus in this theoretical usage, in this transcendental theory of private philosophical languages (at once general and total), from this non-linguistic identity of language, that the problem arises of a translation of philosophies "into" one another, which is to say in-One-in-the-last-instance, rather than an inter-philosophical translation under the ultimate authority of philosophy. Non-philosophy is this translation of Kant "into" Descartes, of Descartes "into" Marx, of Marx "into" Husserl, etc. That is to say under the condition of the vision-in-One as un-translatable Real. To put it more rigorously, no more than it is im-possible or un-symbolizable, the Real is not un-translatable, but is rather that which

2 Ibid., 15.

renders the possibility of translation real-in-the-last-instance, the Real itself being foreclosed, without negation, to any translation and not becoming the untranslatable other than as force-(of)-thought or, in this instance, force-(of)-translation. It is in this manner, through a translation of philosophical decisions or through solely transcendental equivalents of their respective identity, that a democracy that is not a simple transcendental appearance can be introduced into philosophy and between philosophies in place of their conflictual and hierarchical multiplicity.[3]

The simplicity of translation-in-One-in-the-last-instance is perhaps baffling because it is the immanent and non-alienable usage of translation and of philosophy that was always supposed forbidden to ordinary man. In other words, if translation can find the chance—if not the bare means—for its undivided identity and its human and democratic appearance, then the guiding thread of our search should start from non-philosophy's chaos and its pragmatic rules of redescription. We have not elaborated them explicitly here, since instead we were seeking merely to simulate some of their aspects so as to spoil and scramble things from the start. Rather, we have abandoned our sufficiency (our philosophical suf-fiction) for the great wide open of hyper-speculation and philo-fiction (destined to remain empty by essence but open to infinite variation by way of force (of) fiction). This is because translation of-the-last-instance proceeds identically in a non-aesthetic and non-rhetorical register, and from the start it is open to an unlimited space in which to turn-without-return … in which to flourish for itself by not reposing in-itself but in-One-in-the-last-instance. It is up to us, we visionaries-in-One, to take language in its occasional philosophical varieties and incessantly bear it in line with its uni-versality, the only burden that can be borne via radical solitude.

---

3. F. Laruelle *Principles of Non-Philosophy* (Bloomsbury: London, 2013), 224.

A Note on the Text

Perhaps more than a flashy introduction that would vie for the reader's attention against the main work, what is needed here is some historical context that can shed light on the (non-) philosophical trajectory of this text. In other words, it should be noted that *Philosophy and Non-Philosophy* holds a privileged place in Laruelle's *oeuvre* because it conserves the thrust of its origins in Philosophy I (1971-1981) while also looking ahead to developments in Philosophy III (1995-2002). This means that *Philosophy and Non-Philosophy* falls right at the end of Philosophie II (1981-1995), and in truth this text constitutes the most formal exposition of non-philosophy until the *Principles of Non-Philosophy* (1996). However, before tracing our line of flight ahead to the Principles, let's look back to the regime of Philosophie I in order to get a sense of Laruelle's preliminary, intra-philosophical labors of the 70's that provide the framework and outlook for *Philosophy and Non-Philosophy*.

If we had to choose and isolate a book from Philosophie I that would resonate the most strongly with the present work, then it would have to be *Textual Machines: Deconstruction and the Libido of Writing* (1976). There are several apparent reasons for this. First, it will not come as a surprise perhaps that Laruelle has spent at least a full book on the topic of deconstruction. In other words, *Textual Machines* reveals the preliminary work that Laruelle has already invested into the question and problem of deconstruction, which is reprised and taken up in a really non-philosophical way in chapter 6 of *Philosophy and Non-Philosophy*. On the other hand, perhaps this was not exactly obvious due to the fact that Laruelle is merely seizing upon deconstruction as a concrete example for manifesting the non-philosophical procedures of reciprocal redescription laid out in chapter 4. In other words, this usage of deconstruction as an example might misleadingly indicate that this interest is merely arbitrary. This leads to my second point, which is that deconstruction is not merely the example to be reworked in *Philosophy and Non-Philosophy* (toward "post-deconstruction"); instead and prior to this, deconstruction serves as the problematic matrix not only for articulating a general theory of the generalized and the restrained (the Non-Euclidean), but also for elaborating the pragmatic procedures of reciprocal redescription themselves. In other words, deconstruction is not just the example in *Philosophy and Non-Philosophy*: it is the prototype and testing ground for the procedures of reciprocal redescription themselves. Third, *Textual Machines* starts with a question that resonates with where *Philosophy and Non-Philosophy* ends: who deconstructs?[4] In a similar vein, the question arises at the end of *Philosophy and Non-Philosophy*: who exploits? In other words, is it philosophy that exploits ordinary "man" (by making a philosopher of him…), or is it man instead who now is in the position to utilize and manipulate philosophy as an object bereft of authority over itself and submitted to a really "human" science?

On the other hand, the object of *Textual Machines* is not merely the deconstruction of Derrida (and Heidegger, Wittgenstein…). More specifically, it is the twilight and resonance of two series: a mutual disappropriation of the "proper" names of Derrida and Deleuze. As one can already tell, even if *Textual Machines* is not a book "on" Derrida or Deleuze,[5] it is an *intra*-philosophical attempt to *displace* textuality and repetition in what will ultimately conserve the Principle of sufficient philosophy. However, it is less interesting to merely write this text off as not-yet-non-philosophical, and it is more fruitful to interrogate how this attempt can shed light on the pragmatic procedures elaborated in *Philosophy and Non-Philosophy*:

> This is our problem: by what conditions can deconstruction become a sovereign process whose domination over logocentric materials would be a transcendental, and no longer technical, domination? By what conditions does it form a machinic rather than technical process and find in itself a transcendental limit, rather than find outside it a transcendent limit to its functionality? By what conditions is there a transcendental generality of deconstruction, which we oppose to its transcendent generalization in a positivist interpretation? What does the constant reference to the "generality" of writing, syntax, economy signify?[6]

The key to the "generalized" or non-philosophical "generality" involves the way in which philosophical texts, utterances statements, etc. (after being rendered transcendentally equivalent in the non-philosophical chôra) are utilized *against themselves* vis-à-vis the non-thetic *a prioris* (cf. chapter 4 of this work). In

4 F. Laruelle, *Machines textuelles: déconstruction et libido d'écriture* (Paris: Seuil, 1976), 11.
5 "I have merely attempted to make the Delida/Derreuze series resonate, repeating deconstruction in the signs of intensive production, re-inscribing the Eternal Return into textuality, making intensive différance and the textual simulacrum communicate in a reciprocal parody that somewhat displaces deconstruction and intensifies it up to active and affirmative différance," ibid., 18.
6 ibid., 42-43.

a sense, the non-thetic *a prioris* function as an "anti-logos" that provides the co-efficiency and "resistance" through which the reciprocal redescription of the material language must work against itself:

> *Conspiracy or machination against its origins as well as against every origin, this is the sense of deconstruction as différantial break in relation to logocentrism. The problem is not merely that of the break carried out in the logos of Hegel or Plato, but of the immanent break that delimits deconstruction's process and the withdrawal of the logos, or which makes it into a machine of anti-logos.[7]*

Now that we have had our retrospective view of *Philosophy and Non-Philosophy*, let's look ahead quickly to Philosophie III and the transformations that non-philosophy will undergo in the next few years so that we can close this introduction. Already by the time of the *Principles of Non-Philosophy* and the *Dictionary of Non-Philosophy*, Laruelle's language has changed somewhat. Here I will bracket the conceptual changes and merely focus on the language of formulation itself. For example, here what Laruelle calls "reciprocal reformulation" (chapter 4) is already deemed somewhat misleading, precisely because reciprocity (reversibility, exchangeability, convertibility …) is the index of a restrained intra-philosophical approach that, in the end, indicates a Unity-of-contraries. In other words, what Laruelle calls "reciprocal reformulation" (and, by extension, universe-languages) he will very soon elaborate as "cloning." This is important to keep in mind because, despite the confusion that may arise, reciprocal redescription of the material (in its essence at least, if not its description) already encapsulates the major procedures of cloning as laid out in *Principles of Non-Philosophy*. On the other hand, what Laruelle will soon call "foreclosure" (which is a reworking of one of Lacan's analytic terms), can already be identified in the notions of "radical immanence," "DLI," and "force (of) thought." In fact, it is not coincidental that both "foreclosure" and "cloning" are taking up and transforming all of these terms mutually, for they are both notions that indicate a reworking of Laruelle's language. Lastly, and perhaps this is the most important, the notion of non-philosophical "first terms" and of "transcendental axiomatization" is not yet elaborated in *Philosophy and Non-Philosophy*. In other words, even though axioms are discussed here in this

---

7 ibid., 45.

work, they are still treated as transcendent artifacts of empirical/positivist endeavors of the sciences and philosophies. Nevertheless, the scaffolding for this move to non-philosophical axiomatization is already laid out here, specifically in chapter 1 where the One is described in a variety of non-constitutive ways. This is helpful to keep in mind, for it not only situates *Philosophy and Non-Philosophy* in its proper historical and non-philosophical context, but it also goes to show that the text itself is not simply antiquated but still essential (in-the-last-instance) for grasping the trajectory and the principal procedures that will inspire non-philosophy for the following decades.

Taylor Adkins
Atlanta, June 2013

Preface

Rather than a new philosophy, this work proposes a new practice of philosophy that detaches it from its own authority and includes it within a thought whose origin is wholly other than philosophical—a thought of the One rather than of Being—and which is also scientific rather than ontological. Many theses are therefore implicated in the foundation of what we call "non-philosophy." And since non-philosophy is starting to exist in various texts, it is time to define it and to present its ultimate foundations that have made it inevitable from the moment that they made it possible.

The most noteworthy of these foundations is what we call "thought of the One" (in order to distinguish it from the "thought of Being"). More rigorously: vision-in-One. The structures of vision-in-One will be systematically exposited and distinguished from that which constitutes ontology, i.e. philosophical decision itself. Thought of the One, of the nothing-but-One, has never been a philosophy, even if it can evoke certain appearances of it, and non-philosophy is the *de facto* demonstration that an essential thought can and must exist outside the Greco-philosophical and even *before* it. This thought of the real as One rather than as Being is also the essence—the essence alone, not the whole—of science. But the second thesis, which is sometimes invoked in this work, is not, unlike vision-in-One, analyzed and explicated, because here it does not have the utmost importance.

No doubt it will have to be said—it must already be said again: non-philosophy is not a "philosophy of the no" and is even less an attempt at the nihilistic destruction or positivist negation of philosophy. Such a project would be completely absurd and impossible, but above all else we are proposing a positive endeavor. By all accounts it must instead be understood analogously with "non-Euclidean" geometries. Rather than a new variant of the *Copernican revolution*, our project is to introduce into philosophy a *Lobachevskian and Riemannian mutation*.

We all sense the extent to which philosophical practice, such as it has been determined by the Greeks, remains constricted, repetitive and superbly sterile. Without knowing the reason for it, we necessarily sense it, but we almost always deny it, too happy to identify with the mores we baptize as "reason," "tradition," "fact" and now "Being," "Destiny," ontological or metaphysical "Necessity," etc. Without realizing it, philosophy has functioned as a conservative and reactive enterprise. For that to come about, it would suffice for it to do nothing. It simply has to do nothing but repeat the Heraclitean and Parmenidean invariants, no doubt repeating them with the jolts of new "revolutions" or "decisions," but which are almost null gains because they are programmed by these invariants. It is in this agitated, sometimes heroic, always warmongering way that it has remained what it has always been: an activity of thought as limited as the Greek world itself.

The effects of this Greco-unitary closure of thought are well known. On the one hand, there is a perpetual implosion of philosophy within its own limits and prejudices. This allows philosophy to believe it is renewing itself by multiplying its objects and its encyclopedic busywork or even by delving deeper into its history, its texts and its archives, its corpus and its institutions, progressively avowing that it has never been anything but a commentary at worst, or an anamnesis at best. On the other hand, the appeal to what now passes for ethical exteriority and the saving outside: the Other, the Law—in short, Judaism, as if this would change what spontaneous, uninvestigated philosophical faith is. What is contemporary philosophy? It is either that which repeats the most archaic schemata, attempting to adapt them to the situation in the most opportunistic way (Habermas); or that which implodes in its own naiveté to which it lays claim as such (Deleuze); or that which seeks implicitly or explicitly in Judaism for what loosens, and merely loosens, the Greek confinement of thought (Wittgenstein, Derrida and also Heidegger in his own way through Kant).

It has accepted once and for all its Greek destination in these different forms. It only contests this dispatch so as to better acquire its so-called "unavoidable" necessity. It partakes in the clumsiest and sometimes most theoretically inconsistent compromises so as to perpetuate the old Greek claim, that *of the sufficiency or validity of philosophy for the real, the unitary postulate of their co-belonging.* This unitary claim is obviously not rooted out but is rather reinforced *in extremis* by its Judaic alteration.

The history of philosophy is that of the simultaneous or successive codings, decodings and recodings of thought and language in accordance with this postulate. The contemporary expansion of the norms of acceptability—this opening which pins down a minimum of philosophical sense to be conserved so as to prevent the dislocation of philosophical decision and, within these limits, the maximum destruction of the old rational and metaphysical limitations—can produce illusion only for those who practice them by immersing themselves in philosophical sufficiency without distance. Neither Heidegger nor Wittgenstein, and now no longer Deleuze or Derrida, have really suspended the closure of the philosophical; they have not even thought to suspend it; above all they have not even been able to imagine this would be possible. They have done what philosophers have always done: they have spontaneously practiced philosophical faith.

All that would remain to be asked, each in their own manner, would be the following: to what degree does one have the right to go into the dehiscence outside the philosophical, into the destruction of its norms and its codes—in other words: ultimately to what point can one still conserve a philosophical sense, appearance and effect? How can we limit the destruction of philosophy and guarantee the conservation of its capacity to simulate the real? Non-philosophy is not the answer to this question of philosophical fear, as though it were a supplement of deconstruction or critique, a supplementary "push in the right direction" in the decoding of occidental thought; no more than it is simply a brute and spontaneous attempt to compose philosophical fiction, philo-fiction: from this point of view, philosophy indeed suffices by itself. Generally, non-philosophy does not depart—in any sense of the word—from philosophy; it would in that case be merely a mode of philosophy's self-destruction and nihilism. Non-philosophy is instead by its very essence vision-in-One: it departs from the One, and, by its effective deployment, it is the treatment of philosophy as a simple contingent material. Therefore, the usage non-philosophy makes of philosophy suffices for interrupting the attempts to place non-philosophy within an extension of deconstruction.

Non-philosophy is not a new economy of philosophy, which would always suppose the sufficiency of the latter; it is an immanent pragmatics—or a pragmatics that ensues from the One—of simple philosophical material. In breaking once and for all with ad hoc compromises and syntheses, non-philosophy is the experience of thought that is unleashed by bracketing the celebrated unitary postulate—here considered to be transcendent and, within certain limits, globally useless. "Vision-in-One" is what makes this suspension of philosophical sufficiency possible. This is what also makes it necessary to denounce in the spontaneous practices of the Greco-philosophical tradition a strong spirit of conservation and of unitary mastery that incapacitates philosophy and prevents it from carrying out the theoretical and technical mutations which the sciences and the arts—above all painting and music—have carried out since the beginning of the 20th century. This is why non-philosophy will discover in these scientific and artistic mutations if not its *raison d'être,* then at least its strongest encouragement.

Introduction:
New Practices and New Writings of Philosophy

From "open" philosophies to "non-philosophy"

Non-philosophy is one of the solutions that our age must contribute to the problem concerning new writings and new practices of philosophy following the age that came before it.

If non-philosophy is defined externally, its program can be formulated in the following way: how do we continue to practice philosophy without devoting ourselves to its history, without interminably commenting on its works and its doctrines or even without remaining content with deconstructing them? How do we produce new texts and new thoughts without necessarily presupposing others already given as the norm for what must be done? Without supposing philosophy completed and constituted in an authority which one would be content to breach and make tremble? How do we stop treating philosophy as a past yet to be thought, as a tradition which is still hidden, or as a presupposition that the whole activity of thought consists in manifesting so as to open it, simply open it to the future? How do we no longer comment on the forgetting of philosophy while playing the perpetual game of suspicion on its behalf? How do we exhibit philosophy in its entirety as actual, all the while treating it as positive and as sufficiently determined so that it does not need a decision or a supplementary intervention? But if it is defined more essentially in terms of what is new about it, it will be said that non-philosophy is a quasi-scientific practice of philosophy which therefore delivers us from the two relations that philosophy undertakes with itself and within which it immerses itself and becomes paralyzed: its history and its textual labor, the interest in its past and in its text—in both cases, its narcissism, its "philocentrism" and its sufficiency.

Formulated this way, the problem of non-philosophy is the apparent opposite to that of deconstruction: of Wittgenstein, Heidegger, and, above all, Derrida. What is it that motivates this appearance? That reflects a distinction which is indeed real? No doubt each philosophy defines new practices and writings, but they do this within certain general and obvious presuppositions, certain immutable closures and certain norms of validity and of acceptability which are never brought into question. These latter presuppositions ground philosophy in a foundational sense and are then taken up in philosophy's authority over itself in its unique, imprescriptible, inalienable law of legislating on itself, of programming its own transformation and of defining the mutations it can tolerate. *These are the ultimate codes that assure the coherence—despite everything—of philosophical decision and its coherence as representation supposed to be constitutive of the real.* This coherence is expressed by phenomena like conceptual and thematic discursivity, linearity, intentionality and *the very nature of the narrative of the philosophical text, which already seems to be referred to the real, not only in order to describe it but also in order to transform it.*

Philosophy is indeed a revolutionary practice by its very essence. But for this reason it does not wonder how revolution—neither its gesture nor its operation—is possible, for it spontaneously practices it. In the 20th century it has therefore witnessed many ruptures: for example, Wittgenstein's introduction of language games, Deleuze's generalized serialism and univocal chance, Derrida's Other as absolute or Judaic Other (deconstruction). But all these revolutions that transform, distend or impregnate philosophical decision in the last instance continue to guarantee its cohesion and its ultimate coherence, essentially leaving philosophy to be the master of itself and the real, i.e. to be partially autolegislative within these adventures.

How do we explain this continuously revolutionary yet ultimately conservative situation which is the enemy of true mutations? In effect, the structural rule of philosophical decision—which is also a transcendental rule, because it is itself affected by affecting what it organizes and distributes—is Unity-of-contraries, the circular coextension—with some shifting here and there—of the One and the Dyad. However, this ultimate rule of conceptual aggregations qua philosophical regime is not broken; more accurately it is purified and instead becomes immanent in contemporary philosophical serialism and even in deconstruction, where one of the opposites of the Dyad is simply replaced by the Other-who-*is*-not. In other words, this rule governs more than ever when it remains concealed, as for example in a certain "rational" and "critical" practice of concepts, which is merely one of its forms that is obliterated and obscured exclusively by its denegation. *No philosophy can suspend the validity of its rule, which appears "natural" to the philosopher in the same way that harmony and tonality appear natural to the classical musician or capital to the capitalist.* At best it has been possible to breach, incite or distend the Dyad based on an alterity or a Différance: this is to maintain the One in the mode of the Other, instead of being in the mode of Being or of the two. But nothing fundamental has been gained by this.... Such that the more profound revolution, what would no longer be a revolution but would affect the possibility itself of philosophical practice as perpetual revolution, always remains in waiting. Therefore this ultimate traditional presupposition of all philosophy—which would like to be constitutive of the real—along with the phenomena that accompany it and ground its authority over the real and over itself, its necessity, its legitimacy, none of which deconstruction has ever called into question, is what "non-philosophy" must globally attempt to suspend by producing practices and writings of philosophy that are really new: due to their technique, but above all due to their non-submission to these codes of the ultimate coherence or of the non-dislocation of philosophical decision supposed as identical with the real.

If this is not the first time that philosophy is attempting to break or disperse its objects and the corresponding linearity of its discourse, or is attempting to substitute, for example, the thematic description of referents for a labor of the signifier and a whole practice of textuality, the problem is now elsewhere and is more fundamental: there is an invariant and specific linearity and discursivity of the philosophical text which holds to the presupposition that this discourse is constitutive of the real by way of sense, truth and value. There is no philosophical discourse that is not spontaneously split into object or referent (the real as being, essence, substance, spirit, will to power, text, etc.) and into an intentional aim—regardless of how off target—of this referent. Whatever the unsettling [*sollicitation*] may be by which this division is affected, it remains a dyad with which the One is coextensive or a unitary type of duality: that of the real *and* language. This more or less circular intentionality, this more or less overt referential splitting [*dédoublement*] and doubling of philosophical discourse, this teleological usage of language in view of the essential real—which can be language itself—this discursivity and auto/hetero-referentiality must now be broken in order to unleash the real from linguistic hallucinations: in this way it also allows language to flourish definitively for itself and in its solitude. This is what we call "non-philosophy."

Practicing unlimited and univocal serialism (generalization of the series to all the dimensions of philosophy) and destroying the thematism, regionalism and objectivism of traditional discourse will therefore not suffice in order to accede to non-philosophy and radically open, not philosophical decision, but thought, which comes *before* it; nor will it even suffice to articulate, outside any elaboration of their unity, the series as one of the faces, albeit the "metaphysical" face, of a quasi-system whose Other would be absolute, and not simply relative, differ(a)ence. Transversality and limitrophy, seriality and supplementarity, a generalized syntax rather than a theme, object or region, allow for the destruction of certain particularly dogmatic and massive forms of philosophical representation but conserve what is essential to it and its fetishistic usage as unavoidable fact or tradition, i.e. as constitutive of the real. These are just a number of the filters and barriers against a more "liberal" usage of certain linguistic aggregates, those in which one imposes the norm and the *a priori* of "philosophical decision" not only in the form of substance and concept, but also that of series and supplement, difference and différance, etc.—the form of unitary duality, of the circular simultaneity of the One and the Dyad. This is precisely what we call "philosophical decision."

Therefore it is less a matter of critiquing or deconstructing a representation which we would, despite everything, still admit to being constitutive of the One or of the real and which would then be real in its own way; rather it is a question of more profoundly breaking the ultimate bond of reciprocity this deconstruction continues to presuppose between the real and its representation; of liberating the one from the other, liberating the real just as much as representation; of removing them from this aporetic situation in which the Greeks, under the name of "philosophy," have abandoned and devoted them to being opposed to one another.

What is to be done and how do we proceed more concretely? One can no longer remain content with suspending, as limited or exhausted, the average or statistical axioms that ground a given age—such as ours—if not the philosophical community, in philosophical common sense. This is like saying: put philosophy in relation to its Other, in relation to the non-philosophical. Or, better yet and more rigorously: put the Other-without-relation in relation with philosophy; open the Other or let the Other open philosophy. Instead, it is necessary to suspend the *belief-in-philosophy* that supports these fairly massive slogans, the spontaneous belief according to which, for example, *there is* logos or logocentrism, and *there is* the Other or the Undecidable. Rather than practicing them naively, we should question why we uphold these axioms and the absolute authority we confer upon them, how their statuses are due to our belief and what allows them to bind us and requires that we identify ourselves with them. Perhaps it is possible to be even more radical in order to learn to doubt—within certain limits, we shall come to this—the axiom of all axioms, philosophical faith itself: *there is philosophy*. From where do we know it, from where do we get this evidence, *this objective philosophical Appearance, if not from philosophy itself which concludes from its force and from its presence to its reality, from its effectivity to its right to legislate on itself? There is philosophy—undoubtedly—but which mode of existence and necessity hides in this "there is?"*

All these axioms, even the one mentioned above, present the traits of a transcendent empiricism and present philosophy under the traits of a more or less idealized and autonomous factual given, simultaneously transcendent and immanent to things and to man, but not entirely and merely immanent *to itself or to man*: as rational fact or *a priori* factum, tradition and call, destiny and dispatch, history and already prescribed possibility, etc. But it is these axioms of philosophy's transcendence that prescribe the interminable labor of commentary (at worst) and of the text (at best). These operations are thus at the same time secondary or supplementary to a *supposed given* past or tradition and techno-teleo-logical (scission and identification, decision and position, reversal and displacement). Philosophical practice reduces thought to a boring and repetitive mixture of history and technology. However diverse they may be, these practices have in common the fact of *supposing* philosophy *given* in the element of transcendence and consequently supposing it to be accomplished, i.e. real and absolute. Even if a supplement of decision or of alterity is necessary, even if this accomplishment is an illusion, this illusion still defines philosophy's reality or its accomplishment as absolute. Thus in the foundation of philosophy there is this amphibology—another name for the rule of the circular simultaneity of the One and the Dyad, of the real and representation—that founds all of its spontaneous practices: that of the *factum* and of the real, of tradition and the absolute, of the relative and the absolute, etc. Such an amphibology imposes the mutual opposition of the operations of thought and the inevitable paralysis or internal inhibition demonstrated by the contemporary—and not merely contemporary—practices of philosophy. However, these are just some of the effects. The radical critique of amphibology, which every philosophical decision is, will come from further away.

Non-philosophy is not philosophy's massive negation, its (impossible) destruction, but another usage, *the only one that can be defined outside its spontaneous belief in itself, a practice of philosophy which is no longer founded and enclosed in philosophical faith but is positively established within the limits of the bracketing of this faith.* Non-philosophy is a practice of philosophy that is heteronomous to it but no longer heteronomous to man—whereas philosophy's spontaneous practice is autonomous for itself and heteronomous to man. But inversely, it is not, for example, a question of refusing deconstruction and claiming to close the age of the textual, if only in order to substitute new practices of the same order for a supplementary variation or another decision and to repose upon the same belief, the same illusion of omnipotence, the axiom of a factum, a tradition, an unavoidable destiny or an *objective philosophical Appearance* that would enlist us into its service.

The preliminary task is thus to lift this basic belief, the identity of the factum and of the real, of transcendence and immanence, of philosophy and the Absolute; *to reduce philosophy to the state of material or given (whatever material) for a knowledge rather than a technical and teleological auto-transformation*; to make it pass again from so-called *factum* to the state of *datum*; to thus make possible operations that are more fundamental and autonomous than those of Reversal and Displacement or Decision and Position, which are always secondary and prescribed or determined by the factum itself. Non-philosophy is the only usage of philosophy that is not programmed by it. Then by whom or what is it programmed? It will be said: *by the One and by thought of the One or "vision-in-One"—and ultimately by "science" rather than philosophy.*

10

Non-philosophy will be nothing other than what the real experience of thought, what we call vision-in-One, takes from philosophy.

The true advances, ruptures or mutations of thought do not consist in extending the existing phenomena a little further or in tracing the continuities, *in passing from the modes to the infinite or unlimited attributes, from the empirical to the universal a priori*—this is philosophical practice—but consists rather in relativizing the essences, which were presented as real or absolute, to the state of modes, effects or particular cases of a new thought; in treating the elements, ethers and attributes as modes, in treating philosophy's *a prioris* as the empirical; in unmasking the abusiveness of the so-called "universalities" that are always found to be forms of ancient thought seeking to perpetuate themselves. Contemporary philosophy is progressive and "open"; it seeks the Other, the stranger, the "non-philosophical." But it is only so revolutionary because it continues to suppose the validity of ancient thought, and thus metaphysics merely revolutionizes itself at the same time in order to further extend its offshoots into the future. Philosophy creates a "snowball effect," for its entire past is more or less integrally preserved in the memory of philosophers, and it lays claim to each of its decisions in order to re-assume the totality of its heritage. It is not merely a practice of conservation but above all a belief in the value of the past and conservation. Philosophy is revolutionary and, like all revolutions, it persists in re-exhibiting the past and recognizing a normativity in it, assigning it an ultimately absolute validity. Non-philosophy must put an end to this hypocrisy and this conservatism.

Philosophy as non-philosophy's simple material

Non-philosophy has two aspects: on the one hand, it reduces philosophy to the state of whatever material; on the other hand, it announces new positive rules (which are non-philosophical but deduced from vision-in-One) of the labor on this material. By presenting these rules without yet founding them, we are giving a very succinct and elementary idea of their foundation, which is vision-in-One.

What does the following mean: *philosophy treated as whatever material or as whatever given?* As we said, it is a question of suspending or bracketing, from vision-in-One, philosophy's auto-legislation, its teleology that makes it the goal of itself: a question of lifting philosophy's circularity or what must still be called its auto-position as absolute fact, tradition or "unavoidable" destiny.

Philosophy is not just a set of categories and objects, syntaxes and experiences or operations of decision and position: it is animated and traversed by a faith or belief in itself as in absolute reality, by an intentionality or reference to the real which it claims to describe and even constitute, or simply in itself as in the real. This is its fundamental auto-position, which can also be called its auto-factualization or auto-fetishization—all of which we label as the *Principle of Sufficient Philosophy* (PSP). The suspension of these phenomena amounts to a defactualization, defetishization or deposition of philosophical decision, to its reduction to the state of material of philosophical *origin*, no doubt, but which is philosophically inert or sterile. This state of philosophy as sterile material will be called *chaos* or *chôra*—concepts obviously meant to be remodeled. Philosophical decision's general form, the coupling-of-contraries or mixture-form, is here itself given inertly alongside objects, categories, statements, etc., but it loses the function of standardizing this material, of being valid for this material as its rule of interpretation and as theoretical horizon or point of view on itself.

Is it a question of a destruction? Obviously not, but a question of a transcendental reduction, of an *indetermination* qua suspension of philosophical determination *alone* (decision, philosophy-form, mixture-form, etc.) and, in this very sense, of a *chaos*. It is also a question of a ground of decision in a place that secondarizes it, that of a *chôra*—these points will be explained. A nihilistic destruction of philosophy would itself be imprecise or undetermined and limited to the extent that it would be self-contradictory and would reaffirm the power and authority of decision over its claimed ruin. *This chaos and this chôra are not a new decision but the correlate of the One or of vision-in-One and are founded in the latter as their necessary effect, as the already accomplished and radical transcendental reduction that affects the World or Philosophy themselves and not just several particular philosophical decisions.* If the One, alone rather than mixed with Being and Transcendence, is taken as a transcendental point of view, then it implies the suspension of the theoretical authority or validity—and these alone—of philosophical syntaxes, organizations, distributions, norms and economies; it implies *their suspension as theoretical point of view and their conservation as givens or material whose properties must be described.* Unlike deconstructions and more reasonably than traditional philosophical practices, non-philosophy refuses to accept philosophy except as a veritably sterile object, neither as the knowledge of this object nor as knowledge of itself, but—as we shall say—as "support," "occasion," or "given" for a different activity of thought. Philosophy is not breached, prolonged, reversed and displaced, opened, etc.; it changes function, *it undergoes a transcendental change of function*: it passes from a point of departure, beginning or commencement, enclosure or element, etc., to the state of "whatever material" that has its own laws but can no longer impose them as a point of view, which is what happens in technology. Non-philosophy is not a technological process; it will instead be something like a scientific process.

Thus from the outset it is important to distinguish between any labor of serialization or above all the textual labor of deconstruction, which conserve the validity of decision as unavoidable point of view, and *the placing into chaos, the transcendental dislocation of philosophical decision reduced to the state of whatever material by vision-in-One.* From the start, the principle of departure is not at all the same. We oppose these philosophies, which are "open"—by violence or by force—and which correspond with the contemporary ideal of the "open work" and are still obedient to the PSP, with a non-philosophy that does not consist in opening philosophy or even opening it halfway, but in plunging it from the outset into *chaos* or the *chôra*, into a pure indetermination, yet simply in order to formulate rules beyond this chaos, rather than in conjunction with it and in view of saving philosophical pretention and sufficiency once again.

A non-philosophy does not deny philosophy's existence but denounces an amphibology in this term "existence," a conflation between *supposed given existence*, which is that of philosophy, and the *real given*; non-philosophy dissolves this amphibology by distinguishing on its behalf between material-existence and fact-existence, which is already an implicit decision. The objection: "but philosophy exists, it is a fact, a tradition, a destiny," must be critiqued and denounced as the PSP itself, as the process of auto-factualization and auto-fetishization, at any rate as an equivocation concerning the real. For whom is philosophy *supposed* to exist *de facto, supposed given* in transcendence and as what simply needs to be breached? This question has only one answer: for the lone philosopher who identifies with it and auto-identifies does philosophy exist for this reason: not only as material but as auto-position.... This mechanism of auto-factualization by which philosophical decision is given as transcendent, and thus *is supposed given*, must be examined and exhibited as the place of philosophical fetishism and resistance. This is philosophy's autoreference, auto-legitimation and auto-recognition. What will be opposed to this existence as fact, tradition or destiny, etc., is its existence as *non-philosophical chaos* of philosophical decisions dis-located outside themselves and re-localized in the *chôra*. This dislocation of philosophical auto-factualization and philosophical authority unleashes a manifold or a material capable of receiving new rules.

Consequently, non-philosophy no longer posits the preceding external problem in the same way, the question that would invoke a final norm or an ultimate philosophical teleology that proceeds to limit its activity: i.e. *how is this still philosophy? What is the ultimate bond, the final synthesis between the non- and philosophy in "non-philosophy"?* This unitary question of the bond or synthesis still makes of non-philosophy *a unitary simulation of philosophy*. In reality, if it appears to be a *philo-fiction*, this is only for philosophy and from its point of view. Furthermore, the "non-" derives from the One and vision-in-One—this is the "(non-) One"—rather than from Being and philosophy. It shares in the nature of science—this thesis will have to be returned to—and not of "philo-fiction" as simple philosophical fiction. It is necessary to guard against this ultimate teleology that would make non-philosophy a simulation of philosophy. Instead it will be said, even if it means founding this formula later: if non-philosophy simulates philosophy, this is only in the last instance and because its contingent material is philosophy; but this is only due to its material rather than its essence. The reason why non-philosophy is not a simulation of philosophy is the same reason which guarantees that it is a scientific rather than philosophical or technological process.

From Unity-of-contraries to vision-in-One

Non-philosophy's second aspect is more positive. It cannot stop at chaos: the movement of decoding philosophical decision, if it is brought to fruition beyond the closure of the philosophical, shows that, from this radical or predecisional chaos itself, a special set of rules arise that are unknown to any possible philosophy. These are no longer rules concerning the limitation of destruction or recoding; they are not even rules coextensive with chaos, as is the case in generalized serialism where dispersion is itself still of the order of a transcendent norm. These are rules that emerge from the immanent chaos of philosophical decisions (chaos is originary in relation to these rules, since it is itself an effect of the One—all these points will be clarified). In short: whereas the structural rules of philosophical decision, which are founded upon and express it, are teleologically responsible for the circular co-extension of the One and the Dyad, for limiting the threat of an internal and external dislocation of the decision, for rendering it tolerable and containing it (even deconstructions are preventive ways of filtering the menace of the dislocation of philosophical decision), the rules of non-philosophy suppose philosophy's state of chaos to be originary, or first after the One. While philosophies and even deconstructions begin by supposing that philosophy exists (as factum, tradition or objective philosophical appearance) or give themselves the axiom of the existence of a *nondislocated* but autonomous and self-dependent decision and then partially dislocate it (together with an Other which is itself not elucidated while proceeding through a relative, absolute or relative-absolute reversal)—here we apparently do the "inverse." *We begin by supposing that philosophy does not exist or no longer exists, at least in the sufficient and authoritative mode and manner in which it presents itself,* i.e. as a rational yet transcendental fact that teleologically controls the possible operations upon it. Philosophy is only given as material when decision is already dislocated outside itself.

Starting from this material, a text is then built—it can sometimes have a philosophical appearance—via rules that suppose this chaos rather than those that simply limit it, rules that conserve this chaos such as it is rather than those that simply internalize it, reinstate it, surpass it, etc. In a sense, it is on the basis of the philosophizing non-existence of philosophy that the text's creation is constrained. But this current and future production *of a philosophy without a past* can no longer exist, apart from being compared to its auto-position and the image of itself that has spontaneously been its own, except as a "non-philosophy," but which is all the more positive. Since their origin is given in vision-in-One, which from itself imposes this radical dispersion, non-philosophy's rules of production can no longer be limitative, restrictive or normative; they will no longer be rules of organization or of a unitary economy. On the one hand, rules will emerge from the immanent procedure of vision-in-One and the (non-) One as real dislocation of philosophical decision; on the other hand, they will be rules of the greatest opening, of the opening which is infinite as such or as a primary—and no longer secondary—dimension of thought. They will be the *only representation still possible of the chaos of philosophical decisions*, because non-philosophy will simply be the representation of philosophy's real essence, a rigorous representation that will integrate what this essence is for vision-in-One: a simple inert material.

These positive rules will be those of the reciprocal reformulation of philosophical utterances—reduced to the state of philosophically sterile material—and of the structures of the new experience of thought, which we call vision-in-One and which we take as a guiding thread for these new practices of philosophy. It is useless to claim to describe these rules, even summarily, so long as we have not "acquired" the concept of vision-in-One, so long as we are not replaced within it in order to cast an altogether new gaze upon philosophy. Non-philosophy is only what we see in-One of philosophy, but this "vision," far from being a mystical intuition, is formulated by rules and practices which are as precise as they are ordered.

Non-philosophy's essence thus consists in substituting the structural and transcendental rule of philosophical decision, the rule of Unity-of-contraries, of the circular simultaneity of two principles—the One and the Dyad, supposed co-extensive—for a completely different principle, that of vision-in-One, which dismembers the One/Dyad system of philosophical decision and rigorously subordinates the Dyad to the One, which is first of all restored to its real or ante-dyadic essence. Non-philosophy supposes the acquisition of a description of vision-in-One, but it is also a little more than this since it consists in "seeing" philosophy—hence this structural rule of Unity-of-contraries itself—through the One such as it is given (to) self before being supposed given in a transcendent way by philosophy, with and by the Dyad. Vision-in-One thus detaches the principle of Unity-of-contraries from its auto-legislation (philosophical sufficiency). Toward this end, vision-in-One reduces it to the state of inert material and reformulates or transforms it in accordance with the "unary" structures of vision-in-One.

A scientific practice of philosophy

One can obviously be frightened by this radical opening and overwhelmed by vertigo in front of the abyss of apparently "uncontrolled" and uncontrollable possibilities that consequently open up with a renewed philosophical practice. At the same time, one can be indecisive facing so many possibilities and perplexed facing the absence of any standard. But it is not impossible to formulate new rules that permit moving forward in this chaos, for these rules are nothing but those of vision-in-One as science's essence. This abandonment of philosophical spontaneity procures a certain number of new benefits and theoretical possibilities. Two of them deserve to be singled out for their importance: the critical function's change of sense and of truth—which will not be examined here—and the foundation of a rigorous pragmatics of philosophy. Why "rigorous?" Let us suppose that vision-in-One, the mode of thought which remains in the One alone and autonomous in relation to Being, is the real—by definition of epistemology, unperceived—foundation of science, and that, inversely, the One's description is necessarily of a scientific rather than philosophical type: we would then have the possibility of a rigorous (adapted to its object, not "positivist") practice of philosophy. Perhaps thought has too often abused the unitary postulate that leads philosophy to believe it could legislate on the real and on science, which both have their root in the One. Now that this bewitchment is beginning to be lifted or held in check, we can propose a solution which will appear, to the hasty spirits who postulate philosophy's sufficiency in order to think the essence of things, like the simple reversal of their practice but which will simply be the ensemble of the uncontestable points of impact of science, as vision-in-One by its essence, on philosophy: rather than a new but opposite reduction of philosophy to science or a new "decision," this is instead a type of labor upon philosophical material that is scientific in the last instance.

It is understood that one can continue to think in a philosophical regime and that, in a certain way, one is constrained to answer the call of the Principle of Sufficient Philosophy. The history, auto-critique and hetero-critique of philosophy are possibilities by its ample right. But one can also limit the unitary spontaneity and faith that define this traditional auto-exercise. A science of philosophy on the basis of vision-in-One implies, beyond the knowledge of decision's essence which it procures, a sort of "transcendental deduction" of philosophy in relation to science and within the limits of reality and validity that henceforth science alone is able to define. If science, correctly elaborated in its essence of vision-in-One, is now philosophy's transcendental criterion rather than one of its objects, this means two things immediately for philosophy. First, it means philosophy's spontaneous exercise, philosophy's belief-in-itself-as-in-the-real, is a transcendental illusion; it means the call or the seduction of objective philosophical Appearance[1] is a hallucination, not as appearance but as "objective," an objectivity which therefore no longer recovers the real for science detached from philosophy. The other consequence, which envelops the preceding one, is that, on the basis of a real usage of decision, it becomes possible to radically renew its practices, to *found a real usage of the fictional and hallucinatory virtualities of philosophy—non-philosophy.*

Faced with the Greco-philosophical reassessment, with this aporetic, sterile and skillfully conservative triviality, which was and always becomes more philosophy in the hands of its old and new "deciders" and "revolutionaries" who think—the ancients too, although the specification is meaningless—that they renew interest by the perpetual agitation of "questioning" and "reversal," and who are satisfied with reproducing the same norms, it is urgent to assert a *non-philosophical principle* around which the practice of a philosophical *type* of thought could be reorganized upon less conventional, less normalized foundations. The old unitary postulate of Unity-of-contraries, with the infinite games and the more or less "opened" and "displaced" circular aporias of the One and Dyad to which it gives rise, seems foundational and originary to us, natural and unavoidable. But perhaps for thought this postulate is nothing more—and nothing more original—than what the laws of tonal harmony are for twelve-tone serialism or for music that is even more an-archic (there is a philosophical serialism). It is ultimately a particular system that has crystallized to the point of passing for the ultimate nature of thought whose *transcendence* is then discovered, the artificial exteriority that prohibits access to thought's immanence just as the aforementioned laws prohibited access to the immanence of sound. Perhaps "philosophical decision" is merely the state of thought that is as "pre-cubist" in its own way as the laws of perspective formulated in the Renaissance or as those of cubism itself in comparison with "Abstract Art." Even if non-philosophy does not yet represent the broadest basic

---

1   The notion of "objective Appearance" (*gegenständlichen Schein*) comes from Marx (via Hegel) and is most notably associated with the semblance attached to the fetish-character of commodities. In this sense, the phrase "objective philosophical Appearance," which recurs throughout the present work, clarifies both the sense of philosophy's "auto-fetishization"and the sense of non-philosophy's "defetishization" of philosophical decision. It should also be noted that this objective Appearance will be distinguished from the universal Appearance (non-thetic Reflection) that culminates with the sixth rule at the end of non-philosophy's pragmatic procedure (cf. chapter 4). [TN]

mutation—if others are obviously possible and will be sought in any event by generations who, unlike ours, will not allow themselves to be enclosed in their history—nothing ultimate in thought, especially none of the Greek decisions, prohibits us from opening our eyes to thought and from denouncing in philosophy, i.e. in its "sufficient" practice, an extremely conservative and stereotypical activity. The philosophical accusations of a "hostile takeover" will not be able to prohibit this rejection or mitigate this malaise: the description of vision-in-One will show that what is essentially a permanent activity of hostile takeover or of arbitrary decision is philosophy, an activity of transcendence without real foundation, and that it is necessary to recover the ante-philosophical basis of thought.

It is well known that philosophical possibilities can seem exhausted, the resources of the tradition doomed to overexploitation, and that, although they know it in their own way, none of this prevents philosophers from believing them to "work": that they have the unimagined resource to turn this exhaustion into a new possibility from which to draw their effects. In order to escape from this circle or this balance, the powers and usages of thought must be radically revived: there must be an external renewal under the sign of a science of philosophy. Until now, pragmatics has simply been a byproduct of philosophy, but we are seeking a pragmatics for philosophy itself, a pragmatics of the scientific usages that can be made of philosophical games. If we should still complain about philosophy, we will not address this complaint to philosophy but to science. The latter, however, complains about the former only insofar as it has already operated on philosophy with a fully positive usage and has inscribed it in a space of thought that cuts into philosophy's own without appeal.

An attempt upon the philosophical that would be non-philosophical from the start—but nevertheless non-contradictory—is the only chance to "escape" from the narcissism and the historicizing and textual auto-reference within which unitary thought seems to want to consume itself until the end of time. This is not to say that it would be necessary to give up the texts and the problematics of the past for the busy and exclusive pursuit of new objects. The true renewal of philosophy, before passing to the invention of new objects not yet elucidated by it, begins with the discovery of the non-contradictory law of the scientific and "non-philosophical" usages of its utterances, texts and problems. The Greco-unitary reading of the World, of History, of Language, of

Power, etc. is always possible and perhaps desirable. But far from being valid by itself and capable of passing for the ultimate sense and truth of the World, here it will merely be a simple material for another labor of thought that will define a *philosophically impossible yet completely real usage of the properties of this material.*

This means that the invention of philosophy, its non-philosophical invention, does not merely consist in exacerbating the fictional and experimental virtualities which it already contains, since new decisions are in every way *possibilities* producible by the matrix of the open and undetermined rules that constitute them. It requires something other than the imagination, something other than a sense of alterity and of the possible, other even than the sense of the crossing, interference or intercession of series. Contemporary thought has beautifully exploited this latter possibility. But practiced in this way, philosophy remains the object of a repetition—undoubtedly in approximation with its "difference." Contemporary thought practices it, for example—Wittgenstein must also be added here—through a triple repetition of a widening gap: the slightest gap, the poorest but the most assured repetition, is the history of philosophy; the most intense gap, the most fruitful repetition, is its interpretation as an immanent operation or auto-productive machine (Nietzsche then Deleuze); the most distant and heterogeneous gap, the most menacing and hesitant repetition, is deconstruction (Heidegger then Derrida.) But "non-philosophy" is still something other than a repetition or a tautology (in the widening gap) of philosophy. It is one of the most radical changes of usage or function that philosophy can undergo, because this change precedes what is changed, precedes it and, as a new practice, is no longer circularly determined by it, i.e. by what is here nothing more than its empirical "object" or its contingent material.

Perhaps the paradox is that the precedence of science as vision-in-One over philosophy, the "transcendental deduction" of the latter in view of the former, inaugurates for philosophy a new vocation, less sterile than its "repetitions," which are always founded on philosophy's claim to suffice for the real and for itself and therefore *de jure* doomed to a transcendental illusion and sterility. The deposition or de-stitution of the PSP itself is the condition for preventing the auto-paralysis, auto-consummation and auto-consumption of thought in and by philosophy. Science's point of view teaches us to distinguish thought from philosophy's claim to sufficiency. But science ultimately leaves-be[2] philosophy as a material so that it is authorized to use philosophy in its own way and according to its own requirements. Freed from its illusory claims over itself, decision can accept, without fear of falsification or devaluation, its entrance into a new regime of thought and ultimately its subordination to the one it had tried to enslave: man, i.e. man-as-One.

Rather than inventing new modes of philosophical decision, modes of its unitary and sufficient usage, thus leading back to *the narrowness and arbitrariness of the Greek solution which is consequently condemned to overexploitation*, new resources of thought can emerge only from the unprecedented conjunction of autonomous science and second philosophy. It will not be said too hastily that this would be a "new alliance" proposed to old adversaries. Instead, it is a question of a perpetual peace treaty between science and philosophy, a treaty henceforth founded on the former rather than manipulated by the latter on its behalf, as has generally been the case in history. From science to philosophy, rather than the other way around, it has become possible to establish a democratic and peaceful community. "Non-philosophy" is the symbol of this new agreement and of the work that can be done in this community.

Philosophy's change in function and the abandonment of its traditional functions

The *non-philosophical principle* around which we are attempting to reorganize the philosophical type of thought must be grasped in its radicality. Here radicality can no longer signify a simply "revolutionary" character but a thought other-than-revolutionary by its essence. We prefer to say that it is a question of a

---

2 French "laissez-être." This turn of phrase describes the "passive" activity of non-philosophy as science (among other things) that leaves philosophy (its object) to its own coherence (from philosophy's point of view) without blending with it circularly (ob-jectification) by knowing it. This is not only the posture of science but also the posture of the One or vision-in-One, which does not destroy philosophy or decision but merely suspends its authority in a chôra. This renders them not so much indifferent to the One (what they are already, since the latter is foreclosed to them without being opposed) but more specifically renders the One's indifference for them via science's perspective on them (vision-in-One) such that they are indifferent also to one another and for man's practice of them (ordinary practice without war, "democracy in thought," etc.). This indifference does not affect philosophies from within or *intra*-philosophically, but it does describe their determination-in-the-last-instance really. Leaving-be thus has mystical, political, scientific, philo-fictional registers, albeit rendered non-philosophically. [TN]

scientific type of mutation rather than a philosophical revolution. We abandon philosophy's traditional ambitions—for us, these are hallucinations—and assert a "finitude"—precisely the "radicality" or the "finitude" of the scientific posture—which is in any case more modest than philosophy's unacknowledged folly. Non-philosophy is a mutation of philosophy's syntax and grammar rather than a mutation of its objects and themes. This is still an insufficient definition: non-philosophy is at the same time a mutation of philosophy's syntax and of its experience of the real, the foundation of philosophy finally set upon its real base. It is not merely the production of new rules of thought and writing, but the ultimate experience in which philosophy can really be given to man. *Really given* rather than *supposed given,* as is the case when philosophy itself proceeds to its external auto-givenness. These rules are no longer those of *Unity-of-contraries*, nor those of the operations of decision and position, of Reversal and Displacement that are attached to Unity-of-contraries. These rules are not content with saying that there is no longer decision and position; their existence itself proves the fact that these two things no longer function, because these rules could not be formulated within the unitary framework. These rules are far from being formal; they forge the chaos of philosophy, i.e. the abandonment of the old philosophical teleologies and especially the intimate teleology of the philosophical as such, which posits itself as an intervention in the real and in the human real. What does philosophy become? As soon as it functions as material and occasion, it loses its traditional purposes which are all founded on "spontaneous philosophical faith." This faith forms a circle: one is constrained to practice philosophy for ethical, juridical, scientific, aesthetic reasons external to it; but in turn philosophy also profits from these purposes in order to triumph and affirm itself over their subjection as the unique excellent activity, the only one that is "unavoidable" or absolute. All this prescriptive activity—ethical, pedagogical, etc.—this normative, auto-normative usage or usage "for experience," the whole latent or explicit teleology of spontaneous philosophy must be abandoned, i.e. rather than destroyed, treated as a simple material and henceforth practiced within these limits. Non-philosophy is a completely new usage of philosophy toward ends which are no longer those of the comprehension, explication, elucidation, description of objects and regions of objects, nor even those of critique and deconstruction—but toward philosophically non programmed ends of "simple material" for a science and a practice that have a wholly other origin or essence.

Therefore this is also more than simply the usage of philosophy as material: this is a new "vision" of philosophy, a vision so devoid of the "mystical" in the transcendent sense of this word that it is formulated in rigorous and productive rules of "objective" knowledge. These rules no longer serve to better comprehend the World or philosophy *for themselves* or to favor the alienating insertion of man into them, but in the last instance to enjoy the unlimited possibilities opened by and for man-as-One or as subject (of) science. Thus it is no longer a knowledge through concepts, a production and consumption of sense, a rational activity, but the rigorous knowledge that can ensue from a real *jouissance* or from the vision-in-One of "reason" itself. If, for example, structuralism and, in a more founded and more transcendental way, serialism have reduced thought to the exercise of a form without substance, or of the relational and of the positional, non-philosophy reduces it to an experience of forms and of substances, a regulated and founded experience but anterior to the disjunction of form and substance, of relation and position, etc.

In any case, non-philosophy is at bare minimum the refusal of thinking *in accordance with the World*, with Transcendence and its attributes (history, economy, language, etc.), in accordance with philosophy that is already constituted and with its tradition. Vision-in-One contains a transcendental reduction, and it considers the Tradition broadly as a transcendence to be suspended, at least in its claim to validity. If spontaneous philosophy constitutionally refers to its own transcendence, if its current practice is traced, in approximation with some gaps, from that which exists, from its past and from its objective Appearance, non-philosophy on the other hand is a usage of philosophy in accordance with what the One—or man considered in his finitude—can do. This is a thought which only represents the One, which describes it in its interiority alone without claiming to describe the World and philosophy already constituted but which utilizes them as simple material. Inasmuch as philosophy is spontaneously "figurative" in a broad sense, i.e. descriptive of the given figure of the World, of language, of objects, etc. or of transcendent Being, non-philosophy is to the same extent "abstract," i.e. founded in the being-immanent of the One, and consequently capable of procuring a rigorous knowledge, founded in the last instance, of the World and of philosophy.

The "manipulation" of philosophical decision and its limits

To treat philosophy in a non-philosophical way is to combine: 1) the suspension of the PSP, of philosophy's authority over itself and over the real; thus to be given the right to treat philosophy as a whatever material: not "in general" but, instead, from the only point of view where the PSP has been lifted, that of the real and of vision-in-One or of the science that gives it. Non-philosophy will have no sense or possibility for the World or effectivity, it will only have this for the subject (of) science or from the point of view of man-as-One; 2) the consideration, but in their order or only as "material," of the structures and norms of validity proper to philosophical decision and to its multiple modes.

Thus it is not a question of intervening *into* philosophy supposed valid or sufficient, in the sense in which one would claim on this basis *to continually add* scientific processes to it, for example, and claim to dismember it, or better yet to abstractly isolate some of these rules and to combine them with other elements in the hopes of again forming *mixtures* in this way, i.e. new modes of decision. The first solution would destroy decision itself; the second would refuse to use science for the benefit of new decisions. This would then still be a "philosophical" chaos. The problem of non-philosophy must be grasped precisely in its scope or its Idea. It is neither a question of transforming philosophy from within its manner of being given, nor merely of varying literary genres or forms, styles and writings. Above all, it is a question of a *lived mutation—for man or the subject—of our relation to philosophy*, and thus of the preliminary suspension of the PSP. Non-philosophy's sense resides elsewhere than in these confusions of disciplines where philosophical authority alone finds its reckoning. Philosophy must be utilized outside itself; but it must be used on the one hand as material, in the incessantly recognized integrity of its operation, and on the other hand, on behalf of a thought which must no longer have anything philosophical about it.

One therefore has the right to work on decision only if one has the *a priori* means of considering it as a whatever material yet preserved in its integrity—this is only possible from the point of view of science or vision-in-One, which imposes *solely a real rather than an effective transformation onto it* but which can use its effectivity toward this end. The pertinence of this project does not surpass that of a transcendental science of vision-in-One. On the basis acquired from their chaos or from their *unilateralizing em-placement,* it is then possible to treat philosophy's possibilities more freely; possible to intervene, so to speak, in the rules of production of a text and not merely in its rules of writing, but by knowing that this intervention signifies in every way a radical beyond of philosophical decision or a wholly other way of thinking. This is a decisive nuance: rather than producing new philosophies at the heart of existing decisions or producing rules of coherence of decision and of its invariants, of new ontological or even Nietzschean varieties, etc., of mixing or coupling Spinoza with Hume, Nietzsche with Husserl, etc., or the Greek logos with the Judaic Other, it is a question of proceeding to an operation more serious than this: *a "manipulation" of decision itself, not only in the optics of science, but also by and for science which alone can legitimize and found it.* One must be oriented toward the idea of a scientific type of manipulation (or founded in vision-in-One) of the rules of the production or of the grammar of philosophical systems. This will neither be an addition or a subtraction of new rules that would respect the form of decision and of the PSP; nor an inscription of philosophy into rhetorical or literary codes with the production of excessively elaborate metaphorical effects; nor an internal deformation of some of its rules; instead, it will be a heteronomous treatment of decision on the basis of rules which are truly inassimilable to it, i.e. of a scientific type: only extreme "dualitary" heterogeneity, rather than "unitary" difference, only the radical reduction of decision can found the right of this transformation and of this usage of the philosophical. It is a question of a "leap" in relation to decision, since the rules of this usage are absolutely foreign to it: these rules do not consist in adding dimensions to those that already define it. Admittedly non-philosophy is the opening of a new space, but *for* philosophy: *from this opening or this radical possible, it becomes possible to acknowledge decision as a particular case of "non-philosophy."* This quasi-space can be described by the ensemble of effects that it produces on decision, for which it represents an enrichment or a complexification but under conditions that can no longer be called internal to decision itself; consequently, it does not exhaust itself in what is nothing but its material.

An example of a possible misinterpretation resides in the term "philo-fiction." Once the PSP is lifted, philosophy is recognized as being an illusion or even a hallucination, at least concerning the real. If philosophy is a hallucination in which man's essence is not involved, then it is legitimate and possible to treat philosophy, *but from this point of view alone*, as a fiction and even to radically aggravate this character. From this point of view alone: because this is neither a hallucination for the One or for science, nor for the World or effectivity. In effect, philosophy in itself is a consistent and systematic thought that cannot be freely modified or led astray; from its own point of view, it is a rational and coherent discourse. Thus the point of view from which it can be considered a hallucination, namely science's point of view, prohibits modifying it intrinsically and also preserves its spontaneous claim. The lifting of the PSP only unleashes the real and does not permit experimentally modifying decision for itself, which is only modifiable within the limits in which it is fixed. These rules of scientific re-writing represent the only possibilities that we have for an *external manipulation of decision*—since every other rule arises from the PSP. They are not *at the same time* external and internal to it, they are merely external to it; but philosophical decision is not simply external to them, for it supposes them as conditions of the last instance of its *reality*. Likewise, the discourse produced in compliance with them is no longer valid or even intelligible for philosophy, i.e. decodable by its criteria and syntaxes. Therefore it cannot be said that these rules of "non-philosophy" modify philosophical decision itself in its effectivity while also allowing it to subsist as philosophical decision, for science and philosophy perhaps do not have the same experience of what is the "same" and of what decision "itself" is. It is a question of a wholly other usage of philosophy, absolutely heterogeneous to its auto-exercise, because science precedes decision in order or by right, i.e. here, in reality. *And science precedes philosophy even when it in fact utilizes philosophical language: the scientific usage of a word* a priori *precedes the philosophical usage of the same word or what philosophy imagines and believes to be the same word.*

The concept of the non-philosophical usage of philosophy must therefore be limited. This means a usage that is formulated from a thought—vision-in-One—such that philosophy no longer has any mastery over it. It is no longer a question of the play of philosophy/literature, philosophy/art, which is always re-interpretable by philosophy or which ultimately still supposes the PSP, but that of a usage of language, and even of the signifier, which is wholly other than philosophical or literary, wholly other than a literary and textual scene of philosophy: *the scientific scene of philosophy*. It implies a certain labor on decision, and it is this labor that is the real content of the Idea of "non-philosophy."

Non-philosophy as "human philosophy"

Chaos and *chôra* of philosophical decisions signify their equivalence and their indifference, the impossibility of choosing among them. But this loss of *interest in* … philosophy, this indifference to metaphysics, is compensated and more than compensated—this is not an economic problem or problem of exchange, but of truth—by a double gain:

1. The opening of a really unlimited field of possibilities of combination not only outside conceptual enclosure, outside rational norms, but even outside decision itself. This is no longer the opening of a closure and what would of itself close thought again. It is not a question of producing *non-philosophical effects in philosophy*, which would still amount to supposing it valid; from the start, it is the establishment of thought in the universal opening as such, *the opening as essence* and not as simple event, attribute or alterity; in the opening which is not manifested by the means of a reversal and of a displacement as essential operations, but which is always already manifested by the One and whose correlate it is.

Whereas deconstructions work out and moderate philosophical critique, but still practice it and claim to know an author better than he knows himself; whereas they practice the gentle war of suspicion, of the "destructive ordeal," of crafty interpretation, the violence of placing-in-structure and sometimes in series; whereas they detect presuppositions, the unthought, the unsaid and turn this critique into the dominant part of their activity, non-philosophy no longer utilizes critique as its main activity. It treats philosophy in the most positive and most actual way possible, undoubtedly as simple material deprived of authority over itself, as sterile chaos, but without resentment or interminable strategy and in the actuality of its accomplished exhibition. If non-philosophy still has a "goal," it is immanent, i.e. to produce non-philosophical possibles with philosophy. It is a question of "extracting" them directly from the material itself, of making this material serve as their production or manifestation. This is a creative task, an activity which is open by definition rather than by accident or supplementarity. Not a suspicious critique of philosophies, not a war of interpretations, but a usage of philosophy as "material," "occasion" or "signalization" for the formation of other utterances which are more free, less coded and above all less illusory or hallucinatory.

2. The radical humanization of thought, which stops being transcendent as a Factum or a World in order to become the

27

correlate of the One, i.e. of man led back to his essence. Passing from Greco-worldly philosophy to "human philosophy" is not an *anthropo-logical* subjectification, but is to make of thought the simple, infinite, unlimited but scientifically founded representation of man's essence as subject (of) science. What is opposed to spontaneous philosophical Appearance, which is apparently *objective* and *unavoidable* and is the seduction and commandeering of man who must identify with it, is the production of a *(non-) philosophical "subjective" Appearance, by and for man, where it is philosophy that has to identify with man rather than the other way around.* Non-philosophy is the authentic, not alienated, concept of "popular philosophy" and of anti-vulgarization. The traditionally highest usage of language, its usage-of-logos, its philosophical pragmatics, is its *exploitation* in accordance with a set of decisions or restrictive *a prioris* that form the capital of the *logos*. A non-philosophical pragmatics lifts this limitation, redistributes the available material according to a rule which is no longer that of economy or rarity, and therefore distributes it to every man. Philosophy can only really become "for all" or "popular" by becoming non-philosophy.

On the one hand, the value of philosophy for man is invalidated—*at least for man's essence.* While philosophy continues to be valid for man to the extent that he is *also* (transcendentally contingent given) in the World, it is invalidated from the point of view of his essence or of the One; it can no longer claim to modify this point of view, as it has always wanted to do by bringing to man the threefold supplement of sense, truth and value. Philosophy can only serve as material for its description, which is still something else entirely, and can no longer claim to modify man's essence. On the other hand, the new rules founded in science as vision-in-One should be sufficiently liberal to allow for heterogeneous usages and not restrictive, such that non-philosophy would not be a solitary practice facing a tradition, as unitary practice is in a sense. The relation of the supposed given Tradition to an individual decision, which must identify with it as an objective philosophical Appearance, must be replaced with another relation: *that of a body of really universal practices and rules to inalienable individuals who are inalienable or conserve their individuality and their humanity only in this practice.*

Philosophy globally changes function and status in relation to man now defined as vision-in-One or subject (of) science. It can no longer serve to think man, i.e. to "transform" him, to "assure" his so-called essence. In reality man lives an interminable auto-en-slavement through philosophy's spontaneous practice. This is the interested folly that wants to transform not only what can be—the World or *effectivity*, philosophy itself—but the *real* which cannot be transformed, i.e. man in so far as he has his essence in the One. It is precisely because man is un-transformable that he can and must transform philosophy and measure it against the real.

One could imagine the positivist caricature or slogan—it can also receive a historicist and dialectical sense—which is in any case a unitary slogan: *philosophy is dead; the science of philosophy can replace it....* Not only is philosophy beyond life and death, two things it says quite a lot about and conjoins in its own way mainly by ignoring them, but also the subject (of) science cannot pose the problem of philosophy's future in this way. Since this subject is man, ordinary man in his most immanent life, what usage can the most immanent life still make of philosophy offered in this way without science having to posit it and without it affecting science in return? Here we have the new problem that ensues from phi-losophy's vision-in-One. This science does not deny philosophy: it only denies the PSP or the hallucination of the real. Decision remains such as it is, for it is not even transformed in itself; it is henceforth simply deprived of its magical power over man and to the same extent better contemplated by him. If there is a tran-scendental reduction, it is here spontaneous and natural, without operations of decision or position. Science bears this reduction down on decision but leaves it intact, ultimately delivering it to man such that he enjoys it on the hither side of any objectifica-tion or decision. Not only does the scientific equivalence of every philosophical decision deliver it from the hatred of the others and from the guilt it inspires in them, this equivalence also delivers decisions to man in the absolute respect of their claims and their follies, albeit rendered inefficacious. It has sufficed for the unap-parent gesture of science to be revealed (to) self, i.e. (to) man as (to) its subject in vision-in-One, in order for philosophy to fall back completely into *chaos* or *chôra*, to be "dismantled" and of-fered outside any indiscreet auto-exposition. When philosophy is thus ex-posed by and in the One, unleashed from its archaic claims on the real which are tied to its nature of decision and position, it stops expositing itself as a universal continuum of the thought *of the* real. Man as subject (of) science is no longer this philosopher spectator who exposits, decides and positions him-self in logos-games and in *objective philosophical Appearance* as decision's auto-exposition. If man wants a community, it is no longer on the basis of this Appearance that he will find it.

This indifference that the subject (of) science imposes on philosophy is positive and foundational for new relations to it. United by a scientific practice and constrained to renounce spontaneous philosophical war, a community of researchers can still consecrate its efforts to this object and, around it, can invent other usages, other emotions, other games, produce other possibles that would not be programmed by the Greek opening and the unitary practice that it supposes.

Practical and collective perspectives of non-philosophy

Within this introduction and this book, which strives to clarify non-philosophy, it is a matter of dealing with the non-philosophical principle, of its foundation, of its non-unitary sense and of its rules and procedures. At the moment, what is left out is its impact on the practical conditions of thought that it insists on renewing. However, a quick inventory gives an idea of the subversions that will inevitably be introduced into the practice of thought. For example:

1. The individual and collective conditions of the production of non-philosophical texts: it becomes impossible to maintain the respective roles of the creator of the system and that of the interpreter, critical mediator or consumer of texts. All these roles will necessarily be scrambled on the following basis: *if non-philosophy must be made "by" and thus "for" all men, and not solely "by" the philosopher for other men, then the "human" reception of non-philosophy is the* a priori *that governs its production rather than the other way around.* This principle is obviously not possible without philosophical contradiction unless non-philosophy is founded on the restitution of man's real essence. Man, as One, is then the radical subject (of) non-philosophy, completely on the hither side of decision, which goes from "vulgar" man *to* the philosopher, and on the hither side of the philosopher's position as paradigm of the human.

2. The conditions of the writing of non-philosophy: it is impossible, even here, to maintain the old universal *genres* of the philosophical style (system, work, doctrine) and of its writings (dialogue, essay, treatise). Generally, on the hither side of a linearity in philosophical discourse, there is, as we said, a sort of

profound narrative (in all philosophers—here as well, not simply in Hegel ...) which is founded upon the reference to a *supposed* real; a factuality and a representativity that are not eradicated but are fortified by the "post-modern" style; and which only a mutation of philosophy's overall function can ultimately eliminate and whose exercise of thought it alone can unleash. It is the ensemble of the relations of philosophy to art, to literature, to the novel and to poetry, the ensemble of these restricted *decisions* and these "economic" shares which should give way to what we call the *universal non-philosophical Appearance*. It seems that, rather than a total thought which would again claim to synthesize every experience or simply to make them intercede diagonally, non-philosophy is situated at the only point of reality capable of joining without decision or contradiction the effects of philo-fiction, poetry-fiction, religion-fiction, science-fiction, etc.—on condition of understanding that these fictional aspects, far from simply extending philosophy, poetry, etc. in imaginary forms, are instead the image of themselves that the wholly-other which non-philosophy is gives upon the mirror of philosophy, of poetry, etc.

Let us repeat once again that because of its Greco-spontaneous usage of thought, philosophy, which continues its desire to govern the real, man and science, finds itself lagging behind the arts and sciences. Despite its serialist and deconstructionist revolutions, perhaps it has simply passed by the only mutations that could prevent it from sinking into what it has become: a conservative and repetitive activity deprived of imagination, the supercilious guardian of a tradition of which it would like to make us believe that it has "decided" once and for all upon the essence of thought and of man: an exploitation—in every sense of the word—of thought.

Chapter I: Of vision-in-One

From the One's figures to the One's essence

There are a countless number of philosophers who speak of the One. As for the others, if they do not speak of it or merely evoke it surreptitiously, they necessarily think it without always knowing it. They all design their turbines and their flows or deposit their sediment on this continuous current of the One. They make heard the voice of Being or even suspend it on the grounds of this murmur that precedes and accompanies it. Among those formed by thinkers, two communities are particularly attached to the One, seemingly distinguishing it from Being and distinguishing themselves in this way: the cohort of neo-Platonists from ancient times, and now a school of psychoanalysts skilled in the most esoteric of thoughts. It could be that the One, more so than Being, by nature constitutes a school. Yet it would be necessary to know what it is by itself. The guiding idea of "vision-in-One" is that, because they have refused from the start to shed light upon the One's essence, neither philosophers nor analysts know what this essence is, and that they can only do this so as to make it enter into assemblages with Being or even, most recently, into arrangements with the Unconscious which replaces Being. It does not suffice to consecrate to Being an overly serious discourse suffused with gravity, if only to continue the old nonsense concerning the One; nor does it suffice to support Being as the cornerstone for systems, if only to abandon it to the subaltern functions of synthesis or totalization. The forgetting of the One is the condition for the thought of Being, but also for the thought of the forgetting of Being. More important than the "One" of which one speaks, there is its specific essence that always distinguishes it from Being and whose elucidation alone can deliver it from the aporetic situation in which the Greeks have left and abandoned it. "Vision-in-One" is the experience that is no longer solely a functional concept to which philosophy could lay claim at will for its works of synthesis or of the coupling of contraries, but has a positive phenomenal content and forms a veritable "internal world" by itself: this world or quasi-transcendental field has not begun to be explored for itself except by extremely rare thinkers who do not in any way belong to the "great" ontological tradition or who have been marginalized by it. Vision-in-One is neither another philosophy properly speaking nor a vision-of-the-World, which is nothing but a philosophical *intuition* of the World: it is, quite precisely, vision of the One in the One and therefore vision of the World and of Philosophy in the One. Vision-in-One is the experience that the One is the absolutely sufficient element of thought and that there is no need to seek "Being," "ontology" or even the "forgetting of Being" so as to think in a positive, radical and coherent way; that there is no need to assemble the One with Being in infinite aporias and topologies so as to give the One a reality which it instead takes from itself; that it does not suffice to think "about" the One or even to use it if not to really manifest and describe its essence, to do justice to its specificity and not to conflate it with the figures of Being and of the World, which are still external. Against the One which philosophers and now analysts sometimes inconsiderately utilize and against the One's subjection toward ends which are not its own and which make it function with other pieces in the philosophical machine, *vision-in-One* is opposed in three ways: as a thought of the *essence* of the One; as a thought that defines this essence independent of the One's philosophical usages; and lastly as a thought founded in this essence and which thinks, "on the basis" of the One, the new relations or the new order that ensues (for philosophy and for Being) from the restitution of the One's real essence. Vision-in-One is the experience of thought that once and for all remains in the One without experiencing the need or claim to escape from the One or indeed the duty to accede to it, even when it endeavors to regard the World, Being, Philosophy and History "for themselves." In other words, in relation to the traditional philosophical vision of the One as a transcendent, estranged, albeit functional reality, vision-in-One instead presents

34

itself as a vision of philosophy from the One and "in" it, where philosophy is now what appears far off and slightly unreal.

Far from having to be accepted as a new dogma or a new decision stemming from the philosophical will, vision-in-One obviously must demonstrate both its plasticity via the particular usage of language that describes it and that it makes possible, and its liberating power with regard to philosophical norms and closures by its practice of opening up to radical possibles. Texts that describe the One—by commencing through it—are merely some of the One's infinite facets. This includes several of its descriptions, which are possible in an unlimited way, as well as what one can see of language and philosophy in it. The description of vision-in-One is already "non-philosophical" and must be accepted as such. Thus we should exposit the conditions of possibility of a pure thought of the One independent of its entanglement with Being; the possibility of the formulations or descriptions given to it, that of a new usage of language in accordance with the nothing-but-One; ultimately and consequently, we shall have to unmask the sense and the origin of philosophical objections and of the "resistance" that they manifest. In particular, the task brings us back to showing how vision-in-One is not a mystical identification. Beforehand, a finished or completed description of it will not be given—this does not exist—but the matrices of a certain number of the One's possible descriptions, here carried out naively and partially, thus reserving the question of their possibility and only exhibiting it after these descriptions. In other words, from the beginning these descriptions in a certain way will have to appear to philosophers as impossible tasks or wagers that are contradictory in their very language. However, before explicitly posing the problem of their internal possibility, it will be suggested that a description that is unlimited in principle and by right (which is impossible to stop or determine and is at first open like that of the One) must not be confused with a description that is assumed by philosophy to be at least partially stopped or completed, and thus in this way made to become contradictory. We are attempting to lead philosophers, rather than to renounce philosophy, to break through the ultimate barriers of philosophical imagery and even the speculative Imagination and to be provided with the means to think the unthinkable as unthinkable finally without contradiction, to describe what is speculatively indescribable without paradox. We are attempting to pass from the One's transcendent figures to its essence.

These descriptions of the One have a precise "goal": they must finally assure the One's radical autonomy in relation to Being, its merely transcendental nature which is not *also a priori*, only its reality and not its possibility as well; to deliver it so to speak from the constraints of the mixture that it forms in philosophy with Being or Duality. Vision-in-One is the minimal and the radical of every thought. It demonstrates that the mixture state is not an *addition* of reality, but a *subtraction*. Adding a second principle to the One, philosophy does not enrich the latter but impoverishes it and itself. The richest thought is not what requires 2/3 simultaneous principles so as to think the One (the Dyad *and* the One), but what is the poorest or only needs 1/2 principles (the One *then* the contingent Dyad) in order to be as real as a thought can hope to be. Thus, the One must stop being simply commandeered to functional ends which are determined outside it and which deprive it of reality, then attributed to the mixture, i.e. to a process or an operation that does not itself have reality, but which must suppose the infinity of time so as to *realize itself* and which, "meanwhile," has already fallen into nothingness and unreality. Philosophical decision, and the One when it is nothing but a simple piece of the latter, is a machine (which is certainly transcendental) that "runs" to the infinite or the unlimited—supposed given in excess of the One's finitude—: this is the weakness of its apparent richness.

In order for the One (then the Dyad in its mode, which philosophical decision itself can become) to have reality or be the absolute, it is necessary for it, without returning to substance, to no longer simply be functional but first of all real; its reality or its absolute autonomy must be exhibited as containing a special structure through which it refers (to) self immediately; it still must be more inherent (to) self than the Idea is to thought; it must be constituted by a knowledge (of) self that has never passed through the World; by an immanence that enjoys (of) self and solely (of) self without surpassing itself, breaching itself, transcending itself; that it be completely "internal" (to) self without consequently being a transcendence turned around and which would consequently change nothing of the prejudices of philosophy; that it be self-*jouissance* without any relation to itself or any disjunction; that the real be an experience that precedes every decision. *There has never been a decision of manifestation; there is the already-Manifest before any external, dual or dyadic operation of manifestation: this is the immanent state of affairs to be described.* No operation could ever produce the manifest if the latter did not fully exist from the start. The Manifest is the absolute requirement of manifestation; it must be accepted that it precedes manifestation and that it is, as One, already manifest before any "philosophical aid to manifestation." Man does not have to assist the One—as philosophy believes—for it is the One that assists Philosophy and the World.

Possible matrices of description of the One's essence

By its real and no longer simply functional, technological or possible essence:

1. The One is an Identity that is not solely deprived of scission or unaccompanied by a division which would "re-give" it each time, but that positively has no need of such an operation associated with division. Scission is the practical moment of philosophical decision and is conceived as an *aid to the One*, a technological aid to Indivision, and, reciprocally, Indivision is an aid to division, Identity an aid to difference. If the One no longer requires scission nor to be re-given or manifested, this is because it is already manifest or given fully or completely without the help of this supplement, but directly and as though by itself. Not within the interior—*supposed* already given—of itself, but instead forming a given (transcendental, non-psychological) interiority by this manifestation itself, to the extent that nothing—above all nothing outside itself—comes to interrupt and restart it, to extinguish it and render it possible. The One is necessarily the *already-given*, it is not the *supposed-given* as is every given inscribed in the sphere of transcendence.

2. The One is of the order of an auto-affection, of an auto-reception, more precisely of an *auto-impression*, a term which, without yet totally excluding distance, transcendence or the received offer, more faithfully describes its immediacy (to) self. It describes impression as constituting the One's reality, then the reality of every eventual form of transcendent subject, instead of it already supposing this transcendent form that would come to be superimposed upon itself and "make" an impression upon itself. There is impression, and it is the One. It is not alienated from or external to itself, it is what (is) imprinted as self, it is One by and as this (auto-)impression, which is nothing but an impression and the minimum impression required for there to be a given "interiority" and not merely a supposed identity. In the same sense that

Identity did not need scission as its other side, originary transcendental impression does not need an accompanying expression. This is an impression without anything (anticipatory) that is impressed, it is the most radical lived experience from the start, the lived (of) lived experience [*le vécu (du) vécu*][3] or what makes a lived experience possess an inalienable immanent being. Rather than an originary impression, the One is instead the *already-impressed*, it is not the *supposed-impressed* of every false immediacy grasped by transcendence.

3. The One is an "embrace" supposed by every "unity" with itself. Eternal embrace with neither past nor future, neither origin nor destination, and which has nothing, no manifold, to embrace. The One has always-already overcome separation when the latter manifests itself, or instead the One is what necessarily has had nothing to do with separation in that which overcomes separation. The One is *jouissance* (of) self where the enjoying has no object, or no object besides itself. Enjoying which is transcendental or immanent, rather than psychological and intentional, this is Enjoying as radical of subjectivity. Here still, in the domain of the real, there is no, nor has there ever been, a distinction between a matter and a form, a subjective and an objective—no articulation, but empiricism (of the) Radical. Rather than a pre-given subject that would then be embraced, the embrace itself, prior to any external synthesis, constitutes the real kernel of the One's subjectivity, its only possible humanity. Rather than the embrace, the One is instead the *already-embraced*, it is not the *supposed-embraced* of every synthesis grasped by transcendence.

4. The One is a *non-thetic* Identity in general, i.e. simultaneously non-decisional (of) self and non-positional (of) self: with neither will for essence nor topology for existence; with neither combat for its motor nor space or figure for its manifestation. Given primitively with itself, as itself, by itself: it exists in the mode of the *as such* or the *how*, yet such that these no longer express an activity or a practice having *become* immanent or internalized but are presupposed by this activity or practice. An integral identity, internal-without-internalization, the One is the transcendental minimum, the minimal petition of reality, i.e. the reality that every petition in general supposes. It is given from itself without being *acquired* or even "originarily acquired" with the

---

3 The usage of "le vécu" is the French translation of the German word "Erlebnis," usually translated as "lived experience" in its distinction from "experience" (Erfahrung). The past participle form of "vécu" literally means "lived." [TN]

aid of a scission or a repeated operation of manifestation. It is the already-acquired before any acquisition; it is not the *supposed-acquired* of the forms of *a priori* knowledge selected from transcendence. Neither process nor result of a process, but that which they have both already supposed so as to be what they simply are for man, i.e. *as* man or as humans "in the last instance," which is how it will be formulated.

5. The One is an identity already inherent (to) self the moment that philosophy tries to breach it. Its essence is not an active inherence; it is not carried out by an external technological agent, not even by itself. It is an inherence without dis-herence, more internal (to) self than the inherence of an idea or of an essence to reason or to thought's ego, that makes it be what it is. Once again: to stop imagining or tracing the One's essence on the basis of its transcendent figures or usages as supposed given forms of unity to which their modes would be "inherent," i.e. still transcendent. The description of an abstract or non-figurative experience of the One excludes, among other things, its inherence (to) self, the transcendent model of inherence, for example the categorical model of the analytic or synthetic inherence of accidents or modes to substance, or of parts to the whole—the external and unreal category of "substantiality." On the other hand, a rigorous, not vicious, transcendental deduction of the category of substance requires that the One's inherence (to) self already be real, i.e. real before being realized and given as such. The One is the *already-inherent* before any substantialist forcing of inherence, it conditions the *supposed-inherent* which is that of analytic, synthetic or even differential identity.

6. The One is a nothing-but-singular Identity, rather than mixed or singular-and-universal, a singularity without conjoint universality (attribute or aprioritic dyad). Rather than an abstract moment of a totality, it is absolutely concrete and accomplished, to the point that it is not even a part—unless it exists before the Whole; not a moment—unless it exists before the process; nor a point in the set—unless it exists before any aggregate. Whereas philosophy, for example, commences in the couplings that substance, essence and attribute (Spinoza) produce, couplings that are the ingredient of the real but in the sense that its substance, essence and attribute are simultaneously distinct and inseparable, a thought of the One intrinsically or of itself is limited to "substance" alone—to its sufficient interiority. This would be a substance, if one can still call it that, whose essence no longer requires

an attribute or a universal so as to be re-given or expressed, but which is sufficiently real as (auto)-reference or rather as (auto)-impression. Here "substance" is essence (of) self and thus of the attribute, but the attribute is no longer the essence of substance or aid to substance in the expression of its essence. This undivided transcendental experience of Indivision itself will be called individual [*individu*]. And one will speak of the *undivided-dual* structures [*structures individuales*] of the One and vision-in-One so as to distinguish them from the individual [*l'individuel*],[4] which remains transcendent and selected from a mixture supposed more concrete than it. The One is the *already-undivided* rather than the *supposed-undivided* like the transcendent Unity of philosophies.

7. The One is an absolute or intrinsic finitude. Finitude resides in the One's powerlessness to operate on itself so as to auto-constitute itself (it is itself and manifested as such before any constitution) or even to leave itself and alienate itself, to separate itself from itself and, for example, to identify itself with the World or Philosophy. This completely positive powerlessness of the real (over) self—and *a fortiori* of the transcendence of the World and of Philosophy over it—is due to internal reasons, since it is not an external powerlessness. It is strictly and exactly the same thing as immanence-without-distance or as being-undivided. Because we, radical Individuals as One, are obliged to see all things in One, this necessity is our very finitude, the impossibility of abandoning our precedence over the World and of leaving ourselves so as to go along-with-the-World, in-the-midst-of … being, along with an objective noema. This is the same thing as our positive powerlessness to turn back, to survey the plane of experience and to make ourselves contemporary with it; our powerlessness to transcend beyond being and follow the lines of perception or inscription that the attributes form on the surface of the World; it is the same thing as the constraint in which we are to see all things—universals, totalities and envelopments included—in the state of inert or sterile "material," or in the state of manifolds or singularities which are in turn incapable of transcending. This finitude thus delivers us from the operation of transcendence as an inert or unsurpassable point and from the philosophical decision as

---

4 "L'individu" is a noun that is equivalent with "the individual" (as noun) in English. "L'individuel" is functioning as a substantive noun here as well, but the word "individuel" in French is the adjectival form which also corresponds with the English word "individual" as an adjective. The word "individual" in French is a neologism of Laruelle's, and it has been translated here as "undivided-dual" in order to emphasize the meaning of "indivis" (undivided) and that of the "dual," which will be elaborated later on in this work. [TN]

incapable of relaunch, of dispatch, of destination, etc. The One is the *already-finite* rather than the *supposed-finite* which metaphysics ascribes to a subject that remains transcendent and limited by transcendence.

8. The One is a real, i.e. passive Identity, where passivity is not defined in relation to an activity or agent, whether external or internal—the One will never be *causa sui* like substance—but "in relation" (to) self, since auto-impression constitutes the self and more than self: the lived Identity which is that (of) lived experience. Nothing but passivity through and through, without any counterpart or activity: its essence is exhausted in the lived experience of receiving (itself), of already-being-received before any operation of reception, of already-being-passive before the activity of rendering passive. Being-One is to be already passive at the moment of "passivation." The One described in this way is no longer of the order of a *decision*, since it no longer contains transcendence, but of the order of a *proof-experience.*[5] It is necessary to distinguish, without any residual mixture, the style of *experience* (in the pure or rigorous sense) from the style of *decision,* and no longer to believe spontaneously that the real has the form of a decision or operation. The real has the form of an unavoidable experience (due to its intrinsic finitude) rather than that of an unavoidable decision (which is only due to Totality). The One is the *already-passive* rather than the *supposed-passive,* which is that of every event in the World.

9. The One is an Identity which is conflated with its depth, its consistency, its flesh, its immediate (auto-)impression, and which therefore is not requisitioned as *limit* of an operation of extraction, of analysis, of transcendence, as simple *surface* of inscription; as *plane* or plateau of nomadism; as *screen* or *mirror* for a reflection; as *film* infinitely developing, etc.—here one recognizes the externalized avatars of the old universal substance or of philosophical decision put to the test of the Other. The One is not a film or an ultra-flat surface without thickness devoted to the subaltern functions of a tearproof envelope. Instead, the One forces us to suspend this topology and this speculative imagery. It is a (transcendental) body and a *full body,* but forever undivided. It is therefore not expressed in a surface or an attribute. Since it is a

---

5   French "épreuve." This word is generally translated as "ordeal" in this text, but it can mean "trial" or "test" (both in a scientific sense) depending on the context. It should be noted that it corresponds with the German "Prüfung," which is not merely a "proof" [preuve] but the series of procedures through which a proof can be said to arise. Here it is translated as "proof-experience" in order to distinguish it from "decision." [TN]

radically finite body that does not need to be developed toward the World or in the form of an exteriority and of a field of inscription for something else, the One is neither just another universal line among others, nor even their plane of coherence, but the immanent body *within* which we see and assemble the universal lines or aprioritic dimensions of the World. It is the interior thickness, which is itself not dimensional, through which we take enjoyment (from) every dimension. However, the One is not thought-of-the-Inside in opposition to thought-of-the-Outside: in it we see the One's essence and the essence of the lines or of the attributes.

10. The One is a postural rather than decisional and positional identity. Here one must distinguish between the postural and the positional. The postural designates a holding not of self, but *in* self, the *how* this holding (is) held insofar as it has essentially never reposed except in itself. Posture is more subjective, corporeal and undivided than position; more internal, spontaneous and naive than will and decision. Posture is too immanent and completed, it indivisibly involves the individual's entire being too much to reinstate a decision or make it equal to a "position," which is always relative to another position, always alienable and revocable, always to be taken up and taken back up. Hence one can describe the mode of thinking that "corresponds" with the One as nothing-but-One, as a postural and subjective experience of thought from the outset freed from the constraints of the World, from the codes of philosophy, from the norms of transcendent exteriority, from the rules of speculative figuration or the speculative imagination. In other words, it is necessary to distinguish the *figurative*, but also the *figural*, *relational* and *positional*, from the *postural*, but as the necessary kernel of reality that precedes them absolutely and instead constrains them to be distinguished from it as mediated by unreality.

These are some of the possible descriptive *models* of the One. Before examining the "logic" proper to these models and their conditions of theoretical validity, several interconnected remarks will be made concerning the One thus described.

As an unreflected experience—non-decisional and non-positional (of) self—the One is a completely singular immanence. It obviously has no equivalent in the forms of immanence that are always more or less figured and idealized, transcendent or supposed, i.e. those which philosophy as a unitary thought has elaborated. It is given (to) itself without alienation; it is a lived experience (of) self that is precisely experienced in its own mode, the

42

specific mode of the One. It is indeed necessary—without it, there wouldn't be anything, if not any reality in general, and above all no philosophical reality or reality of philosophy—that the One be experienced in its own mode and in it rather than, as unitary thought always wants, in the mode of something else: of Being, i.e. of transcendence (break, scission, distance, nothingness, etc…—decision) or even that of the Other. These are deconstructions, insofar as they give up elucidating the One's essence, that postulate without any proof that the One is given in the mode of the Other and, in every way, with the Other.

Thus the One is not "transcendental Unity": it is as transcendental as a lived experience (which is merely immanent) can be, but it has no specific essence of Unity, which is always a blend of immanence and transcendence. This is not the One such that it prolongs and overcomes Being (the scission, for example, between Intelligence and the Intelligible). It is undivided (dual) through and through; it is not founded in a universal, a law, a rule, an *a priori*, upon any transcendent support whatsoever or a Dyad with the goal of "arriving" at itself—all of this will be reduced to the state of simple "occasion." It is ontologically indeterminable but already self-determined. The real is the determining or individuating instance; it precedes all forms of universality and *determines them immediately without passing through their mediation* because it is already intrinsically determined sufficiently by itself.

It is indeed a question of a *real* rather than ideal immanence, but, to be more precise, this is not at all the reality of a *res*.[6] The One reconciles within itself both the real—insofar as it is distinguished from effectivity (the latter's principle is the mixture, the blend of the real and of the possible)—and truth in its essence: *veritas transcendentalis*. "Transcendental realism" so to speak, but not what the idealism of the same name has always fought against by confusing it, through a necessary abuse, with a mixed realism, simultaneously transcendent and transcendental.

The One thus conceived, or experienced rather, is what must be called the real or the Absolute: the only ultimate experience that we can have of the Absolute. It is indeed here a case of saying that the Absolute is "alongside us."[7] Truly speaking, this

6 The Latin word *res* ("thing") is the etymological basis for the word "real," which derives from Latin *realis* ("actual," "of or relating to things"). Here Laruelle is evoking the etymological roots of 'real' and 'res' so as to dissociate them, at least insofar as "(the) real" is elaborated in a non-philosophical (non-empirical, non-phenomenological, non-objectifiable) sense. [TN]

7 See G.W.F. Hegel, *Phenomenology of Spirit* (Oxford, Oxford University Press, 1977), 47. "… das Absolute ist an und für sich schon bei uns." [TN]

Hegelian formula is still deficient: it is not "alongside" us, simultaneously near and far, for it is instead an "immediate given" in the definitive sense of the term—we prefer to say: a "postural" given, what we are intrinsically in our essence. *This is the givenness, but now itself immediate in turn, of the immediate*—something wholly other than the immediate abstracted from the "commencement," filmed and looked over by the dialectic. It is the *already-immediate* before any *supposed-immediate* and its necessary mediation. This is prescribed by its unreflected essence, which distinguishes it in the most irreversible way both from a structure of consciousness *of* self and from a presence *to* self, from the *cogito* and from being; which also distinguishes it from the various contemporary forms of the "Simple," which are not as simple as the One because they merely have the simplicity of "Difference" and because they have had to overcome the Dyad.

Is it a question of a return to "logocentrism?" Logocentrism—supposing that it exists but only for its deconstruction—has by definition never been able to conceive an immanence as rigorous, minimal and poor as it. The "deconstructive" conception and practice of language completely devote it to Being and to the Other together, but they prohibit its adequate posture for thinking the One. Logocentrism and deconstruction have always understood One as presence *to* self, which is the operation of mixture and therefore contains duality or transcendence—or even Indivision which is given in the mode of the Other. The metaphysical One can be deconstructed, but not the nothing-but-One which no longer falls into logocentrism and which is instead the real condition of deconstruction. If the totalizing One is bound to a philosophical decision, vision-in-One no longer is. And deconstructions, including any metaphysics whatsoever, are the active forgetting of the One's essence.

This proof-experience of the One implies several consequences: 1. the real in the immanent and rigorous sense, distinct from the mixtures of effectivity, is self-determined and does not form a process co-produced by philosophy; 2. the real is completely and thoroughly determined; 3. philosophy does not have to identify itself with the real so as to determine it and to be determined; 4. philosophy itself is only sufficiently determined by the real; therefore it will no longer be an under/overdetermined process, but absolutely determined—what we call a "non-philosophy." All these formulas describe the *kernel of phenomenal truth* which is that of an old Marxist thesis on the real—aka "matter"—an anti-dialectical and above all anti-metaphysical thesis, but whose real sense Marxism did not know how to elaborate or transcendentally found because it had, due to a residual Hegelian obsession, founded it on matter, i.e. on a transcendent concept of the immanence that constitutes the real.

Contingency of language:
the suspension of the unitary postulate

Thus there are multiple possible descriptions of the One. Their plurality permits the struggle against the great unitary danger, that of hastiness or the objectivist complaint: "but then what is the One? Wasn't it dealt with definitively by Plotinus and several others?" Hence one imagines a sort of supplementary object on high in the World or in accordance with the World and arbitrarily supposed given as fact; an entity transcendent to the neighborhood of Being, the Other, the Soul or the "grand genres." But then one is thinking about philosophy's One and—for good measure—it is still projected a little too high and a little too far. This fetishist habit can and must be globally abandoned. This does not mean that the One is therefore ineffable—this is the problem's unitary position—but that its description, which is completely possible, is indifferent for it or does not itself constitute it. In describing the One, it is a question for us of struggling against this "worldly" hastiness and this obsession with transcendence, against this operation of abstraction that expresses philosophical resistance to the encounter of the One. This is the first rule for dismantling the unitary drive: these descriptions must be multiplied and diversified in accordance with the thematics, whether *philosophical or otherwise*, that are available and chosen as material—rather than as means or procedure—of description. A second rule concerns the usage of these thematics or models: it prescribes to summon them, let's say provisionally, "against" themselves and in view of making them describe the One's autonomy, self-consistency and indifference to philosophy itself.

We will come back to these rules, above all the second one. They respond to two fundamental requirements, which are requirements of invariance. The first stipulates that the One must be described by one material or another, on this specific "occasion" or another—but as autonomous, as an Identity that reposes in itself, as that which has no need of a transcendence, a manifold, a scission, etc. *There is no privileged description, since what is essential is this invariance which* a priori *structures the material utilized.* For the remainder, if a multiplicity of descriptions is *de jure* possible, it is because these descriptions of the One, and language in general, are contingent in relation to the One, not constitutive of its essence. This is precisely the second invariant requirement to be considered for whichever material utilized for description: *the absolute, unreflected precedence of the One or of the real over its description,* and the "subordination"—according to a certain determined order—of the description to its "object." *These two correlative requirements express the coherence proper to the thought of the One, the only coherence on which it must be judged, rather than on philosophy's abstract objections.* In all the descriptions already given, the essential was not the content of the local representation of these descriptions but their invariant rule. This does not mean that the One does not exist or that only a matrix of formal rules exist. On the contrary: the One-real "exists" such that its description and it alone is contingent or would not exist save through these *a priori* rules of invariance. On the other hand, the One "exists" as that which can only be real and which is presupposed by everything that is merely *supposed*—by Being, by the Whole and by the World. For example, it will be said that it is experience or affect, posture, inherence (to) self, lived experience non-decisional (of) self, etc. But what will be described in the last instance by these multiple languages—none of which should be privileged—will no longer itself be an effect of language (or of metaphor).

Hence the necessity of an ongoing rectification of these descriptions. For example, one can be tempted to describe the One instead, or simply, in an already unitary way as lived experience, affect, life, etc. But then one risks reducing it to this language, to the transcendent philosophical experience of the lived and affectivity; this is again to conflate the One with language and to fall back into the old philosophical amphibologies. This description is not false in itself, it becomes so *if it is not pursued and rectified incessantly* under the pressure and function of this specific matrix of the One. Furthermore, this coherence is no longer that of a system (the reciprocity of the object and its discourse), it is that of the One and of its non-relation to language upon which it imposes a radical contingency by depriving it of every constitutive capacity. No longer unitary or systematic, but dual or dualitary, this coherence implies that all language must always be in second position or unilateralized in relation to the One. Taken as our immanent guiding thread, this is a rule that works the descriptions from the inside and particularly requires their constant recasting. Philosophical objections arise because language is autofetishized and autofactualized spontaneously. Philosophy reposes in this auto-factualization which it never notices, reposes in its *supposed real* auto-reflection. Thus it cannot relate language to the One and practice it in accordance with these invariances or with this coherence that is a coherence of what we shall soon call "Determination in the last instance."

There will be a hesitancy in saying that all language betrays the One, because language would always manipulate couples of opposites and would be the nourishing element of unitary dualities. That kind of thought postulates that language is a specular reflection of the One and that it has the same structure as it (cf. the argument of the *Tractatus Logico-Philosophicus*) or is isomorphic with it. This is the postulate of ontology and negative theology and is above all a supplementary and useless presupposition: language can describe the One, which does not at all have the same structure as it, without exactly reflecting or reproducing it. It will be said that language is *a non-thetic Reflection (of the) real, a non-specular or mirrorless reflection, or a description "in the last instance alone" of the One.* Language does not betray the One, it can never betray the One because they do not share an origin and because it is found in the World—but in a sense, language always represses the One, simultaneously because it presupposes the One and because it does not belong to the One in a constitutive way. On the other hand, a description must not be determined but indefinitely rectified, for the preceding descriptions are already ongoing processes of language's rectification or of what it spontaneously conveys, the unitary couples of opposites. It can be admitted that no term or attribute is "suitable" for the One or does not describe it *adequately* (in the mode of a non-thetic Reflection) if it is not at least accompanied by the suspension of its virtual opposite, a suspension which must also be thought as positive rather than as opposed to what it suspends. But that means that if one rectifies the description in accordance with the rules imposed by the One, then it can adequately be described.

Perhaps, from another angle, one will try to generalize the philosophical objection in the form of an alternative and say that the One alone, the nothing-but-One, is either unthinkable and ineffable, or in every way requires language so as to describe it (not to mention philosophy ...), a language which must be "contemporary" with it in a "Same" that envelops it with the One. There is no doubt: language is necessary. But what we mean by the nothing-but-One is this: language is necessary for the One's description and *if* one proposes to describe it; on the other hand, it is not necessary for the One itself or for its intimate constitution. Philosophy precisely conflates—in approximation with several nuances or differences—the object and the thought of the object, the real and the knowledge of the real, the real's essence and the description of this essence, the description—and it alone—being in need of language. Philosophy conflates—this is its amphibology par excellence—the real and language in the mixture of the *logos*. On the contrary, for what is here called vision-in-One, language's necessity is conditional (in the case of the description or "science" of the One), and language is itself contingent. The amphibology is dissolved dually or in a static duality and without scission; it is aligned with the project of a science or a description of the One, but the science of the One is contingent in relation to the One itself. This is the suspension or the radical reduction of the *logos* itself: language has no other function but description, it no longer has a constitutive function; the description of the real, i.e. the thought of the One as non-philosophy, is contingent in relation to it; indeed it has its essence in it but only in the last instance. Vision-in-One is therefore the thought that states that language, philosophy and even non-philosophy do not determine the One's reality, but that the One affects them with an absolute transcendental contingency, that they are not necessary for the essence of the One, i.e. (although this will not be taken up yet) of man.

Philosophy, including all the deconstructions (Heidegger, Wittgenstein, Derrida), have never been able to accept this radical contingency of language for the real. Philosophical decision, or Being in the most differentiated and least substantialist sense, is merely the same as the arbitrary yet unthought presupposition of language's co-belonging not merely to the description of the One, but to its essence or intimate constitution. Vision-in-One definitively plunges language and philosophy into the depths of what we call a *chôra* and then treats them as simple transcendent given. Non-philosophy exists at this price: there will be no radical opening of thought, save through the complete sacrifice of the Greco-philosophical horizon. The abandonment of the oldest philosophical or unitary postulate—clandestinely present in classical metaphysics, but whose thematization as such will have constituted the obsession of 20th century philosophy, namely the presupposition that language is co-determining or co-constituting of the real—can and must be carried out in order for thought to be unleashed from its philosophical or unitary confinement. Philosophy can continue—for example, it could be said it will continue in the way that Euclidean geometry continues and remains valid within certain limits now determined from the standpoint of non-Euclidean forms. It will specifically continue only within the limits of this presupposition which posits that language is constitutive of the real, and which is henceforth nothing more than a unitary postulate unnecessary for thought and whose contingency is now evident.

More generally, what matters is not the way in which philosophy will automatically represent the One of which one speaks. Philosophy will necessarily represent the One as abstracted out of the mixture of Being where it is, for philosophy, normally included, and philosophy will believe that we are attempting a hostile takeover. This would be a falsification of the One's essence, and this is its own affair. In reality, the "One itself" has never been abstracted from philosophy, it is instead that from which an order is determined that unilateralizes every duality or eventual Dyad. The latter represents the possibility of "speaking" about the One and "describing" it, but the Dyad is contingent and now comes *after* the One irreversibly. It is no longer blended with the One in a mixture which would be that of philosophical decision. Duality is second as well as contingent and is founded in the One which only dispatches to itself: if its description is made, this will not affect the One's essence. The knowledge (of) the One includes or postulates that its object absolutely precedes it and does not depend upon it; for immanent reasons, this knowledge rigorously "submits" to its object without claiming to totally or partially constitute it.

Against the falsifying and abstract objections stemming from philosophy and its resistance, a single argument, a single rule can thus be valid: that of the "theoretical" coherence of the relations between the One-real and language, i.e. the *Determination in the last instance*. Everything must change simultaneously in relation to philosophy: if the One in question is no longer what philosophy has always known, if the One's content or essence is different, then philosophy's relation to language must change, along with the very conception of language that is formulated by a pragmatics. It is no longer our philosophical and transcendent practice of language that modifies the One's nature, it is the One as immanent transcendental experience that implies another conception and another practice of language, i.e. of philosophy. Because the One is not philoso-phizable, it imposes a new practice of philosophy. The grand rule is this: *the One is the ensemble of the One's effects*. Even more rigor-ously: the One is the One, and *more so* the One's effects (upon language, philosophy, etc.).

Three specifications concerning the preceding should be added:

1. Even though the "non-philosophical" descriptions of the One are structured by rules which are imposed by vision-in-One, this does not at all mean that these rules are a structure that is mu-tually shared by language and the real to be described, a structure in which the former and the latter would again reciprocally deter-mine one another philosophically. On the one hand, this body of rules *ensues* from the One in which it has its essence, on the "occa-sion'"—this concept will be taken up later—of language, and does not reflexively constitute the essence of language but is imposed upon it as what prescribes its reduction to the state of simple ma-terial or language-of-description and as what determines it in the last instance. It forms the exercise of the last instance that condi-tions the usage of language and of its philosophical artifacts in view of the One.

2. This "dualitary" coherence, or the order of Determination in the last instance, has only been described here schematically. It is explained in a certain number of more precise rules correspond-ing with the different phases of this determination of the One's descriptions by the One that they describe. These rules will obvi-ously be none other than those of the "transformation" of philoso-phy into non-philosophy, more precisely rules of the treatment of the former as simple *material* or *language-of-description* in view of non-philosophy.

3. The One thus described is unthinkable from the specula-tive point of view alone; it challenges the speculative imagination itself as power of synthesis of contraries, as transcendental power of philosophical imagery. It reclaims a thought without image, for, in a sense, it is always absent, at least invisible within the horizon of the World or philosophy. *But it is not because it is unimaginable, non-projectable into the element of transcendence, that it would be unthinkable or ineffable.* The philosopher wants to fold the real onto his thought and decrees through idealism that the real does not exist if he cannot think it. Vision-in-One constrains us to do the opposite: fold our thought onto the real by modifying the concept in accordance with it; no longer to be able to be willful, decisionist, idealist, but to be necessarily naive, experimental,

realist, and to modify our traditional practice of thought and language in accordance with this experience of the One-real that we take as our transcendental guide. Descriptions—in their own finitude, i.e. their powerlessness to constitute the One to which they refer in the last instance alone—are there for proving "*de facto*," on the grounds of the immanent necessity of vision-in-One, that it is possible to think the One in a specific, unreflected mode, that there is not only a thought or a non-thetic "vision" which ensues from the One or is formed in it, but that this vision-in-One of the World, of philosophy and of everything that is found there, is equivalent to a non-philosophical representation of the One itself and to the most positive representation whose immanence would thereupon be accepted.

Determination in the last instance, specific coherence of a thought of the One

The system of rules that we shall spontaneously practice in the descriptions of the One can now perhaps allow us, if not already to explicate it in detail (i.e. the rules of "non-philosophy"), then at least to give its principle and distinguish it from that of philosophy, thereby distinguishing in this way more precisely between the order of philosophical decision and the order of vision-in-One.

Here is the founding Parmenidean equation of metaphysics: "The Same is Thinking and Being" or, to simplify, thinking=Being. Let us juxtapose it against the foundational equation of vision-in-One: thinking=One, an equation that also expresses thought's immanent claim to attain the real in-itself but as One. Perhaps it is simpler than the philosophical and therefore just as transcendental: these are not mathematical equations, but real or transcendental. To the question "what is thinking?", philosophy replies: it is to think Being, by and for it; vision-in-One or science replies: it is to think the One in the One and from the One.

Philosophy's founding equation obviously does not posit a flat indifferent equality, but rather the Principle of analytic identity, which at worst is deficient as Same and at best is the Same. In turn, the latter is a possible example and can be experienced as *co*-(respondance), co-presence of the system, or even as (co-)*respondance*; sometimes as "difference," for example, sometimes as "*différance*." Whatever these variations may be, they emit an invariant: philosophical identity is not immediate; it is a relation, be it "without relation," a relation mediated by operations of decision and position, of scission or alteration and identification, of reversal and displacement, etc., or by the semi-operation of a "withdrawal." *In every case, a certain reciprocity, reversibility or simultaneity between opposites is supposed, whether central or residual, and this is without considering the delay, difference and irreversibility contributed to identity by certain interpretations of the equation, some altering it more than others.* This is verified concerning two Platonic principles: the One and the Dyad, which both suffice for the integral constitution of philosophical decision. The problem is that of the *order* between these "principles"—there is always an order, be it more or less irreversible. The Platonic order, which is also that of the philosophical in general, instead departs from the Dyad to go to the One, from duality or from the coupling to go toward its unity. *More accurately*: the order here is also circular and goes in both directions at the same time. Unity is already supposed given as internal to the coupling or immanent to the relation, but it is also external and transcendent to them. It therefore fulfills the conservative function of gathering, unification, synthesis and struggle against the risk of dislocation that duality holds. On the other hand, duality represents the empirical side of the departure, the diversity that must be overcome. Thus:

1. Philosophical thought necessarily takes its departure in an external given, in the supposed given exteriority of the World—Transcendence. Not only is there a scission "between" the two terms, a reciprocal transcendence toward one another, but transcendence is itself inscribed in the sphere of what is already given as a transcendent and autopositional "fact"; philosophical thought is of the order of a decision, which is partially factual and empirical or necessarily tied to the empirical, like the *a priori* always is, a decision included in a system, that of the *supposed given* "fact," "tradition" and "destiny"—a system of autofetishization or what we shall call, in opposition to the One, Transcendence.

2. Unity—ultimately a function of immanence—is here already presupposed by the pairing of opposites where it exists "in itself." But Unity comes after this pairing and requires it so as to conquer its own effectivity and in some way become "for itself." Unity, despite everything, is thus aligned with and subjugated to it. The transcendental is subjugated to the metaphysical or the *a priori*. It is a consequence of the essence of philosophical decision that the transcendental be devalorized, just like the One is by and for Being.

The order of vision-in-One is inverse and still something other than inverse. Whereas the order of philosophical decision is *simultaneously* irreversible and reversible, always a mixture like that of the blend of the One and of the Dyad—*a mixture that is necessary the moment one commences instead through the Dyad*—the order of vision-in-One is only irreversible and necessarily departs this time from the One and from the One alone in order to go to the Dyad eventually, *if* the latter presents itself. If it must have a sense, i.e. a specific truth that distinguishes it from the equation thinking=Being, the equation thinking=One can and must be interpreted in another way than as a mode of the philosophical. Even in the latter, there are indeed two terms, but this Dyad is no longer arranged by and in a cloven Identity or a Same, submitted to a Unity which would be internal and external simultaneously and would guarantee the co-presence or simultaneity—even peripheral—of its members. In the philosophical, each of the two terms is divided—by one procedure or another—and each identifies with the other: the Dyad (or decision) and Unity then form a system that is reflected in itself or is indefinitely auto-affirmed. *Another solution can be imagined*: Identity on the one hand, and Division or the Dyad on the other, could be redivided otherwise between the two terms of thought and of the One. Otherwise, i.e. without blending together, without reflecting themselves within one another and surveying one another, without forming mixtures. For the real, there is Identity alone, without Division; for thought or for the Dyad, there is not only Division but, since the latter is unthinkable and unreal without the Identity of the real, also *this Identity as well*. But this thought would not and could no longer then be a divided Identity like the philosophical. On the one hand, by its real foundation or its essence, this would be nothing-but-an Identity; it would be rigorously identical with the real without passing through a division or a Dyad; and, on the other hand, this would be a pure Dyad, a radical duality; it would also not be obtained by division and then blended again with Identity. The Dyad would have its foundation in this Identity but would ensue from it without being reciprocally determined along with it. This economy distributes the One and the Dyad without a chiasmus or a fold, without making them recover one another and reflect themselves in one another. It founds the Dyad in the One but without the Dyad then determining the One in return. Whereas philosophical decision supposes 2/3 principles, vision-in-One no longer supposes but 1/2.

Such a distribution is possible only if the terms at hand obviously have a change in nature and not merely in relation. Thought can depart from the One alone (rather than from the Dyad or from the circle that the latter forms with the One) only *if the One is sufficient by itself,* if it does not require this factual (empirical or aprioritic) relation as support, i.e. the Dyad, and if the One is not blended with it. The real as Identity, absolutely not divided or associated with a division, has no philosophical sense, but it perhaps has another sense (scientific, for example). Philosophy thinks the One *with, by* and sometimes *as* something else: Transcendence or the Other, Scission, Nothingness, Decision, etc. Philosophy is given the One to subjugate it to the Dyad—to subjugate the transcendental to the *a priori*—and utilizes it in this way, supposing its reality without having elucidated it; philosophy is given the real, its Identity, without having elucidated its essence for itself. On the contrary, vision-in-One—this is what its grounded or postural realism (in order to oppose it to philosophy's voluntarist idealism) is called—does not suppose the One, or at least does not refer in the last instance to the real without experiencing it, without "postulating" that it experiences the real as a radical immanence (to) self, deprived of operations of decision or of transcendence; as an Identity that does not need to be divided and then related to a superior Same. The real's identity is lived, experienced and consummated by remaining in itself without having to be alienated in a representation.

Vision-in-One is the experience of this real. The real grounds representation within it, but it does not require representation to be what it is: this is a statement that philosophy would refuse. On the other hand, representation is now a duality that is immediately rooted in the real and its transcendental Identity but which, on the one hand, does not determine it in return and, on the other hand—this is the inevitable consequence—is no longer a scission. Whereas philosophical representation is a cloven Identity or rather the scission of an Identity, "non-philosophical" representation is a primitive duality, an originary dyad that is not obtained by scission and is thus not susceptible to an identification with the real; a representation that is not produced by an operation on the real but "accompanies" it from afar without claiming to make it return there, to re-integrate it or to make it arrive at its essence; a transcendence that is not obtained by an operation of transcendence, that cannot be generated and is grounded in the real statically. Such a representation of the real, which does not derive from the latter by scission or which is founded in it without co-determining it in return, is in general called reflection but is here non-specular: unilateral determination, by the real without reflection, of a reflection without real. Such a reflection is neither decided nor divided nor positional. It will be said that, in vision-in-One, representation is a non-thetic or non-positional reflection (of the) real, that it is descriptive, in the last instance at least, and not constitutive like philosophy claims to be.

This particular, strictly irreversible order—which ensues solely from the One's essence in which it is transcendentally founded and which renders the Dyad contingent while transforming the Dyad's nature by detaching it from "unitary" scission or difference, thus reducing philosophical decision on its side to nothing but an occasion and a material—can be called: "Determination in the last instance." For this irreversible or unilateralizing causality of the real on thought, of the One on the Dyad and on the One's descriptions, is nothing but the irreducible phenomenal residue of what Marxism understood by the formula "causality of the real," which is opposed to the reciprocal Determination that governs in philosophical decision. Thus thought (of the) real is not the contrary of the real, i.e. still a part of it: the real is without contrary, and the thought that describes it is the simple correlate of Determination in the last instance.

The condition for guaranteeing that this minimal real order subsists, anterior to the laws of the World, is therefore that the One be a sufficient reality; that it be an immanence no longer impregnated by transcendence or by scission and thus by unreality; that it be a Unity absolutely without Duality and which no longer reposes upon the World, on the supposed fact or the auto-positional fact; and that the latter be empirical or rational and *a priori*. What matters is that this Immanence, this Indivision, which would already represent in philosophy the authentic real for scission-division, now be recognized as *absolutely real by itself*; that it no longer share reality with transcendence and no longer need to be fortified and guaranteed by it in a mixture that would be the absolute alone. This Identity is already transcendental in philosophy, but in the latter it is both *real* and *possible* (idealizing scission). How is Identity solely real rather than a mixture of reality and possibility, solely immanent rather than a process of Identity and Difference? Vision-in-One as an absolutely real and finite thought responds by its own immanent necessity or its finitude. It is criterion (of) self—and thus criterion (of the)

55

non-philosophical representation that utilizes philosophical decision as a simple material.

The developed concept of vision-in-One

"Vision-in-One" means first and foremost that henceforth one sets off from the One rather than from the Dyad; that the One is taken as the immanent guiding thread of research; and even that one remains within this immanence from which we can no longer, not even by the World and Philosophy, be made to leave. But it is acknowledged that we also see the World. Vision-in-One then means that we no longer see the World from itself or from a being-in-the-World, but from and in the One's immanence; that we see an object no longer from its objectivity but from and in the One; *and that we see philosophy no longer from itself but from the One* ("*non-philosophy*"). However, in the One—this is obvious—there can no longer be a simple "image" of the object, furthermore supposed "in itself," no image on a surface or a mirror looked over by a third person, but, in a certain way, the object's "in-itself" itself, i.e. that which in it arises from the One: both its being-immanent and its aprioritic structures. The One can no longer be a surface or a screen redoubling the object; it is the reality or the thing itself, the *thing* (of) thought, its "in-itself." This extension of vision is therefore possible because, more profoundly, the One sees the One in the One. Here we have the concrete concept of this Identity, which is real rather than logico-real, the concept of this knowledge, non-decisional and non-positional (of) self, which is only demonstrated of and by itself. Because the One is in itself vision-in-One, it can be vision of something else in-One and under its laws, which are no longer the vicious laws of perception and of its auto-factualization. *We should now describe the plane of Transcendence or of Representation which we also call the Dyad of the (non-) One; the aprioritic structures of representation.*

"Vision-in-One" supposes that the One is an "exploitable" immanence or interiority; that it is not absolutely "confined" in itself, repulsive and exclusive of every other reality, and that this would be a false problem, a transcendent problem. We have described it in a quasi-phenomenological way, extremely careful to do justice to its positivity—to its reality—and to exclude nothingness, the negative and all their modes from it. Since it is immanent (to) self without any transcendence or any nothingness to constitute it, the One "excludes" exclusion from itself, which it does not require. Because its immanence only depends upon itself and is not inscribed in a third element (transcendence) in which it would become exclusive and repulsive, it has no reason to deny or destroy the World, Philosophy or anything that could be presented as Other than it. The One's real Identity is not a logico-real identity, impregnated with transcendence or with decision that would smother alterity. The One therefore has no reason—since it is neither abstracted nor even extracted from the World, but absolutely precedes it—to refuse that the World be presented to it of its own authority and that the World be seen or thought from the One. Precisely, and this is the only thing that matters, the World can be seen from the One and by the One only on the sole condition of the World's radical "transcendental contingency." This is nothing but the effect of an already accomplished transcendental reduction that is absolutely primitive because it depends on the One alone and not on the World.

What then is the positive reason that apparently forces us to go "beyond" the One? The first reason is obviously because—without us having to *exit* the One (this would be a purely philosophical appearance)—the One's essence excludes that one exit it, which itself exits from and reenters into itself, and because its immanence remains our guiding thread—something other than what philosophy effectively presents here, for example. There is philosophy—the One does not prevent it from presenting itself, as we said—and it first manifests itself by resisting the One: *this is what we call th*e "*dual*" *as condition of the* (*non-*) *One's existence.* Philosophy resists if the One is taken as a point of view on philosophy itself, which is what philosophy already does automatically. Resistance to the One is the very way in which it presents itself from the start, presenting itself only in the form of protestation, refusal, objections, etc., a resistance to the One which is *exactly the same thing as its auto-sufficiency and its "factuality."* But seen in or from the One, this resistance is lifted, at least sterilized, i.e. also manifested as such. Neither philosophy nor its spontaneous resistance is destroyed in their effective constitution: resistance is made futile by the simple fact of its manifestation as resistance. *This is what is now called "duality," the* (*non-*) *One's form, and which contains a "terminated" or completed transcendental reduction. Its effect is to inhibit philosophy's validity as "theoretical" point of view of legislation and interpretation of itself.*

A few remarks on this effect of suspension: this effect of reductive emplacement, carried out by the (non-) One as the One's correlate and grounded in it, can be called *chaos* or *chôra*, albeit not in a transcendent or cosmological sense but in a transcendental sense. This is obviously not a chaos in the vulgar or empirical sense, however near or far it may be from anything whatsoever. It merely implies that philosophical decision, Unity-of-contraries or the One and the Dyad's circular simultaneity stops governing the philosophical given itself, stops organizing and managing its economy; that there is no more filtering and coding of the given, no more interpretation possible. Philosophical decision itself floats alongside what is apparently non philosophical as an element that is in turn inert or sterile.

This "free" state of decision and of its members therefore does not correspond with the residue of an imagined or fantastical chaos; not even with a regulated but limited chaoticization of certain philosophies by an operation of *Reversal,* as is the case in philosophies and above all deconstructions. An empirical and transcendent chaos is still a mode—albeit deficient—of a decision: still a nihilistic chaos, always inscribed in Being, thus self-contradictory and limited, destined to conserve decision's ultimate authority, cohesion and coherence. On the other hand, the *chôra* is the suspension of this authority itself in all its forms and tricks, but a restrained and precise suspension: it does not bear on decision in its effectivity, but only in its claim to *be valid* as theoretical, unique or exclusive point of view. This is because decision subsists; it is at least conserved in the state of simple material or inert manifold. Even philosophical reflection subsists in the state of unreflected given, the state of material or of philosophy's effectivity: in a sense, everything is conserved; all the mechanisms of decision are still present in their concretion, in their complicated combinations. But we "see" all of this in the One, i.e. from the depths of the *chôra,* from an absolutely philosophically disinterested vision that would no longer know how to do anything philosophical with this material. This is more than skepticism, which always risks being yet another decision.

This reduction, then, has the effect that we have supposed and begun to describe as "de-factualization" or "de-fetishization" of philosophical decision, as its reduction to the state of contingent material, of inert and sterile given. Reduction and destruction, sterilization and negation are not conflated: the World or philosophy can always be there and present themselves; they are not consequently destroyed in their effective reality. And nevertheless they are henceforth there only *for* and *by* the One, i.e. as contingent or—this is the same thing—"seen" from or in the One.

However, the suspension-effect or reduction-effect is nothing but one side of the (non-) One or of the Dyad, which has another more positive side, one that will have to be described. Philosophy seen in this way instead of from itself, perceived under conditions of the purest transcendental truth and no longer from its own mechanisms, is the same thing as non-philosophy, at least one of the conditions of its production. Non-philosophy therefore begins with the reduction of philosophy to the state of inert material, with its insertion into the (non-) One which from the start fulfills the double (philosophically divided) function of *chaos* and *chôra*, but it is richer than this state of material; this is what the material "becomes" through the One or, instead, that in view of which it serves. Non-philosophy is what the One—and it alone—sees of philosophy, rather than what philosophy sees of itself when it would be seen from the viewpoint of the Other. But, what it sees must still be described now, a description which will give fullness to the concept of non-philosophy, its reality and effectivity simultaneously. The analysis cannot stop here, for the material is not simply inert; it is seen under the One's conditions which must have an effect, this time "productive," on it. This is the "positive" aspect of Determination in the last instance. The term "material" already indicated it: with the chaos of philosophical decisions, we are not at the end, but only at the very beginning of non-philosophy. What does this entail?

Two paradigms: perception and vision-in-One

Let us consider perception in its psychological and philosophical sense. On the one hand, it is a supposed given fact and even a factum: "perception" is already its own theory and this theory of our relation to the World, or to the object that supposes that this relation presupposes itself (factum) as given but universal, necessary and total; as auto-interpreting fact and as supposing itself already-there, already real at the very moment of its genesis. On the other hand, and this coincides with the above in terms of division with auto-envelopment, "perception" is that which describes, concerning our relation to the World, a foreign and superior observer, which can be us, the self[8] in us. Both the self and the object are in a state of splitting. Perception is simultaneously the given of this relation and—in approximation with a scission or a decision, in approximation with a philosophy—its interpretation and its thematization. Like all the "facts" of philosophy, and primarily like philosophy itself, "perception" is a split and redoubled entity, a unity-of-contraries or a coupling, a unitary dyad, a phenomenon that is vicious or circular by essence. This is what explains its triple or quadruple dimension: the object as *perceived* and *perceiver,* or as dyad; the subject as *perceiving-being* and as *disinterested observer,* as One internal and external to the dyad. Or furthermore: the *represented* and the *representation* on the one hand; *the representing being* on the other hand, as *representation* and *observer of representation.* In this system, the perceiving subject is split into perceiver or condition of perception and into observer of perception—into mirror and gaze. And the perceived object, in turn, is divided or split into transcendent object and into image ("idea") of this object, a more or less idealized and more or less specular image according to the philosophical decisions or theories of perception. Whatever decisions may be considered—this is an invariant—there is a specular relation between the object and the mirror, between the object and its reflection-in-the-mirror, between the represented and the representation-act, etc.—a unitary dyad. And another dyad, also unitary or by scission, of the subject, which is simultaneously representation or mirror and the mirror's observer.

Vision-in-One is the pure and simple abandonment of this paradigm of autopositional decision or factum. In relation to this auto-fetishizing schema, it functions like an Occam's razor: too many non-simple, non-radical identities obtained by simple splitting and redoubling of division, by useless agglomeration and multiplication—the philosopher's busywork in its entirety. On the one hand, the subject or the One is no longer split into a mirror or subject that would be subjectively inert, technical, "unconscious" and dispossessed of knowledge, surrendered to objectivity—and into a contemplative subject supposed to know, but this time technically inert. They are no longer split into "phenomenological consciousness," which is constrained to experience and closed off

---

8   Depending on the context, the word "le moi" usually means "me" or "self," but in the discourse of psychoanalysis (Lacan) or German Idealism it can mean "ego" or "I" (cf. Ficthe's I=I). Here it has been translated merely as "self," but it is important to note that parenthetical phrases (such as "immanence (to) self") always use the French "soi," which also means "self" but reflexively in the grammatical sense. [TN]

to the sense of this experience, and into "philosophical consciousness" ("we philosophers" …), which reads the sense of experience without doing it. That these two consciousnesses be the *same*, dialectically or not, here has no importance or does nothing but confirm what vision-in-One destroys, for the latter is the contestation that there is any difference, scission or duality whatsoever in that which is no longer consciousness but the One-subject. The entirety of perception must be explained as a possibility—if not as a mode—of the immanence (of the) One, as what the One immediately sees in it: not by means of a transcendent and contemplative ego looking at a worker ego or a mirror. Such an empiricotranscendental division of labor is produced the moment there is the slightest crack or scission in the One, the moment the subject is barred or cloven again by a philosophical decision. The ultimate reality of perception, that which makes it so that it must be at each instant *finite* or *completed* by itself, *positive* and *absolutely successful* in every way, and no longer primarily knowing itself and by its own force without appealing to a supplementary theoretical structure of it—this sufficient reality is grounded in the One as immanent posture that sees everything "in" its immanence without needing to be split, i.e. without needing to be made object, without needing to identify with the perceived and to identify the perceived object with the perceiving subject. This immanence of the One must suffice for perception, if at least the latter is itself real and sufficient from the start, even when it is also involved (this is the problem of the *order* of experiences) in a process.

We have already described the One-subject. What the "object" becomes in vision-in-One now interests us more so in accordance with non-philosophy. What can this One-subject, without presence *to* self and beyond-cracking, henceforth really perceive, if this would no longer be the World, the fact or the object, if it would no longer be these fetishes? This is the moment that corresponds with the Dyad after the One. The object—philosophy, for example—in effect still appears in the form of a duality or of two states but which will no longer correspond with the philosophical usage of the Dyad: neither in themselves nor in their intimate constitution; neither in their mutual relation, which will no longer be that of scission or decision, of difference and the circle, nor in their relation to the One "in" and "from" which they are now "seen." In effect, we are now describing the object philosophy such that it is "seen" in-One and no longer from itself, its tradition and its auto-legislation. In relation to the non-philosophizable One, it is now philosophy and its decision that occupy the place, henceforth contingent and second, of the Dyad, and of a dyad which can no longer be philosophically conceived because it is instead a "transcendental" place, matrix or economy *for* philosophy. First the content of the object, *that which* is seen in-One via the object, in some sense vision-in-One's noematic content, will be described. Then its relation to the One, its transcendental sense or its noetic side, will be described. From this point of view, non-philosophy or its rules are in this way merely what are described in this double register, vision-in-One's noematic and noetic content (we obviously employ "noematic" and "noetic" according to a slightly different distribution than that of Husserl).

What is seen in-One or vision-in-One's noematic content

What remains of the old "philosophical" object appears in two forms:

1. There is definitely the auto-positional and auto-normative *object* such as it is supposed given to a perception, a common sense or a philosophical decision. The One, we know, does not destroy it, but merely suspends or sterilizes its auto-position or factualization. It thus remains there now, for the One and in every way, in the state of residual given or inert material; it is selected from the horizon of the World, still having the structure of this horizon, philosophy-form or mixture-form, but the latter in turn being rendered inert. This both is and is no longer the *perceived* or supposed-to-be-perceived object of philosophy and of common sense. A radical transcendental reduction distinguishes between them, but it is the same object in approximation with this difference of transcendental status. In relation to the object such as it is given in spontaneous and transcendent perception, this first change is considerable. *There is this inert material, the first side of the Dyad*, the farthest in relation to the One but not the most external: this is an *a priori*, the *chôra* is the *material's a priori*.

2. Then what happens to the reflection or the image in the subject of the perceived or represented object, namely the second side of the Dyad? No longer external object, it is not denied or destroyed by the One: it is simply and also transcendentally reduced and transformed in accordance with the One-subject that serves as immanent guide. We have distinguished with Husserl, also with philosophy in its entirety, between *what* is perceived and perception as "image" of the perceived; between *what* appears, the

62

appearing object, and appearance as image of the appearing, etc. It is well known that Husserl "worked" on this dyad in order to try to radically distinguish between the reflection or the image and its object; in order to put the greatest distance and most qualitative heterogeneity between them, between appearance and the appearing, the perceived and perception. Already his goal, which is more than ever our own, is to subtract appearance or the *phenomenon* from the psychological, empirical, transcendent status of the object's simple *image*, of its simple specular double. Decision, the type of decision structuring the dyad, is obviously in question here—it will be examined with the "relations" of terms between them.

It is slightly more obvious now that Husserl has not entirely managed to subtract the *phenomenon* of perception from the object perceived. This is because he still put a *decision* between them, a unitary and thus definitively specular duality, and because, like all philosophers—like Kant in particular, who is merely an example here—he remained empiricist from the point of departure. He set off from the Dyad, from the *fact* of the perceived object or of perception as supposed given, and proceeded analytically through a series of decisions on this fact. This occurred to such an extent that the aprioritic or pure structures of perception—what constituted the "phenomenon"—remained applied onto the empirical supposed given (auto-factualization), instead of first being grounded, as they should have been in all scientific rigor, *in* the transcendental. Here this is veritably nothing but what philosophy itself does. Vision-in-One instead requires—insofar as it is not philosophical—that the transcendental deduction of these *a prioris*, after the *chôra* which is already an *a priori*, really be first, sufficient and constitutive of the *a prioris* themselves, that it precede every aprioritic analysis; that the *a priori* be simply founded upon a transcendental experience of reality rather than first and also founded upon a transcendent experience, like that of "perception."

This then means—and we are already in the analysis of the noetic side—that the "reflection" or the "image" of the "object," perception or appearance is not produced by analysis or idealizing abstraction on the basis of the perceived object which, in every way, is now nothing more than material (although necessary, albeit in another way that will be affirmed), and that it is not produced continuously and circularly by a decision of analysis. Rather than *abstracted* by an operation, the reflection is from the outset *extracted* from the material by the One itself and for the One alone. Certainly the material is still necessary, but what matters here is that the reflection or the phenomenon-of (the object) is immediately grounded in the One which is its essence or its condition of reality. What the One here sees "in" itself or from itself is therefore indeed the pure or aprioritic *phenomenon* of the object, more exactly, here, the *a priori* of its objectivity (rather than of its reality). By definition, this can no longer be a transcendent specular reflection which would have the same formal characteristics as the object or which would mutually share a structure with it: having its essence in the One absolutely distinct from the transcendent object and philosophy-form, it has nothing in common with the object, it is limited to "designating" or "seeing" it, that's all. If this situation is thought out radically, it implies that the "image" of the object (of philosophy-form) is so non specular that it excludes philosophy-form from it, i.e. the mixture of decision and position: it is non-decisional and non-positional (of) self. Consequently, it is *a priori* "image" of this object, of philosophical decision, simultaneously of its transcendence and of its immanence. In other words: upon the foundation of the One and for it, for us-as-One, we have a real transcendental experience of the *a priori*, i.e. of universal and necessary knowledges, but insofar as they are the *a prioris* of objectivity, of philosophical decision and position themselves in their own generality.

As for the types and total number of *a prioris*, they are deduced from the number of dimensions of the philosophical decision of which they are the *a prioris*. There are four of these dimensions—there will therefore be four *non-thetic a prioris*, including the *chôra* which "corresponds" on its side with decision's auto-position or auto-givenness. In philosophy, this auto-position is there from the start. Afterwards, there is scission or decision, or even transcendence or exteriority. Then there is the dimension of position as "base," "generality" or even as "attribute," dimension of position-as-universality or of being. Lastly, there is Unity, internal or external to the dyad of the preceding, the mixture itself as Unity. These invariants of philosophical decision correspond with the four *a priori* deprived of the form of their philosophical unity or blend, of their entanglement in a mixture. The *chôra* first of all; then a *non-thetic or non-mixed Transcendence* (without scission and without an accompanying position); a *non-thetic or non-mixed Position* (without the position stemming from a scission or decision; absolutely indivisible and globally given); lastly, a *non-thetic or non-mixed Unity* (respectively: NTT, NTP, NTU).

We thus have—on the contingent condition that there is a material (and no longer on the necessitating condition of a factum's existence)—the transcendental experience, for example, of a transcendence or of an objectivity, which is itself without scission or decision, *before* the latter, of which it is simply the *a priori*; but also without antecedent or subsequent position, without open, horizon, etc., deprived of the mixture-form in general. Similarly, we have the transcendental—more than *a priori*—experience of an *a priori* plane or of an open deprived of mixture-form, i.e. the coupling of decision and of position, and of the effects of reciprocal "distortion," paralysis or inhibition that this coupling implies; this is the *a priori* condition corresponding with position in its philosophical usage of the attribute. Lastly, we have the immanent experience of an *a priori* of unity, which is also freed from its mixture-form and which constitutes the highest *a priori*, the Unity that does not yet completely exhaust the (non-) One itself or non-thetic representation, which will be taken up later on.

It is important to already grasp the noetic style of these *a prioris*. It is a question of an experience where they are given in an absolutely non specular way or in a way that is not itself still *a priori*, or divided-redoubled. It is transcendental or is made from and for the One and in the One's immanent mode. This is not an *activity* of idealization or of ideation, this is an *extraction* by the One—this word will be taken up again. Here is what reflection-in-the-mirror and the object being reflected become, the "appearance" or "image" side and the "object" side of the dyad of perception. It is a question of the *a prioris* whose transcendental experience we have or which have an experienceable phenomenal content for the One-subject: the *chôra*, objectivity, universality and unity are not already given as reflected in themselves but in the mode of immanent phenomenon. This is vision-in-One's aprioritic content or bearing and what it sees or "represents" of the object, the non-mixed dimensions of reality, universality, objectivity and unity through which it relates to its content and takes it into account, a certain accounting that forms a system with its reduction to the state of material.

It should be noted that this layer of "intermediary" reality of the *a priori*—i.e. of representation—indeed exists, and that the supposed given fact and the One do not remain "face-to-face," since the fact would then be on the verge of falling into a radical contingency; that when it is considered necessary, this is obviously for the existence of the *a priori* itself rather than of the One; and that in a general way, faced with the perceived, the specific phenomenal reality of perception must be guaranteed, faced with the appearing that of appearance must be guaranteed, and faced with the "seen" that of "vision" must be guaranteed. The idea of "vision-in-One" cannot designate an act or an empty and therefore mystical operation. It designates a real phenomenal content, a precise structure which, without "articulating" vision properly speaking, assures it a specific autonomy between the object, then the material, and the One in which vision is formed as in immanence which is its ultimate essence. If the *a priori* draws its *reality* from the One, it also has a "reality," this time in a less rigorous sense of the term: a certain "content" of its own—transcendence, immanence and unity (not to mention the *chôra*) in their non-mixed form. In effect, the One does not solely "serve" to "see" them, it does not see them except on condition of extracting them from mixture, thus on condition of suspending this state in which decision and position are mutually conditioned, transformed, impeded, redoubled, etc. Freed from the form and constraining weight of their blending, the experiences of a universal and necessary knowledge are unlocked, ultimately untethered from philosophical limitation. These are possibles qualitatively heterogeneous to philosophical possibles, because they are both infinitely "vaster" and also simpler insofar as they are no longer condemned to mix and inter-inhibit themselves; they are static possibles given to the One which manifests them, because they are no longer condemned to be mutually determined and transformed.

This experience of the possible can be taken further in other directions. It permits—this is an example—the recovery of the Leibnizian and Kantian theories' kernel of reality and of truth. But the discovery of the radical positivity of the possible has its absolute condition in the One's reality, which distinguishes between this conception of the possible and of the understanding from that of Kant and that of Leibniz as well. Possibles are unreflected noemata, they have the One's phenomenality in the last instance as noetic essence and are deprived of positionality or of being, more exactly of the form-of-mixture. Consequently, they are not analytic or grounded in the principle of contradiction in a Leibnizian way, nor synthetic like Kant's concrete essences which are mixtures, *real possibilities* that have their site, rather than in the divine understanding, in a transcendental imagination (whose essence itself remains ambiguous or of the order of the difference between Reason and sensible Intuition). Non-thetic noemata are grasped-produced *before* the disjunction of Reason and Intuition, they have their common basis only in the radical, unreflected or real experience that we have of Reason, i.e. in the One, then in the *nous* as non-thetic-Transcendence and non-decisional-Position, in what could be called *the non-onto-logical experience of Being*.

Possibles fulgurate in this human understanding which is the region of the Other, the Stable and Unity. They fulgurate as the modes of these latter, inhabit their region and are the inexhaustible *a priori* sources of the ultimately rigorous or scientific representation of effectivity; they are in every way the reality of the last instance of philosophical decisions. They form a veritable correlation of Intelligence and intelligibles, a non-positional correlation without worldly or divine horizon. The site of non-philosophy as thought (of) the Other, (of the) Stable and (of) Unity is the real or concrete understanding insofar as it is lived by the subject or man in the mode of being-immanent or of vision-in-One.

The understanding, in the non-thetic sense of the word, denotes the opening that does not illuminate any open already there, thus re-illuminating it. It undoubtedly manifests itself "in the void" or "in the loss" of the point of view of the World and of History because, in the night of the understanding, the obscure static fulguration of the possible does not illuminate any earthly or celestial dome: a "rift" so intense that it remains in itself and is only unleashed as pure event of sense. However, it is immediately filled up by non-positional noemata, by possibles or events of sense in itself that never enclose, exhaust or confine it. The non-ontological understanding is filled with possibles that do not objectify it, do not render it "effective" or "realize" it. The absolute, unreflected opening is "full" *as opening*, and the transcendental understanding does not need to be related to the World and History, within which it would be inhibited in its operation: this is not a project in general; it remains what it is, i.e. Exteriority, Base and Unity, and all of this before "the-world."

These *aprioritic Images* are the real or phenomenal content of the imagination—even that of the speculative Imagination. The pure Imagined precedes the imagination's operation; aprioritic Images are therefore not themselves imaginable, even speculatively, because they are already imagined, albeit in an unreflected mode—but merely describable through a labor of language upon itself. These four *a prioris* are the noematic content of appearance or representation "in-One." They give rise to the practical rules of non-philosophy. The exposition of the latter will be the occasion to return to these *a prioris* and to specify their content.

How the One sees or vision-in-One's noetic content

The relations of the *material* and the *a prioris of non-thetic objectivity* remain to be described: both the relations between them and those between them and the One, i.e. the whole "noetic" side of vision-in-One.

1. *Between the material-object and the a prioris of its non-thetic objectivity*, there is no longer, as we said, the circular relation of reciprocal determination, which is the essence—if not the entirety—of philosophy's operations in general, and in particular of those of the abstraction of the *a priori* form (Kant) or of the ideation and intuition of idealities (Husserl). On the one hand, because the object has shifted from the state of auto-positional fact to that of simple occasion, and then that of signal incapable of still determining the *a priori* itself in its essence: the very condition of abstraction or ideation has been abolished from the outset. On the other hand, because the *a prioris* have not formed the object of an operation of production by a transcendent subject *ex machina* but have been "passively" manifested or phenomenalized by and for the immanence (of) the One alone. *What is called "transcendental extraction" is this non-operation through which it is their essence or their being-immanent that makes them appear or emerge, no doubt with the support or on the occasion of "empirical" material but without there being an operation upon the latter which would be of the same nature and originarily identical with it.*

The radical "interruption" of all circularity, of all "technological" and unitary continuity between the object supposed given and its *a prioris,* but also, afterwards and within the *a prioris,* between the material and the other *a prioris* that have a different function, is the same thing as the transcendental extraction of the *a prioris* by the One. Together they establish these different levels in a *radical duality,* a static duality or without scission that breaks the continuity of the philosophical dyad. This type of duality derives directly from the *dual,* i.e. the One's absolute, irreversible precedence over the World's resistance, a precedence that now is reproduced in the form of this originary duality, anterior to any operation of scission or of difference of the two sides of the noema (the perceived (and) perception, the appearing (and) appearance, etc.). The One, philosophically undecided or unengendered, statically "engenders" a Dyad that is also philosophically unengendered or undecided. *This non-unitary Dyad, non-decisional and non-positional (of) self, provides the future "sides" of the contradiction or opposed terms of the coupling in their real and primitive form. This is the Dyad's content of phenomenal reality which philosophy supposes given and in which it commences.*

Nevertheless, the fact that no philosophical or unitary type of circularity exists does not mean that resistance is unnecessary for the extraction of the *chôra*, nor that the *chôra* is unnecessary for the extraction of the following *a prioris* and that the originary phenomenal duality is as rigorously irreversible as the dual itself. If the "object" (philosophical resistance) and its "material" state are both contingent for the One which does not require them, the "object" is necessary for the unleashing of the material, and the latter is necessary for the unleashing of the following three *a prioris*. Yet precisely all this is no longer required except in the mode of occasion (for the "material") and signal (for the other *a prioris*): the "object" or auto-positional "fact" is no longer required in its mode by the One. The material, for example, is necessary in the precise sense that it alone can contain something like transcendence or decision—in excess of immanence and blended *a priori* with it in the primitive form of a mixture—and that the material alone can *signal* it to the One which will extract it from this mixture in the form of non-mixed Transcendence. All these non-relations and residues of relations, everything that happens outside the law of reciprocal Determination and of decision, can be gathered in the formula that describes the material's function as a triple and identical function: 1) *of occasion* (for the *chôra*; it is not the real or essential cause of the *a priori*—the One alone can be this—but only its occasional cause); 2) *of signal* (for non-mixed Transcendence and Stability, it signals their existence to the One); 3) lastly, *of support* (it serves as an empirical "support" for non-thetic Unity and all the *a prioris*). This is what will implicate that philosophy as material serves as occasion, signal and, more importantly, a support for non-philosophy.

Thus, due to the noetic relations that structure them on the different levels of the *a prioris*, the two opposed sides of the noematic dyad, the perceived and perception, stop being contemporary or even simultaneous within a unitary philosophical hierarchy. The famous *Unity-of-contraries*, the structural rule of philosophical decision, is dismembered *a priori*—transcendentally rather—and stops being valid for the real as philosophy claims. Unity-of-contraries is manifested as a transcendent structure, the spontaneous and consenting victim of the transcendental appearance that makes it claim to be able to reflect and determine it. It has never had validity except for the sphere of transcendence or the mixed, the sphere of the World.

2. What "relation" or non-relation is there *between the* a prioris *of the object and the being-immanent of the One*, for example, between the perceived or perception as *a priori* and the One, and how is it described?

Here the description must distinguish precisely between the auto-positional fact and the *a prioris* (the material is already an *a priori*) and also between the *a prioris* and the One which is their essence. From the start, the One is what *extracts* them rather than what *abstracts* them. The *a prioris* therefore take their reality from the One or are phenomenalized by essence alone. They do not circularly phenomenalize themselves but are manifested by the One itself. The One is the source of every real phenomenalization, every non transcendent manifestation, because it is the Manifest *before* manifestation, the already-Phenomenon before any supplementary operation of phenomenalization, i.e. of prop-to-the-phenomenon. Nothing phenomenalizes itself (*causa sui*), neither the One which does not require it, nor the *a priori* which is instead phenomenalized by the One. The One therefore "determines" it in the full sense of this word, or makes it emerge in reality, by only requiring the *supposed given* or the transcendent in this task for its "second" functions of signal, occasion and support. In other words, the *a priori*, whether "appearance" or "representation," will be completely grasped or "seen" in the One, within the indivisibility of its immanence, and nowhere else.

It is important to grasp the phenomenal status of these *a prioris* exactly, the way in which they are given or lived in the last instance. They are given to the One and in the mode of the One but without themselves being the One. In other words, without having the One as their specific content (since it is instead that of transcendence in general and of its quadruple dimension) and without it constituting the One in turn, this content is nevertheless received in the mode of the One. The non-thetic *a prioris* are seen in the One without constituting its reality; they are lived "in" it without at all "entering into" it and structuring it from within.

If we experience or gain access to transcendence, then it is in the mode of a radical being-immanent.

Without a correspondent within philosophy, this situation gives a new and more rigorous sense to the formula of Husserl and of every philosophical decision: "transcendence in immanence." On the one hand, rather than a blending by division and redoubling and an unthought blending or a knot which is itself still transcendent, the *in* henceforth indicates an absolutely non-thetic and non-decisional being-immanent and forms the real basis of transcendence. The One's immanent phenomenality replaces the transcendent being of the *knot, chiasmus* or *fold*, which is philosophy's ultimate secret. It frees thought from its divisions and its redoublings, from its useless foldings and stand-ins. It also simplifies transcendental or real causality: transcendental immanence is the real cause of transcendence, and the latter exists *by* as much as *in* immanence. From its reality, the transcendental instance thoroughly supports transcendence and its quadruple aprioritic structure, i.e. the plane of the (non-) One or of Representation.

On the other hand, the subject accesses it immediately and without passing through its own mediation; man accesses intentionality directly without being grounded in a relation once again mediated by intentionality itself. Transcendence or intentionality is thus globally given and manifested as undivided without having to be divided up, partialized, redoubled, etc. Philosophy, on the contrary, is condemned to be established *in the midst of* transcendence supposed given, thus auto-divided; philosophy departs from transcendence in order to return to it; philosophy is constrained to open—merely open—the amphibological mixture of transcendence and of the transcendent. It is given—this is what it calls Being—the blending of intentionality and of the transcendent object. The philosophizing subject not only lives this intentionality but is at the same time *really divided by it, barred by transcendence*; he is *also* alongside the object or alienated, separated from himself and identified with this object. Here one recognizes the fatality that shackles philosophical decision to the presupposition—which is also transcendent—that the object is given by itself or given in the mode of an auto-factualization. This empiricist fetishism of philosophy, which makes it conflate the real with transcendent existence, condemns it to analyze and divide a given which it supposes consistent by itself and prohibits any real and rigorous genesis of objectivity or intentionality—of transcendence or representation. This does not even take into account that this abyssal fetishism of the fact, of the object and of the mixture obviously prevents it from freely treating philosophy as what it is: a simple occasion. The causality of the empirical given is in effect merely occasional, it is not essential or real. And, on its side, transcendence is simpler than philosophy imagines; it no longer has the structure of the knot, chiasmus or fold with which philosophers, believing to think the real, remain content with passionately augmenting the aporia.

Ultimately the dissolution of the two amphibologies, that of the One and of intentional transcendence, that of intentionality and of the object or material-being, allows for the deliverance of intentionality itself from its conflation with the material of the World or of Philosophy. This dissolution frees it from its ontological and positional limitation and even from its little opening-by-the-Other, from its new confinement by the Other. The moment that intentionality is detached from the transcendent ground of consciousness or of Being and the moment that it is grounded in the One's posture, it stops being intention-of-the-World or of-the-object, stops being an ekstasis which is opened *as* World, which is filled by it or completed with it. It becomes by itself—this is its non-thetic structure taken as a whole—a radically unlimited open, what we can call a *non-thetic Universe* or an undivided Appearance in distinction from the *Cosmos* as correlate of the *Logos*. An infinite transcendence that acknowledges neither the division nor the fulfillment by an object or a World, neither the gift and withdrawal nor the rarity and false abundance of philosophical doublets. The Universe is lived in a completely immanent way by the One which is its ultimate basis. The One reposes in it without constituting a "bridge" between subject and object, which would both be supposed given or transcendent, a bridge whose continual collapse fuels the philosopher's heroic engineering. This is also to say that the Universe, correlate of the One-subject's aprioritic representation, passes—if one can phrase it this way—"alongside" the World, brushing against it merely to lean on it for a moment, selecting from it what will be a material rather than an object, finding a signal, occasion and support in it, rather than these fetishes of the universal "ground" or "foundation," the archi-Earth, etc. The Universe in the rigorous transcendental sense, compared with the old *Cosmos, Polis, Physis,* etc. in which philosophy keeps turning like the rational animal in its cage, is acosmic and utopic.

The restitution of the One's essence therefore produces a chain of effects upon intentionality and the object; it clarifies the latter's constitution by ultimately separating what in the mixture of *phenomeno-logy* would be mutually impeded: namely, on the one hand, immanence, which becomes *that in which* or *how* intentionality altogether is seen in a sufficient way; on the other hand, transcendence or the intentional open itself, noematic objectivity, which are finally freed from their closure by the transcendent *object* or the World's *horizon*. Henceforth they are thoroughly undivided and rigorously infinite, and they are such in a mode which excludes the apportionments, decisions and distributions that constitute philosophical economy.

A transcendental deduction of philosophical transcendence

If there is a diversity proper to the *a prioris*, to the internal content of appearance insofar as it is distinguished from the appearing, and if this specific reality or this variety of the possible guarantees vision of the object and of the World and assures it by reducing them to the state of "material," then this material itself, as we said, cannot be auto-manifested, because the root of every manifestation is forever in the One. On the one hand, this specific reality of the possible is heterogeneous to the One, since it does not enter into the One's undivided essence; it neither conditions nor structures it in turn. On the other hand, it is conditioned by the One's essence and can only be visible in it and by it. There is no contradiction here—in what is precisely Determination in the last instance—for a contradiction would suppose from the start that the *a priori* can determine the One in return. Instead, so as to dissolve the appearance of contradiction, it suffices to describe the *a priori's* phenomenal state of affairs by taking the immanence (of) the One as guiding thread or transcendental guide. These *non-thetic Images*, these *a prioris* which constitute the real authentic content of every "imagination" labeled "transcendental" or even "speculative" by philosophy, do not at all have the One's form as their content, but they are consequently visible from it and in it, which is their essence. It is useless to imagine a continuity and another circularity between the transcendental and the *a priori*, between these pure possibles and the One: none of this exists. And nevertheless, although heterogeneous to the One and precisely because of this, they are given to it without mediation.

The whole paradox, or appearance of contradiction, stems from the manner of philosophical thinking—and from its resistance—which "ascends" from the supposed given *a priori* toward the transcendental, from the Dyad toward the One. In reality, it is necessary to depart—this is precisely "vision-in-One"—from the One or the transcendental, to be held within this immanence and, because they are not exclusive of the World and even less so of the material, to be satisfied with describing what is seen instead of fantasizing "philosophy," "unity of contraries" and "contradiction." Concerning the completely "passive" non-operation of the transcendental extraction of the *a prioris*, the question of its operative effectivity is not posed, because it has never been—if not simply for philosophical resistance—an *effective operation* of the transformation of the World or of philosophy. This extraction—i.e. manifestation of the *a prioris*—is solely real and only real by the One and for it: it is necessary to the strict extent that it is real rather than effective, and arises from essence rather than from the World and its philosophical mechanisms of decision and position, of reversal and displacement.

Thus there is necessarily—once given the World's *occasion*, philosophy-form or the mixture—an activated *transcendental deduction* of the non-unitary or "dualitary" *a prioris*. On the one hand, it is "passive" in its "possibility" as much as the One itself, for it is the real's own "non-operation," that of the already-Manifest which remains content with manifesting the *a priori* in turn. On the other hand, it is carried out by and for the One, and not the World except as occasion, by and for immanence and not transcendence, by and for the One's transcendental experience, and not "empirical" experience except in view of the latter and its resistance. Thus all the aporias of Kantianism and of phenomenology (the empirico-aprioritic circle, then the apriorico-transcendental circle), their "idealist" and "post-Kantian" generalization, ultimately their latent form in "difference," are lifted in vision-in-One, which brings about the "bracketing" of all of philosophy's fantastical aporia. If the *phenomenon* must be reserved for the One and described as strictly immanent, if it is not the *appearance* of the appearing, as Husserl still believes by philosophical objectivism, i.e. by-faith-in-transcendence, if appearance or representation is simply of the order of the *a priori* and if the phenomenon precedes phenomalization, then the extraction or manifestation of the *non-thetic a prioris* within the One itself, and despite their heterogeneity to it, must be described as necessarily "included" in vision-in-One—depending on the occasion—even if this non-relation remains contradictory or impossible to think for philosophy. Philosophy's first error is obviously to remain unable to imagine something besides a relation where there is none, where there is no longer even a "relation-without-relation." Every idea of relation or rapport—even if "deferred" or "breached"—renders the phenomenal state of affairs (which must be described in the most "passive" way) unthinkable or contradictory each time by realizing the posture of immanence and the suspension of philosophical activism. This is because the "logic" of thought-by-immanence, the rigor of vision-in-One, is strictly without common measure, without a structure in common with philosophy's logic. This certainly does not mean that it is "superior" to it, for it is a question of another order, and perhaps of the origin of every order, of the real-as-order.

The ensemble of this causality outside-relation, the content of the transcendental deduction of the non-thetic *a prioris*, will be summed up by a formula: *the One is the determination, solely in the last instance, not of the World and of philosophy as supposed given, but of their scientific representation or of their non-mixed* a prioris *or possibles and, consequently, the determination in the last instance of their combination and composition with philosophical material—i.e. of non-philosophy as philosophy's rigorous representation.* The phenomenal content which "determination in the last instance" must describe is nothing but that of the phenomenalization and extraction of the *a priori* by the One, i.e. by essence, and nothing but their transcendental deduction. Vision-in-One is this deduction enacted.

From vision-in-One to the theory and practice of non-philosophy

This reconstruction to which one will proceed from the concept of vision-in-One, from its quasi-ontology, is obviously not everything, but it is the absolute foundation, the real infrastructure of any form of thought whatsoever, even of science labeled "empirical" by philosophy. It will be asked: is that real? We reply: this is precisely the real itself. This description is an immanent or transcendental auto-description and signifies that vision-in-One is an absolute thought; that its immanent causality and its structure of reflection or of description-in-the-last-instance, i.e. the descriptive and not constitutive usage that it imposes upon language, suffice to render it capable of auto-describing itself on the One's unique basis and without philosophy's help. This description explicates its basically realist character, but realist only in the last instance and by its foundation rather than by its local objects. This also explicates the One's *de jure* opacity, its unreflexivity, etc., everything that renders it unintelligible to philosophy which then throws it back into a transcendent realism or an alterity at the limits of intelligibility. Vision-in-One's immanent or postural realism therefore functions as an absolute limit of philosophical re-appropriation.

Philosophy's reality or real base is an evidence that has never been elucidated and which can only be elucidated by the discovery of vision-in-One. Several characteristic phenomena of vision-in-One, and thus of science, are in effect "forgotten" or rejected as uninterpretable by philosophy: 1) a basic or "postural" realism, a realism of the last instance which can be accommodated by the dissolution of the transcendent reality of the perceived object; 2) an opacity of representation that makes it seem like there is no proper thought (of) the One, but a blind manipulation of symbols; 3) an immanence of the criteria of description that renders thought (of) the One autonomous—in its essence at least—with regard to philosophy. Whereas philosophies tend to deny these phenomena and to separate the unreflected type of knowledges (sciences) from thought (philosophy), we have proposed to explain them by taking vision-in-One and its immanent realism as their own rule of interpretation or their criterion of immanent description. We have thus described:

1. *The radical identity* that is at the foundation of all thought in the last instance: its realism, its claim to attain the real itself, supposes that it is from the start founded on the existence of the *immanent or pre-objective phenomenal givens* that explain its "opacity". This real Identity is not logical and does not contain any essential philosophical operations, for it is non-decisional and non-positional (of) self. Realism precedes objectivity (but does not destroy it).

2. *The real object* (the unity of the *a prioris* of exteriority, of stable universality and of unity with the material), to which vision-in-One relates the knowledges that it takes from the material: it has this radical realist foundation as its essence; it is thus a transcendence, a stability and a unity given *a priori* or before any ontological type of objectification.

3. *The object of knowledge*, of which we still have not spoken and which "contains" the preceding, with the ensemble of the empirical representations selected as occasional material from the World,

but which distinguishes it by its transcendental status marked by a new intervention of the (non-) One. The transformation of this object is not that of the real; vision-in-One transforms its object and its knowledges: it does not claim to transform the real. In this case, it is the effect of the (non-) One upon the real object.

The ensemble of these descriptive givens demonstrates that: 1) a "blind" authentic thought really does exist and does not remain content with being manipulated; an autonomous thought which itself has the claim to know the real in itself and, consequently, to think, contrary to what philosophies postulate concerning the sciences, for example; 2) the philosophical descriptions of this paradigm of thought are possible, but: either they are automatically reduced and emplaced (*chôra*), or instead, as "sufficient," they do not attain the real's essence but merely the object of knowledge which they mistake as the real object. On the other hand, this description, made in a spirit of submission to the demands of the most naive and most radical thought, is not anti- but ante-philosophical and describes a realism of the last instance or an already-manifest ante-philosophical ground.

Since it is a science (of) the One, or transcendental science, this description alone is capable of constituting philosophy into its empirical object—its "material"—without empirically degrading it. Not only, as we said, does vision-in-One's Identity enjoy a transcendental autonomy, i.e. a validity for the real as well as the philosophical; but it is still more originary than the latter. It is first of all more primitive, because it renders the One autonomous in relation to the Dyad, identity autonomous in relation to scission, the real autonomous in relation to its representation, the term or individual autonomous in relation to relation. It is also simpler, because vision-in-One is not, like philosophy, a superior blending that governs other blendings, but a poor minimal thought, that of the non-specular reflection (of the) term, a simply descriptive and purely "theoretical" reflection. It is also more passive, because, if it works, it does so only within the empirical content of representation or of reflection: it does not work *between* the real and reflection, it ignores the fundamental philosophical operations of decision and position, of scission and identification, and all the operations of constitution and deconstitution, of construction and deconstruction that follow from this.

With these transcendental and aprioritic structures (including the material and the *chôra*) of vision-in-One, we possess the essential "tools" of non-philosophy, if the latter is at least nothing but what the One sees in it of philosophy itself. Non-philosophy's practical rules are the development and specification of these structures in accordance with the philosophical "material" and its language. But first and more precisely, it will be necessary—this is the object of the following chapters—to describe the *concept of non-philosophy* on the basis of the structures of philosophical decision grasped in One. Afterwards, the technical problems of non-philosophy will be addressed. From this latter point of view, the description given to the *a prioris* will also have to be continually rectified. Here—despite their great proximity, save when it would be a question of the One—the real states of affairs or the givenness of the *a prioris* to the One in the last instance will no longer be conflated with their description, with language which is always particular and which always conveys the prestige of transcendence. This conflation would reconstitute the philosophical circle and transform radical being-immanent, which is that of the non-mixed *a prioris*, back into an intuitive givenness that would be transcendent and somewhat "mystical" in the onto-theo-logical sense of this word. Thus one will no longer remain content with a single description supposed definitive; but one will systematically exploit the necessity of supposing a linguistic material (language *as* material and *of the* material) as descriptive occasion for the *a prioris*, and no longer as cause of their real unleashing which is the work of the One, or as that through which it is necessary to redescribe them; and one will exploit the possibility of working on this language, of recasting or rectifying the description in accordance with these *a prioris* which are already-there and which then function as the descriptions' immanent rules. This double labor—double but not circular—is already the entirety of "non-philosophy."

Chapter II: Non-philosophy's theorem

Non-philosophy's first dimension: its effectivity, or the philosophical

The previous descriptions of vision-in-One have constantly evoked non-philosophy. Now it is time to describe its new status and its concrete dimensions in vision-in-One systematically.

The non-philosophical practice of philosophy reposes on a single theorem:

The One, understood as vision-in-One or as transcendental experience non-thetic (of) self, is what determines philosophical decision in the last instance as non-philosophy or in view of it.

For this to be understood, it is necessary to remember what was said earlier concerning the One and its immanent givens. It implies a threefold interpretation corresponding with the three dimensions of non-philosophy as effective, as real and as possible. The somewhat apparently constructivist aspect of the path set forth can now be dissipated only by the "phenomenology" of the immanent givens of vision-in-One.

Philosophy must therefore be "related" to this absolute experience, that of the One "in" itself. Even if the One is precisely unable to involve any "relation" to it or unable to let itself be determined by it in return: it suffices that philosophy be manifested by its resistance to the One and for us to take it into account.

This first interpretation does not say whether there is philosophical decision or not, since it simply says that *if* there is one, if such a thing is manifested, it must be put in relation with the One from the One itself: this is the "dual." Philosophy presupposes itself or auto-posits itself and is announced in this mode. It will no doubt be unilaterally determined, in totality and without return, by the One. But this first effect supposes that there is an effective philosophical decision or that it is presented. At least in History—the World and "the facts"—one finds a type of decision that is called necessary and more than necessary: it is called "unavoidable" and christens itself "philosophy." For example, there is an ensemble of invariant distinctions: of Being and being; of the supreme being and particular beings; of the sensible and the intelligible; of ordinary, vulgar, everyday experience and the *a priori* facts or essential experience, which is philosophy's "true" point of departure; or distinctions which are "real," "formal," "transcendental," etc.... None of this is the real in the sense of the One; this is a mixed form of the real, its blending with ideality and possibility: effectivity, i.e. the extremely variable mixtures of empirical givens and ideal forms which are always inseparable from one another by definition. Among these mixtures that form the "World"—what should be called "the-world"—we first come across philosophical or unitary systems, which are both particular, reflected types and the general form of these empirico-ideal doublets. Philosophies, as well as metaphysics and their contemporary deconstructions, are therefore one of the conditions of non-philosophy, even if they are revealed to belong to a secondary, derived, not "real," order of these conditions—an order of effectivity which, as we already know, will serve as the support, signal and occasion for the manifestation of the non-thetic *a prioris* yet without constituting their essence. They are indeed a necessary condition within this order, but only as one condition alongside others that are not specifically philosophical, even if unitary philosophical blendings and scientific or technological blendings, for example, involve the closest relations with one another.

But don't we have the right—this is the true question which is not that of the *de facto* existence of any particular philosophical decision in history—do we not, we transcendental thinkers who are "replaced" in vision-in-One and who take its unreflected immanence as our guiding thread of the order of thoughts, have the right to take empirical events or determinations into account and introduce them into a general calculus alongside the Absolute and the sufficient One? Without immediately denying the ante-philosophical One, can we bring ourselves back to philosophy such as it exists and such that we stop denouncing it as "unitary" and "sufficient?"

We can. This possibility is sustained by the theorem: the One itself does not say, but no longer denies, that there is philosophical decision, at least "empirically," presenting itself as "outside" the One and claiming to be given as absolute fact, tradition, destiny, etc. However, is it not a contradiction to sometimes invoke the One's radical immanence, devoid of all transcendence, and sometimes a decision transcendent to the One? Only unitary prejudices, i.e. a falsification of the One's experience and of its specific sense of immanence, its conflation with an always transcendent supreme Unity, can make one believe in a contradiction here. There would be contradiction if the One were a Unity (for example and "in general," the neo-Platonic One) and if it possessed Unity's completely empty and functional immanence: half-real, half-ideal immanence. There is nothing of the sort here; in any case, no mixture, and since there is no mixture, there is necessarily a certain originary duality. The One is not an object, whether spiritual or even intellectual, which is always transcendent: it has no path of approach and does not support any pedagogy, commentary, conversion, critique, deconstruction, etc. We are here in it, we are of it, we are it. There is consequently no reduction, suspension, negation, annihilation or exclusion of an eventual given necessary—other than the One—so as to attain it. The One does not say that there is a "second principle" (classical formula, but false within this problematics), of which it has no need, but it no longer denies the latter.

On the other hand, the One's radical immanence implies the reduction, emplacement or unilateralization of the transcendent empirical given (of the World, of History, of Power, etc.—of philosophy). The *a priori* of the *chôra* is not their destruction, the abolishment of their effectivity, but the suspension of their sufficiency alone. This is the One's liberality and its sufficiency. Therefore it is always possible, but for reasons proper to and only relevant within the World, History and Metaphysics, to assert these latter as such. The duality (or, rather, the "dual") of the One and its contingent Other does not at all lose the One which, not having been obtained by a philosophical decision, can no longer be lost by another philosophical decision.

All these relations and non-relations can be condensed in the following way:

a) The One does not necessarily imply another term—or dualism, consequently—of which it has no need: the One is not unitary, vision-in-One does not survey the Dyad or is not co-extensive with it.

b) But due to its essence, which is not that of Unity, the One is such that it is not completely opposed to another given. The One makes such a given possible or "tolerates" it without requiring it on its own behalf—this is the "dual"—even if the One reduces it or emplaces it as "material," a state we then call "duality" and which we distinguish from "dualism," just as we distinguish dualitary thought from the unitary thought to which "dualism" still belongs.

c) The passage from the dual to dualism involves the result of a term other than the One and of its claim as absolute or sufficient, a passage which supposes the One in every sense and thus does not nullify it by being carried out.

d) Dualism is itself unilateral: it involves the One but is not the philosophy of the One, which does not philosophize. This is a type of philosophy stemming from effectivity instead of the real and to which unitary thought in general, but also the World, History, etc. are constrained when they attempt to maintain their privilege "in front" of the One.

Non-philosophy's second
dimension: its reality, or the material

The theorem must then be determined directly in accordance with the One itself. The One, as its correlate of representation, has the (non-) One whose first immanent pole is a radical reduction or *chôra* which signifies that philosophy, as the transcendent pole, is contingent—uncertain and useless—for accessing the One's essence. As unitary thought, it has always claimed to access the One, to prepare an introduction, to develop a pedagogy, calculate a strategy ... in view of the Absolute, i.e. of the real. The sense of vision-in-One is that one does not access the One or commence through it but that one remains in it: that the real is completely and always already sufficiently experienced such that the question of a reactivation, reactualization, reaffirmation, repetition, etc. of the experience (of) the One is not posed. The only question still pertinent is that of its rigorous, i.e. immanent and scientific, description. This is what immediately suffices to invalidate philosophy's most secret ambitions. With a countless number of consequences, the paradigm of vision-in-One breaks the blending of the real and of philosophy and denounces the appearance of their alliance. The real, on condition of being understood or described as already determined from itself or as One, is accompanied by an effect of reduction, here and first of all an effect of unilateralizing emplacement, and is no longer the difference between the real and philosophy, not even the specific difference of the latter. The Unconstituted, the Undecided instead determines philosophical decision in the last instance as non-philosophy and therefore no longer forms a sort of circle or reciprocal determination with it. In determining decision by an unreflected or absolute lived experience, which is here from the start the *a priori* of the *chôra*, one begins to give it a *base or a real (and no longer simply logico-possible) essence*. This unreflected does not imply a rapport or relation—all of that is constitutive of philosophy which alone could elaborate and elucidate them—and the insertion of decision into the real of vision-in-One is carried out according to the law of what is no longer a rapport (for example, a "com-portment"),[9] which is always somewhat reversible in whichever way it is worked upon and undone, but according to a determination called "in the last instance," i.e. rigorously unilateral or not circular.

The Undecided can by no means enter into any *relation* in general. Its unreflected essence is *absolute* in the full sense of the word, even though this Other is also a transcendental experience.

This more-than-withdrawal of the One—its effect of (non-) One or of unilateralization in this first mode, *the chôra*—suffices to invalidate philosophy's classical claims on the real, namely its determination; and on knowledge, namely its foundation, legitimation, constitution, production, etc. Unilateralization belongs to this very special type of "causality" or of efficacy: of the One "on" philosophy, but in such a way that nothing of philosophy "turns back" on or recurs on the One. *"Last instance" is the mode of determination when it is strictly unilateral and undivided and when the effect cannot determine its cause in return—when it is not shared between two terms.* Thus it will no longer be believed that we have simply regressed from the category of "reciprocal determination" or of "reversibility," so fundamental for certain systematic philosophies (Fichte, Nietzsche), toward the category of causality, whether physical or not, according to whichever one of its four traditional metaphysical forms. Despite everything, philosophical causality always implies a certain reciprocity, reaction, resistance, etc. and ultimately a *unity* of cause and effect.

---

9   "Rapport," which is usually translated as "relation," here is translated simply as "rapport" so as to resonate with Laruelle's hyphenation of "com-portment," which correlates with Heidegger's "Verhalten," meaning both "relation" and "behavior" (i.e. comportment). It should also be noted that by hyphenating the "com-" in "com-portment," Laruelle is emphasizing the prefix as indicating philosophical reversibility and reciprocity. [TN]

Determination in the last instance is the point of view of the One or of science; it says that philosophical decision does not react upon them, because it is not required so as to—really—"define" their essence: the mixtures of the real *and* of philosophy are, if not dissolved, at least invalidated. Non-philosophy itself—correlate of this determination—also neither prolongs nor develops (explains, comments, reproduces, elucidates, etc.), neither delimits nor even "critiques" these mixtures in which it is not already included. Non-philosophy ensues, absolutely and without return, from the One. No doubt it will be determined on the basis of the material (of philosophical decision), but by the One alone and without this determination conversely signifying a philosophical intervention in the One's essence. The One, as immanent lived experience, does not even acknowledge—one would have to imagine it—a "procession" without "conversion," a conversion destined to be sustained and retained alongside it. Thus non-philosophy will not be an alienation or a degradation. Sense is unilateral, there is a unique direction of real causality, and not two: philosophical decision is therefore emplaced or *unilateralized* after the real—but this is in turn how it becomes real for non-philosophy. It cannot go back toward the One, it is deprived of nostalgia and stops being this operation of "leaping" or "jumping" in place which would, for example, allow it to "correspond," in approximation with a "turning," with the One. Everything must be reversed—or rather: can never reverse again, not even to reverse the reversal once and for all. Everything must be "uni-lateralized" and thought in a rigorously irreversible way. There is no chance of finding a true duality—this is perhaps a secret thought of Descartes—without a rigorous order of thoughts which, precisely because it must be irreversible, can no longer be that of reason and its reasons. This general effect of uni-lateralization will have several modes and will be specified in accordance with each level of the *a prioris.* This is what will guarantee non-philosophy's specific reality.

The notion of Determination in the last instance is now a little more precise. Philosophy exists; even the One's transcendental, absolute lived experience *can* encounter it in the places it ordinarily frequents: in the World and on the edges of the World; in History and as the opening of History itself; in the history of philosophy and on its margins where, by dint of effectivity, it manages in turn to utter one last interminable sigh. But what has changed after we stop being a Greco-unitary philosopher in order to think in vision-in-One? It is that the One encounters philosophy only in the "emplaced" state of material which is in turn philosophically incapable of determining it. The One does not prohibit that there is philosophy and resistance—this is what philosophy wants, at least when it is presented to us in this way, and the World and History want it too—but it determines philosophy as real in the mode of simple material, because it is not a simple "real possibility" but a thoroughly real essence deprived of possibility or of decision on its behalf. It is the *occasion*, and only the occasion, of this determination, even when it wills itself or when it experiences its existence as a self-willing. But the One *only* determines philosophy in the last instance; it is not the One that wills it and is commanded by the philosophical drive, but philosophy that "detaches" from the One its function of transcendental essence for … experience. The One is first of all transcendental "for" itself: it is as immanent and as concrete a lived experience as something can be, but it "becomes" the real condition or base for the sphere of effectivity in general and for philosophy in particular—*on the occasion* of the latter. Nevertheless, the One does not "recognize" the effectivity in philosophy's spontaneous claims, because it is History, Metaphysics, the World, etc. that resist the One the moment that the latter is taken as thought's guide, and it is these latter that need this guide, in the sense, however, that they must be thought by man and insofar as man is by definition inalienable for himself.

Non-philosophy's third dimension: its objectivity, or the possible

To understand the possibility of a third dimension of the theorem, it will not be imagined too quickly that philosophy and the One form a contradiction that requires a resolution. Something similar happens; but the second time, if it has the appearance of a contradiction, this is only from a transcendent point of view: the One does not see any contradiction but only a chaos. From its own illusory point of view, unitary thought is no doubt constrained to experience this situation as a fragmentation. There is then "contradiction" between the radical contingency that the One henceforth inflicts upon it—it is true without this being a manner of negation—and its claim to take from itself not only its right and its existence but also its real essence. Yet the point of view of philosophical faith is merely that of resistance; this point of view cannot be our own, which is vision-in-One and it alone. This is why the production of a new instance alongside the real (the One) and effectivity (existing philosophy, history, relations of power, etc.), the instance now of the *possible* and of the non-thetic *a prioris* in general, which is finally found insofar as it ensues irreversibly from the One, cannot be the resolution of a "contradiction," no more than it would be the result of an "abstraction."

What is the mechanism of non-philosophy's extraction? Let us recall that if we remain in the One alone (but the problem is not posed in this external way: one does not "remain" in the One because in general one cannot "exit" or "re-enter" it: it excludes all these operations by its inherence (to) self), the problem would not be posed, since no effective philosophy would be taken into account. To take a philosophy into account, as is always possible on the grounds of the *chôra* and its indifference to philosophy (or to any event whatsoever that takes place in the region of effectivity) is to now consider it as an inert material: even its resistance, which is not destroyed, is "emplaced" and sterilized. It is thus always present in its effectivity, and this is what is taken into account as "signal," not resistance itself. Then what is this new experience which, without being the One itself, is as unreflected in its essence as the One but which contains the *a priori* principle of the knowledge of effectivity?

Distinct from the One and its radical immanence, this experience can merely be that of *transcendence* or of *decision*, i.e. of any type of separation, scission, rupture, divergence, dis-ference, etc.; merely that of *position,* i.e. of any type of open, plane, base, project, etc. and merely that of *unity—but freed from their mixture-form.* In philosophy, all these dimensions are traditionally employed on behalf of a mixture-form, a form of unity, of synthesis and of reappropriaton, such that transcendence and position only intervene as blended together and thus blended with the One, which in a single stroke would become a simple transcendent unity. Effectivity is the region of mixtures wherein philosophy as unitary thought finds its place; it is the variously governed blending of the One and of Transcendence (the Other), of the real and of the possible. It is only when, as in non-philosophy, thought is established "in" the One and thinks according to an irreversible order that the One acts upon the mixtures and thus extracts a transcendence, a position and a unity (all of which are unreflected) from all of them: they are no longer blended with the One and among themselves as thinkable on the basis of their own redoubling but are an immediately "simple" or immanent exteriority, base and unity.

In opposition to redoubled, duplicated position and decision, which are those of effectivity and unitary events in general, their state of *a prioris* has been called "non-thetic" or "non-mixed," and expressions like "non-thetic transcendence" (NTT), "non-thetic position" (NTP) and "non-thetic unity" (NTU) have been utilized.

Their description is a difficult endeavor. It is a question of pure possibles, absolutely unleashed from the mixture-form and not simply from forms of unity, of position, of synthesis or of correlation. These can only be freed from effectivity because they are real by their being-immanent. Rigorously thought, the possible excludes the false real of effectivity, but it is real in the rigorous sense of this word by its essence. For example, it is true, in a still very external way, that one can think NTT as a scission or a rupture but which would immediately remain in-itself without exiting itself or prolonging itself—this is what usually happens—in a continuity, a rapport, a relation; a sterile break that engenders nothing and revives neither unity nor movement; a *dis*-junction that is immediately experienced as such without passing through the mediation of its effects of synthesis or of junction; an ekstasis deprived of the movement of fusion and of identification; an opening that neither gives place to any "open," to any place in general, nor produces any horizon in which it would come to be reinscribed and upon which it would fall back; an inaugural rupture that inaugurates no project, no history, no world, etc.

We shall manage to acquire the non-philosophical element beyond philosophical decision with this third dimension of the dualitary order of thoughts. The non-thetic *a priori* in general—including the *chôra*—are the real content of decision but definitively remain in themselves: this is the essence of philosophical decision *before* its unitary adventures and its misadventures in effectivity. After the *chôra* and as en-suing[10] from the One, we have acquired the experience of a non-thetic decision, position and unity, i.e. absolute in their order and as "absolute" as can possibly be imagined. What is called non-philosophy does not pertain to forms of philosophy simply reworked or altered, for it is what really and objectively conditions philosophy's mixtures; this is decision described as unreflected or sterile, without effects of blending, of synthesis or of relation, decision which remains in itself because it never left itself and because it is non-positional (of) self. Against its vicious auto-positions, a theory of philosophical decision therefore

---

10   The French word "dé-coulant" describes the irreversible movement of water flowing from the source of a river. [TN]

87

proposes to bring it back to its ultimate conditions of object (the *chôra*) and of objectivity (the three "objective" *a prioris*).

Non-philosophy's genetic code

The dualitary paradigm offers a new experience of philosophical decision. It is both a question of describing and transforming decision by reducing it to the state of material for a thought of another origin, and then, at this point, by impressing upon it an absolute possibilization that consists in the articulation of a triple *a priori* dimension more powerful than philosophy itself.

Let us return to the *a prioris* of objectivity. On the one hand there is an opening-without-open, an ekstasis-without-horizon, an unreflected transcendence that remains in itself without giving rise to a space, a horizon, a position in which it would seamlessly come to re-inscribe itself and inhibit itself. This region of objectivity can also be called *the non-thetic Other*. It is indeed a question of de-cisions, crises or breaks, of exteriorities, but deprived of continuity, of unity, of a binding synthetic property and even of simple association—thus deprived of production and reproduction in general. On the other hand, there is a non-thetic position—or position non-positional (of) self—in a general non-mixed way: the *a priori* of a *non-thetic Being* or of a *non-thetic Base*. Lastly, there is a *Unity* that is also given in the mode of a being immanent. These are the three "objective" dimensions of the representation or of the (non-) One correlative with the One.

The consequence of their determination in the last instance by the One, which bestows a real or unreflected essence upon them, is that these givens of the *a priori* are deprived of the transcendent effects in which philosophy attempts to reproduce them and in which philosophy attempts to discover a shred of reality; that they stop being mixtures so as to become the kernels of a possible without equivalent in "the-world." This real essence renders useless that these ekstases "exit" themselves effectively or that these positions repose themselves effectively. By their essence, the *a prioris* are freed from the "World" and from "History" (even if they need them as "support"), and they always already repose in the Undecided itself. They do not find the latter in front of or behind themselves as a destiny or a death; they do not entangle themselves in the events or rules that weave the compact fabric of the World or of History. Thus non-philosophy contains a transcendence, i.e. an opening, utterly opaque in virtue of its unreflected nature, but also a position and a unity of a phenomenality that is just as unreflected. It is an experience (of) the Other, (of) Being and (of) Unity that would have ultimately found their foundation in the One.

Because they appeal to the Other as though to an instance peripheral to Identity and combine it with the Same, philosophers lay claim to the Other, as well as the other *a prioris*, just as they lay claim to the One: they remain content with making them "function," with including them in relations, leaving their ultimate essence undetermined. The contemporary deconstructions of "metaphysics," for example, relate the latter to an experience—which is itself without relation—of alterity, but which they suppose capable of being effectuated without discerning anything in the Other except its supposed effects (rupture, breakage, dissemination, withdrawal, etc.). At worst, one then imagines that transcendence is always formed *in relation to* … a preliminary given (for example, a whatever identity), that it is a withdrawal *relative to* …; at best, that it is an absolute *withdrawal* or Other, but always inevitably combined with the first scenario. A term of departure assigned with ambiguous functions is given in this way: functions of *withdrawal's* support or reference, but also of what is broken, fractured by the Other, wrenched from itself by this simultaneously internal and external withdrawal. This second function belongs to unitary thought and must be abandoned if we want to think the Other as absolute or unreflected. As for the first, it also belongs to the dualitary model no doubt, but on condition of being rethought as simple *support* or *occasion* of a non-thetic Other.

When the Other is instead founded in the One as such, when it stops being required and used for "critical," i.e. circular and metaphysical—at the very least "unitary"—ends, the conditions are brought together for thinking the Other in its intimate constitution. If non-philosophy is a new experience (of) the Other, (of) Being and (of) Unity insofar as they are determined in the last instance by the One, then this is where one has some chance of grasping the ultimate real ingredients of effective philosophical decision. On the one hand, although, rigorously speaking, there is no "chain" or "correlation" here, the ensemble of the *a prioris* is the equivalent of a veritable *genetic code of non-philosophy*. Other, Being, Unity and *Chôra* designate a specific content, an internal variety capable of being described; this is a *non-philosophical* code of experience in general, of the World, of History, Technics, Language, etc. and is destined to be substituted for the philosophical code. If it can be called "genetic," this is then on condition of not understanding it as a claimed real genesis of the real itself (the One) or even of effectivity (the-world, the-history, etc.) on the basis of the *a priori* possibles or essences. This is an aprioritic genesis of representation or of non-philosophical knowledge that only has sense from the point of view of the One or of science.

In their function as transcendental *a prioris, these* a prioris *are not constitutive of the effectivity of decisions itself,* but they are to be described as the scientific representation of the real condition or real base of the last instance of these effective decisions. If they are not constitutive (in the sense that unitary thoughts can comprehend philosophy as constitutive of the real), they remain required but forgotten and denied by philosophy like the One itself which in the last instance allows for them to be established and described. In relation to systems existing in effectivity, they are both immanent to them, since these systems cannot keep from supposing them so that they can at least be rigorously thought, as well as anterior to and precedent over them, as much as a "last instance" of immanence can be. From this point of view, the elaboration of the non-philosophical code is the non-circular, unilateralizing "critique" of unitary philosophy, of the belief conveyed by its effectivity and its institutional forms, etc.

It should be noted that non-philosophy is the (terminal, not constituting-genetic) universalization of the various regions of effectivity; each time there are several complementary types of *a priori,* because they determine both the ideal elements of every effective-worldly experience and the empirico-ontic elements of this experience insofar as they are all included in a unity-of-mixture. The endeavor of comprehension that drives non-philosophy is definitively terminal: not at the end of the "process," but at the end of the order of realities. Rather than "lagging" behind the real, it is therefore always posterior to it and also, in another inessential way, to effectivity. *This is why the same reason that seems to deprive philosophy of all efficacy upon the real is what opens it to the field of non-philosophy's specific reality and transforms it into a particular order of the real, an activity that is absolute in its order and no longer accountable to the World, History, Politics, Language, etc.* In this new sense of the autonomy of non-philosophy—*as real in its order and no longer as inter-vening in the real*—the *a priori* code is indeed a "genetic" code. But what it produces is neither the real properly speaking, nor even effectivity, but a radical possible, non-thetic and thus absolutely real in its mode. The genetic code produces a representation (of the) real: it is not the real of the "last instance," but precisely the order of its representation.

This non-philosophical experience (of) philosophical decision will allow for the recovery of a power of invention and of fiction which it has lacked. Not a power of the imagination: there is simply nothing at all "fictive" or imaginary in this "operation" of non-thetic *a prioris* which no subject, will or consciousness can claim to enact. Thought (of) the Other can recover, conquer rather, what it has never had as philosophy: an activity of radical fiction, of creation of sense, and of a sense freed from its inscriptions in the objects, texts, representations, blendings of the "effective" world. This possible is absolutely unleashed from its variable blendings with the real, is itself deprived of all position and is an indivisible and necessarily plural event.

Another interpretation of the *a priori* code can be found alongside, for example, concepts which have received a usage in linguistics but which overflow it, here in particular due to their real or transcendental content. Non-thetic Transcendence is the ultimate kernel of transcendence that defines every paradigm: non-philosophy as thought (of) the Other finds its irreducible paradigmatic dimension in it. From this point of view, it supplies unitary philosophical systems, including Greco-occidental metaphysics and its contemporary deconstructions, with their resource in transcendence, in experience of the Other, in alterity and heterogeneity, in difference, in allergy, etc.—their paradigmatic resource. As for the side of the non-thetic Base or Universal, it is the ultimate, irreducible syntagmatic *a priori* that the genetic code supplies for unitary systems, i.e. for their mixed and transcendent experience of the Attribute, of Being or of the General. Lastly, the *a priori* of non-thetic Unity supplies philosophies with the primitive dimension or the real base of their auto-position or of their "speculative" auto-factualization.

The method of dualysis (the unitary and the dualitary)

What is the operation that "analyzes" in this way a whatever philosophical decision in its three dimensions? It is less an "analysis"—a new decision—than a "dualyzation": why not speak of a "dualysis," of the dualytic function which is the labor of a radical dyad, the dual which is without operation of scission? As non-unitary but dualitary deconstruction, it reduces an effective decision to its determination in the last instance (only) by the One; to its mate-rial of mixture that fulfills the function of occasion and support; ultimately to its standing as non-thetic possibility (transcendence, position and unity which are non-decisional and non-positional (of) self). These are three heterogeneous, interchangeable ingre-dients because they involve two-by-two relations (the One and effectivity, the possible and effectivity, the One and the possible) and from the start, above all, non-relations which are characteris-tic of the dualitary style when it is founded on the One's radical autonomy in its transcendental truth and on Determination in the last instance.

"Dualysis" simultaneously frees the real, which is no longer encumbered and hindered by philosophy, and philosophical deci-sion or at least its essence, which is no longer prevented or inhib-ited by itself and by the faith bound to its spontaneous practice. In the last instance, dualysis roots decision as such in an Undecided and, reducing it to the state of material, it aligns decision with a non-positional possible, fating it in a certain way to fiction, giving it a space and a respiration that it has never had, aligning it despite everything with the real in the only founded, not illusory, relation that decision can undertake with it.

What is called non-philosophy is a scientific practice of philo-sophical decision; it is the order of thoughts that relate decision to its transcendental truth, to its ultimate condition in the One and therefore to its other conditions which are those of the dual, then those of duality. In order to find something like a non-philosophy, it is necessary to have been constrained to give up deciding on phi-losophy philosophically, on turning it into an act of self-mastery-of-the-real. Non-philosophy is no longer a principle beginning (*Beginn*), nor is it summoned in a commencement (*An-fang*), i.e. by what would leap in the bound (*Satz)* of a principle (*Grund-satz*) or in the difference of an origin. It is instead "at the end," if it can still be expressed in this way, because the irreversible order of dualitary economy excludes every teleological, unitary and recur-rent process, but also excludes its "interruption." Non-philosophy supposes before it the real (of) the One and, in another way, the philosophical effectivity of the events of the World, of History, of Technics, etc. It has stopped being first (*prima philosophia*) and stopped being inhibited in what comes after it and what it helps to produce. It is not simply an activity of the production of possibles, a philosophy-fiction in a new sense of this word, but a definitive, ultimate activity *after* which there is no longer anything that can manage to recover it, capture it, limit it: it is the great wide open [*le grand large*].

It has thus appeared to us that the unitary knot of the One and of philosophy is an illusion and that it was already cut by vision-in-One. Philosophy *is* determined, it does not determine itself, and even less so determines the real. This is the condition for thought to stop being underdetermined and to stop compensating for this insufficiency with its overdetermination and its activism, such that it will at last be integrally and thoroughly determined as universal: to first make way for the real so as to also make way for (non-)philosophy.

"Determination in the last instance" makes it possible to free non-philosophy in philosophy. It is as real as it is undecided, but not in a relation of self to self, a relation of blending of self and of its essence. Such an illusory blending with the Undecided is exactly what dooms the unitary paradigm to its paralysis. Here one opens a precise space to thought in which it is free, in which it is also limited but without being hindered by these limits, without being inhibited in itself because these two limits (which are moreover very heterogeneous: the real and effectivity) precede it. It is better to walk straight into the wind of the future than to enter into the future backwards or to head straight back into the past. The real is no longer limited by the possibilities of philosophy (it will never be said just how much philosophy, under pretext of "critique," is a simple operation of halting, quite reactionary but also suicidal) nor by effectivity in general. Correlatively, thought is no longer bogged down in its effects or in its works or in this product par excellence which is the absence of all product, work=0 as a tendency toward the diminution of its output. Instead of a simple critical distinction of domains, for example, a Kantian type of decision which implies reciprocal determinations, a whole economy that veers, despite everything, into exchanges, into negotiation and quickly into interminable conflicting relations of *mutual* debtors and creditors—here one puts a rigorously unilateralizing distinction between philosophy and the real, and not simply half-unilateral and half-reversible: a "dualysis" of philosophy.

By no longer claiming to legislate on the real, non-philosophy frees itself for other more inventive tasks. This "dual" divorce, *de jure anterior* to its claimed coupling with the real, undoubtedly deprives philosophical decision of one of its favorite operations: critique; surpassing and overcoming; internalizing turn; destruction and deconstruction; therapeutics, care and concern.

But this is how it becomes as "real" as it can be in its order. Half-Samaritan, half-Pharisean, philosophy has distilled the pharmakon of auto- and hetero-critique without being able or without wanting to go further toward the only positive critique: a *dishallucination of philosophical decision, its absolute dependence in terms of an undecided real.* Dis-hallucination is not the nihilism by which unitary philosophical decision is infected (with) itself. "In itself" or unreflected, the One has not withdrawn from philosophy bleeding to death and abandoned to the shores of the World, for it has not produced the non-thetic possible by withdrawal into itself: this operation is also excluded by its essence, and the possible on its side is sufficient, absolute in its order such as it is, "deprived" of all power of position, unification or synthesis in which it would come to be re-inscribed....

"Why not philosophy?"[11]: it is not, will no longer be and perhaps has never really been necessary. Not for our experience of the World, of History, of Power, etc., of which it is co-constituting and in which it has massively intervened, but for man. Does the real exhaust itself in the philosophical work and the philosophical operation, or from the start has decision indeed been emplaced and unilateralized, rendered irrelevant by an instance which it had denied in a hallucinatory way so as to be established in its unitary and warmongering form? This expression "why not philosophy?" states that the passage to philosophy is undoubtedly always possible, even necessary from History or the World, but that it is no longer necessary "in itself," that it is formed upon the grounds of a radical contingency. Such a question supposes that one abandons it as point of view upon itself, that one, for example, renounces a decision of the "not philosophy!" type, which is always somewhat willful, domineering, overly unitary and classical, and that one undertakes a science of philosophy (the true critique), a science that will be immanent (the true "affirmation": that of the real, the Determination in the last instance, rather than that of effectivity)....

Several specifications concerning the terms *unitary* and *authoritarian* become possible. Here, *unitary* no longer, as is the case with philosophers, merely designates forms of massive (analytic and synthetic) unity in opposition to Multiplicities and Differe(a)nce and in general no longer designates prior "metaphysical" and "representative" decisions proceeding with means as homogenous

---

11   Cf. Laruelle's self-published works from 1983-1985 under the same title: *Porquoi pas la philosophie?*. Some of the material from these six self-published volumes was used by Laruelle in the writing of *Philosophy and Non-philosophy.* [TN]

as "substance," "totality," etc. in opposition to more "heteroge-neous" procedures. All these distinctions are modes of philosophi-cal critique and thus no longer have value for us, since we want to conduct a critique of philosophy as such. *Unitary* instead desig-nates the type of unity that has run its course and is underway in any possible philosophy whatsoever of which it is the main invari-ant; it designates any Unity that is combined with a Dyad and has become "synthetic" in a broad sense or is acquired by procedures of scission and identification, decision and position, etc. Even if this Unity were that of Difference and the Heterogeneous, Multi-plicities and Becoming rather than Substance, it wouldn't change the problem: it always supposes recourse to mixed modes of deci-sion and position—Transcendence in general or the mixture of immanence and transcendence—and is always a "superior" and anonymous unity, an "exploitation" of labor of the terms it puts in relation, and thus in conflict, so as to better extract from them a surplus value of sense, value and truth—and authority. The *unitary*, the *circular* (reciprocal determination), the *authoritarian* (philosophical sufficiency) are strictly the same thing and define philosophy's specific invariant; they are the philosophical as such, rather than one of its historical modes that could be "critiqued" or "deconstructed." The philosophical critique of unity's representa-tive forms remains an authoritarian critique, and philosophy is the paradigm of the unitary style in thought, even when it ap-proaches, like deconstructions, a quasi-dualist thought.

The unitary is therefore no longer opposed to the differential, the multiple, the heterogeneous and even the dualistic, which are all species of it, but the *unary* and the *dualitary*. Deconstructions, which are unitary dualisms, are distinguished from an authenti-cally *dualitary* thought, that which the autonomy of vision-in-One necessarily implies concerning the status of the World and philosophy. On the one hand, the *unary* designates the One non-positional and non-decisional (of) self, which cannot be gauged by the philosophers' transcendent and transcendental Unity be-cause the latter supposes and denies the One's reality from the start, whereas the One has no need of this Unity which remains a functional and possible-real mixture. On the other hand, the *dualitary* designates the primitiveness of a static duality or duality without-scission that ensues irreversibly from the One, without really being elicited from it by a decision, and that does not re-flect itself in it; in a sense a duality as primitive as the One itself, because it is transcendentally founded in the One and *founded so as to be conserved as duality*, as anterior to any procedure of transcendence exerted upon a preliminary Unity (scission, decision, reversal), as impossible to be resolved by an identification in progress. This duality is from the start that of the One and of the World or of philosophy (what we call the "dual"), then that of the residual non-thetic *a prioris* and of the pole of transcendence which is set outside-the-real each time. Such a duality that escapes from philosophical operations is manifested in the form of contingency, or of the outside-real of the World or of philosophy which is globally affected by the (non-) One. But this radical suspension is both what leaves-be philosophical decision and no longer claims to intervene in it one more time.

The expression "dualitary or minoritarian philosophy" is thus ambiguous and must be rigorously recast. It leads one to think that "radical Minorities"—which we call ultimate individuals or One(s)—are insinuated where Unity reigned, or that the concept of minority has been introduced into philosophy, to the place which has hardly been displaced and which has been solicited by *Cosmos*, *Polis*, and *Physis*. Minorities are no longer the object (there would be a philosophy of minorities as there is a philosophy of language, sciences, technics, etc.) because they are not the subject of another way of philosophizing. They are instead the radical subject (of) science and then (of) non-philosophy. It is not even certain that it is above all a question of a *way* besides that of the unitary. There is indeed a dualitary or "minoritarian" paradigm of thought, but it is scientific: there is no "minoritarian philosophy." The displacement of the philosophical operation, literally an irreversible deduction and an irreversible derivation, is absolute: it is the primitive transcendental em-place that ultimately affects it. The project is therefore not to find dualism *in* (unitary) philosophy again (it exists in Plato, Kant, etc.), but instead *to put philosophy to the test* [épreuve] *of duality, non-philosophy as proof* [preuve] *of the "dual" of the One and of philosophy*.

For the same reason, it cannot be a question of a philosophy of the One, namely a "first philosophy," because the One is that which, by its own existence, condemns first philosophy to be em-placed and displaced. The One is philosophy's real condition of the last instance, but not reciprocally. It acts in/as the World and History, but here one refuses to conclude with it from its effectivity to its real essence, and even to its *real* condition (the One) of *possibility* (the possible non-positional (of) self).

Chapter III: The "non-Euclidean" mutation in philosophy and non-philosophy's scientific foundation

The scientific or "non-philosophical" practice of philosophy

Philosophy acknowledges just as many systems as self-critiques. It invests a large portion of its energy into its own examination, which includes that of the World and its objects, of culture and its values, of knowledges and their encyclopedia. In one last twist, it has recently even claimed to renounce carrying out its own critique so as to offer itself to the efficacy of the Other and to abandon itself to alterity. Nevertheless, up to the last moment it will be explicitly or implicitly arranged so as to remain master over this precariousness and to turn it into a game. This is the age of philosophy, an ageless age that will perhaps never end.

None of this, along with "being done" with philosophy, is in question here anymore. After Wittgenstein, Heidegger and Derrida, it has become urgent to pose the new problem to which they will not have led us. Not: what can we still do with the philosophical? But: what can we do with philosophy globally? Despite certain contrary appearances resulting from an insufficient analysis of its tricks, this question has never really been posed by philosophy, even in its most contorted auto-critiques. How would philosophy, which has always claimed it was unavoidable for every possible thought, have been able to simply *isolate itself globally as such*? Whether it be a question of willing it or of deconstructing this willing, philosophy has always sustained that it was necessary, that man could not avoid it, that man must assume it and identify himself with it when this would only be in order to deconstruct it.

We call this bewitched belief, which philosophy has known quite well how to plant in men's heads and which no thought still laying claim to it as its ultimate horizon can get rid of, the *Principle of Sufficient Philosophy* (PSP). It states that philosophy suffices for the real and for the thought of the real and thus that it is unsurpassable like the real itself. It is now also a question of this more crucial problem: is philosophy the Necessity or Destiny that announces itself to man? Or is it man who must and can announce himself to it? And *who* is man: the man of philosophy, or instead the one it did not beget and which it has in reality never known, man who can now be declared to be the One itself and, consequently, since vision-in-One is the essence of science, the subject (of) science? *Homo sive scientia*: the discovery of their radical or immanent unity in vision-in-One ultimately makes it possible for us to affirm that philosophical decision is globally contingent, that it exists without real foundation for the most human of men and that it is up to the latter, if not to "reappropriate" the discovery, then at least to treat it in a spirit of freedom and without the prudence of emancipation that is almost always manifested when confronting it.

Measured against the practice of philosophy that this man in question can still take charge of, the recent deconstructions of Wittgenstein, Heidegger or Derrida seem like restrictive attempts still doomed to philosophical sufficiency because they have internally willed this ultimate submission to the PSP. After them—so long as it is a question of an after and so long as this historico-ontological logic has the slightest significance here—the only things admissible are the following thesis and its foundation: philosophy is not simply an illusion, localized in one of its sectors, "metaphysics," "representation" or "language"; it is through and through a hallucination—transcendental, certainly not empirical—at least when measured against another paradigm it has always repressed, namely that of the *thought* which is also science. Relieved of its empiricist interpretations and its philosophical and epistemological reappropriations, founded in the posture of vision-in-One which is certainly not its entirety but its element, science makes it known that it is indeed an autonomous thought which possesses a transcendental truth that it derives from itself, but a thought more primitive than philosophy due to its simplicity. This earthquake in the general economy of knowledge does not leave philosophy intact: it can only be globally "put back in its place" by science, its authority over and claims about the real thus being invalidated and the PSP lifted or suspended. In this way, several similar attempts in the history of philosophy are radicalized (Kant, Marx, Husserl and the Vienna Circle) that had still remained within the PSP.

It is only in this gap, which is so deep that is has never been delved, in this crack so obscure that the light of the *logos* cannot illuminate it or can only do so by concealing it and making it disappear again, that a new and henceforth "non-philosophical" practice of philosophy can be developed. Restored in its consistency of thought and its transcendental claim to primitively know the real, science can found such a new usage of philosophy. "Non-philosophy" is the positive practice of philosophy—but it is also the only practice that remains for us—once science settles into its place, which is "first," and philosophy is put back into its own place as second.

Among other things, this practice is defined as a generalization of thought beyond philosophical decision. If science also really has a transcendental power of truth distinct from the philosophical, i.e. power of manifestation of the real and not simply a technicist production of knowledge, then it must be presented with a specific capacity of generalization or universalization superior to that of philosophy. And since, as vision-in-One, it contains in itself an experience of the Other, of Being and of Unity in the form of *non-thetic a prioris*, and it also knows alterity in particular (in the form in which it understands the exteriority of its object, which is now nothing more than the philosophical object), it is presented to philosophy with a capacity of alteration more general than that of which the latter is capable. *Non-philosophy is the scientific or "generalized" practice of philosophy, the non- here expressing the positivity of this Other which science knows and which has its being-immanent in the One.* Thus to take the example that will largely preoccupy us later on, philosophy's deconstruction, which is still enacted within the limits of the Principle of sufficiency, will from now on have to be characterized as *restrained*; and what is enacted by the means of science and is the true hetero-deconstruction, its real critique by the ordeal of the non-thetic Other, will be called *generalized* or, for example, "non-Heideggerian." From this slightly external point of view, non-philosophy is this practice of a generalized deconstruction of philosophical decision, on condition that this generalization consequently receives its model supplied by science, which is completely different from the philosophical model. In relation to this non-philosophy (which is an endeavor as positive

99

in its order as the "non-Euclidean" and which must be interpreted in this spirit), philosophies (including deconstructions) can be henceforth grasped as particular cases of a more radical and, under this condition, more general thought: philosophy is to non-philosophy what the "restrained"[12] is to the "general," if at least science, grasped as vision-in-One, imposes upon us its concept and its practice of this generalization that reduces an anterior thought to being a more restrained or more elementary case. Philosophy's scientific or non-philosophical *generalization* will be opposed to the philosophical *reappropriation* of science. It alone bears witness to the claimed commencement of thought in the mode of philosophy which was in reality a constriction—its Greco-philosophical constriction—and to the fact that another and more expansive experience of thought is completely possible.

Since philosophers are the voluntary victims of an appearance which they have foreseen—the *objective philosophical Appearance*, which is unitary thought's own transcendental illusion—the only possible struggle against this bewitchment requires taking things in their real order, to be established in the scientific posture of vision-in-One, i.e. in the *Identity* of the object that one wishes to describe and that must be given in its identity and its reality before any philosophical division; then it requires describing it by taking its immanence as guiding thread and, on this basis alone, to describe the relations it can involve with contingent givens like what philosophies now are, relations which are no longer first but second and no longer circular but unilateral. In this way science describes *the real content of what should be called "superstructures,"* on this side of or beyond their auto-interpretations which are always unitary (but these terms poorly describe the non-philosophical mutation).

What is more important than any new "decision" is therefore first the task to rediscover the great unknown of epistemology and philosophy: *science in its veritas transcendentalis*, in its being-immanent which is vision-in-One, consequently in its precedence over Transcendence or philosophical decision. If the introduction of the non-philosophical style into thought corresponds with the need to "generalize" the possibilities of decision, then this need cannot itself be of philosophical origin, because at each moment philosophy in a sense always draws out all its consequences,

---

12 Cf. the French translation of Einstein's special theory of relativity as "relativité restreinte." Thus what is being opposed here is the "general" and the "special" (restrained) in the (non-)Einsteinian sense. [TN]

produces the effects it can produce, manifests all its virtualities. This power of generalization can only have its distant origin in a wholly other experience of thought: in the immanent experience according to which science does not take its transcendental consistency from philosophy but harbors it in its own depths and, for this reason, instead of still being submitted to philosophy's authority, precedes it and affirms itself as more originary. The consequence of this putting back in order is not simply the extension of science (in the form of a "transcendental science") to philosophical decision itself: it is a new practice of the latter. When philosophical decision is thought through this optics and viewed as a simple contingent material submitted like any other object to the structures of scientific "objectivity" that transform it (an objectivity of the non-philosophical type, which will be clear by virtue of the initial thesis): this is what is called non-philosophy.

In effect, this is the only real or immanent chance of transforming philosophical decision: real, and not simply effective or internal to the World and philosophy. It is advisable to distinguish carefully between these two types of transformation in accordance with vision-in-One or science. Real means several things: in view of science; by its means alone ("real object" and "object of knowledge"); beyond any auto-application or circular intervention of philosophy; without any of the latter's procedures or operations (Decision and Position; Reversal and Displacement); lastly, without any finality or teleology, but by man himself as One-subject (of) science. The effective elaboration of the material in accordance with the non-thetic *a prioris* transforms philosophical decision into simple occasion, then into simple scientific representation of decision as real object to be described. Renouncing any intervention into the effective structures of philosophy, it leaves-be philosophy and produces new effects with this material only beyond its "sufficient" validity and usage.

The science of philosophy proceeds globally to what could be called a "transcendental deconstruction" of philosophy in accordance with the absolute subject (of) science or of vision-in-One. It is confined to describing this subject's real essence. But, by inscribing decision into objectivity of the scientific type, this deconstruction inscribes it into a new order that is heterogeneous to philosophy which is no longer constitutive (of) the real, i.e. in the occurrence, no longer constitutive of the real states of affairs that are at the basis of decision. Decision—its utterances, its language—thus serves to represent itself, or rather *to be* represented or described by itself, but henceforth in a non-constitutive way as non-thetic representation (of) self, outside any relation of co-determination or co-constitution. The possibility of this real practice, which is that of knowledge of the scientific type, is opened to philosophy in this way. For the most human man, this is not only the de-logicization of thought and the destruction of its fetishistic appearance, but its insertion into a different usage that is heterogeneous to its spontaneous and sufficient usage and therefore enables its ongoing rectification. A new usage of decision both inaugurates its unlimited transformation in view of man as well as the critique of the circular, auto-interpretative and "philocentric" relations that it habitually involves with the real and with itself.

The Greek constriction of thought:
the unitary or Heraclitean postulate

Philosophy is only pertinent for a limited type of experience: the *supposed given* or the given in the mode of transcendence. This is what philosophy reflects, analyzes, synthesizes, interprets, transforms. It has no validity for another experience which is transcendental, real, immanent or non-thetic (of) self and which is given rather than supposed given. It decides *a priori* on the first experience, on the World, History, Language, Art, etc. It is thus not surprising that philosophy discovers next to nothing and that it is consecrated to commenting interminably on its own activity of decision, to displacing it, to critiquing it, to investing in and capitalizing on it. Its self-interest, its philocentrism is identically these games in which it reproduces itself in an ultimately limited way. When they slave away at problems, texts, aporias, differences and multiplicities, networks and exchanges, when they deconstruct their tradition, philosophers do it with respect to a closure that is even stronger than that of "Representation" or "Logocentrism," the unitary closure or the Unity-of-the-Dyad, which is the same thing as the principle of sufficiency to the real. Philosophy's traditional practices, the history of philosophy, textual and philological labor, but also the invention of new philosophical decisions (language games, deconstruction and schizoanalysis) remain, from this new point of view and from it alone, enclosed in themselves, wrapped and encysted around the fundamental postulate that defines Greco-occidental thought and its most internal limitation. This postulate, which goes unnoticed by philosophers at least in its real essence and its contingency, is either called "unitary" or "divided Unity." It signifies that when it takes the form of subjectivity, of the Other or of any other figure, the real's essence necessarily possesses *one and only one structure: that of Unity coextensive with the Dyad, a unity which proceeds by self-division and by coupling of contraries.* This postulate defines the opening, the little bit of opening, of Greco-occidental thought in its "philosophical" mode. It is so deep and concealed by what was founded upon it that philosophers are only philosophers—including deconstructionists— so long as they work within the space opened by it and ignore it in its real essence. For them, this is not a contingent postulate; it is the ground or foundation that they establish in thought.

Philosophers then necessarily remain content with operating a machine that they have already found at work. They can vary the regime, speed up or slow down the movement, give it new first matters and make it produce new objects; they can complicate it and add pieces to it that defer and delay the necessity of production. *But they all respect the diagram of its spontaneous functionality, the system of the simultaneous One and Dyad.* They modify the machine without modifying its most general functionality. Their activism stems from this, a functionality so confined within the limits of its Greek presuppositions that it cannot see them. It would be necessary, for *one moment*—but this is impossible—to stop this machine from functioning in order to observe, without modifying, the most concealed presuppositions of its regime; they are all concentrated in the "unitary postulate," which is the same thing as the PSP or the existence of this very machine. The consequences of this internal limitation are countless. Let's consider two of them. On the one hand, this limitation explains that only "applied philosophy" has ever been done—this is the Greek constriction of thought. It is simultaneously applied to problems which are said to be "concrete," political, scientific, aesthetic etc., and which come to determine it in return. And when philosophy is applied to itself while claiming to then determine the real, it becomes auto-applied (as archive, history, deconstruction). Since these two usages always come together, it will be necessary to oppose them to their dis-applied usage of the real's scientific representation rather than that of application to the sciences. Whence the possibility of a "fiction" or hyperspeculation that will put an end to this restriction of philosophy at the limits of transcendent experience. On the other hand, philosophers poorly support their multiplicity, whether *de jure* or *de facto* and even when they turn it into an object of affirmation. A unitary drive forces them to want to mutually integrate and hierarchize themselves. The couples of truth and error, of the authentic and the inauthentic, of the already and the not yet, of the noble and the gregarious, of affirmation and nihilism, etc., serve to organize these countless hierarchies.

Hence this pitiless war they wage against one another, these meticulously planned strategies, these triumphant affirmations and, for the subtlest of them, these claims of moderation and sobriety. Philosophy's enclosure upon itself and into its own war-mongering or unitary multiplicity forces it to be exploited as a supposed inexhaustible but basically rare stock. There is a rarity of decision that stems from its unity or its circularity, from its auto-reference or auto-sufficiency: *all philosophies—the manifold of the Dyad—share the unique prize of Unity, which is in itself indivisible, and this rarity is identical to the war that they all wage reciprocally.* Every rarity implies an overexploitation, and that of sufficient philosophy leads it to over-utilize and expect too much from itself—and not merely in its contemporary forms. This is why there is a relative decline of its productivity in proportion to the growing rage that it seeks to exploit. In this sense, the "history of philosophy" is the dominant practice in which all philosophies reconcile for a moment through the need that they have of making peace in view of their mutual auto-exploitation.

The auto-description of vision-in-One has shown *de facto* the contingency of philosophy returned to its unilateralizing emplacement in the (non-) One. We can pursue this demonstration more precisely by isolating a fundamental consequence of the unitary postulate and by revealing its contingency for thought. In effect, the most elementary matrix of philosophical decision, the unitary coupling of two terms or the system of the One-of-the-Dyad, first of all is manifested from the angle of the Dyad as dominant. Consequently, philosophy is founded more precisely on this obvious and never reconsidered cause that *for each term=x there corresponds one and only one term or type of term, along with a relative, opposed or even contrary term. Greco-philosophical thought completely holds to this "Heraclitean" postulate which says that for a given term there corresponds one contrary term and one alone*, a postulate which in every way does not lack a somewhat distant analogy with the spirit of Euclid's fifth postulate concerning parallel lines. We shall prove the limitation of this Heraclitean postulate as well as the possibility of suspending it in order to open thought radically.

The suspension of the unitary or Heraclitean postulate

We have the feeling—but perhaps it is no longer of philosophical origin—that the auto-warfare which animates philosophy's "unitary" life assures it nothing but a truncated history, a confined atmosphere, an increasingly difficult respiration; that its traditional practice since its Greek invention is so diversified that it is nothing but one possibility among others; that what we call its "unitary postulate" turns it into a restrained or restrictive practice, a simple particular case of a more universal thought. It matters little that it acknowledges none of this: it suffers from an excess of authority over itself and from a sufficiency that it cannot perceive how it does not suffice, how it in-suffices for this other thought which is more universal and primitive than it, i.e. vision-in-One as thought (of) science, "science-thought." The perception of philosophical malaise is thus an effect. The extenuation of philosophy, overexploited, worn out and slow to react to what happens outside the reference to its tradition, is no doubt a disturbing symptom for its future in a regime of "sufficiency" where it invests an increasingly considerable energy into a rare material and into tools with weak theoretical possibilities. But the effects, rather than the mere causes, of why it does this and does it unknowingly, since its blindness is the same thing as its sufficiency, cannot be known and discovered except from another experience of thought which reveals that philosophy's sufficiency is but one of the particular possibilities of thought and that other practices of it are possible; that in particular it reposes on a presupposition of unity which, by assuring philosophy its sufficiency, also marks a limitation rather than an opening for it, a condemnation to rarity and war, and ultimately, instead of freedom, the powerlessness of omnipotence.

It is impossible to question this postulate except with the discovery of vision-in-One which does not repose on it and which renders it contingent, if not useless. Since vision-in-One forms the substructure of scientific thought in its difference that is irreducible to philosophy, science is the mode of thought par excellence that does not need this postulate. Therefore it shows that the requirement of divided Unity, of identifying Scission, of reversible Coupling of contraries, of the One and the Dyad as simultaneous (with the restriction to a single relative term) is transcendent. It is not only "possible" to rigorously think without this postulate, but the realest essence of thought requires its exclusion as transcendent, particular and non-originary. With vision-in-One we have the conditions that "bankrupt" this auto-limitation of philosophical practice in the regime of the PSP and that allow for the lifting of its authority without destroying decision as such. By impressing upon decision a radical or "non-philosophical" opening that eliminates any possibility of auto-reference, it transmits to decision not only a multiplicity of unitary usages (what it already does by itself) but a duality of usages (under the PSP and "under" science), so heterogeneous that this multiplicity takes on a completely different scope. Greco-contemporary practices are so various that they are nothing but a typical or even average case of this multiplicity or of this non-unitary generalization of its usages, and the PSP is an illusion bound to an overly restrained practice of thought. This is perhaps a fundamental case for treating certain problems of the World or of effectivity which is historical, political, linguistic, aesthetic etc., but it is merely one possibility of practicing philosophy among others that together form a more expansive experience of thought. Above all it is not Representation, Presence or Identity that must be critiqued once again: these concepts have been produced ad hoc for a goal that remains autocritical. More profoundly than Representation in general, there is this invisible element of the PSP in which philosophical decision mutates after its origins. Its role, its claimed necessity, its action within the internal operations of decision which it encloses on itself must be replaced by a more liberating presupposition. We shall not take the time to reexamine the finalities or operations of philosophical decision, for the latter is what must be suspended globally in order to examine this universal presupposition at work in each of its operations.

If there is a real or dualitary opening of philosophical decision in opposition to what must indeed be decided to be called its *Greek constriction*, then it could not be the activation of its current opening, the effervescence of its unitary alterations. The problem can only be posed in a radical way: the new space offered to decision must be absolutely freed—freed without remainder—from the PSP. When it is a question of the experience of science-thought and of man, it is not decision itself that is destroyed, but its authority.

Perhaps it is understood more clearly why the expression "non-philosophy" must be interpreted with the intention that distinguishes, for example, between the "non-Euclidean" style and the "Euclidean" style in geometry. This formula is just as metaphorical as that of the "Copernican revolution." And perhaps less so if it is accepted that, in this formulation, it is no longer a simple, analogical and mono-paradigmatic transference from a scientific revolution to the interior of philosophy's supposed autonomy, as is the case with Kant who still at least finds philosophy (if not metaphysics) quite "sufficient." Instead of such a transference which leaves the most profound Greek postulate intact, it is a question of directly confronting philosophy's unitary essence with the non-unitary essence of vision-in-One and science; to confront philosophy with its "Other" or rather with what it can only resent and reject as its Other. If there is a transference, then *it takes place in science alone*, from a particular form of the latter—"non-Euclidean" geometries—to its essence of science. And by all accounts, metaphor for metaphor, we shall require, rather than the Copernican, a "Lobachevskian" and Riemannian metaphor, which is also scientific but which would be more than a vague analogy, for it would express a real scientific mutation. Greco-contemporary thought, i.e. "philosophy," is so to speak "Euclidean" because it is founded upon a supposition of unity, unicity and sufficiency which seem obvious to it but which is no longer obvious for us, because this supposition limits its practice. Against the occurrence of this Euclidean or Heraclitean limitation, we can thus oppose a non-Heraclitean mutation: that of "non-philosophy" or more universal practices of philosophy. *For whichever phenomenon, one should be able to propose a multiplicity of equivalent interpretations, a multiplicity which is no longer simply unitary but "dualitary" and such that it escapes from the Principle of sufficient philosophy; an infinity of equivalent philosophical decisions for the same phenomenon to be interpreted.*

Science's essence therefore implies a radical reevaluation of the sense and truth of the claimed "Greek opening" of thought which philosophers never stop celebrating in the most stubborn blindness to the real thought of science. Founded upon this unitary postulate, which it has become possible to limit without consequently destroying thought, these are all philosophical practices (within the University or outside, this split is no longer pertinent here) because they are contaminated and restrained by it, for it is not a question of suppressing them, but a question of freeing them from their unitary claim to exhaust thought's essence.

Vision-in-One as generalization of the
metaphysical operation or of the Other

In order to suspend the unitary postulate concretely and to define a "non-Heraclitean" thought, we have to isolate the two fundamental philosophical operations that must be transformed in accordance with vision-in-One which serves as our guiding thread, and they must be generalized from it and not from themselves.

Philosophical decision is a supplement of articulation to the ordinary language that its linguistic articulation requires in order to produce sense, truth and value beyond itself. But, similar to linguistic articulation, this supplementary articulation of language in the form of a *logos* or an ontological opening is also a double articulation. That the *logos* be a double articulation of natural language is explicit due to the very structure of philosophical decision. It is a mixture, a space with two coordinates, Transcendence taking the vertical axis, Immanence the horizontal. Each level of articulation makes both dimensions or, in a more originary way, their mixture intervene each time, but the first time *mostly* from the angle of Transcendence, which is then dominant—this is *the metaphysical articulation* ("Reversal") or the Dyad; and the second time *mostly* from the angle of Immanence, which is then dominant—this is *the transcendental articulation* ("Displacement") or the One. These two articulations form a system, for they are inseparable and together represent language's usage-of-logos, a usage that wants to be constitutive of the real and from which a scientific usage, a descriptive usage or that of "non-thetic reflection," has already been distinguished.

The metaphysical articulation articulates empirical language and the philosophical *a prioris*, ordinary significations and the categories, sense and signification, etc. and divides up the *a prioris* that it isolates. The transcendental articulation articulates these universal structures and the unifying or unitary structures, the effects of transcendence produced by the first articulation and the rules of immanence which are the object proper to the second; it thus articulates the Other and the One. Whereas the first produced the Other or was the discourse of the Other, the second produces or reproduces the One and forms the discourse of the One. The complete philosophical decision is this double and single discourse of the Other or of the Dyad (and) of the One that commandeers and over-determines the ordinary language which serves as its vector.

Then what do we have when we no longer generalize decision on the basis of itself but in a non-philosophical mode? It would then be a question of reworking each of these operations or articulations[13] and modifying the first form of decision in a *non-unitary* sense, generalizing its experience of the Other via the scientific model of objectivity supplied by vision-in-One; it is also to modify the second in the same sense, transforming its experience of immanence or of the One via the scientific model of immanence also supplied by vision-in-One. Thus, from the start one will seize upon the meta-physical operation of dismantling the universal or *a priori* structures of experience in order to modify its concept; then one will seize upon the second operation in view of substituting the most radically immanent One of science for the One of decision. In both cases, one will have bankrupt the ultimate internal limitation of philosophical decision and what prevents it from becoming non-philosophy. The Greco-philosophical will be made to appear like an originary "constriction" of thought. We shall now proceed to this double labor.

Here is the "Heraclitean" postulate that we formulated above. Completely understood, the opposed term that corresponds with a term=x can be multiple, but it will only be multiple within a genre, species or generality. It is thus necessary to reformulate the Heraclitean postulate so as to give it the fullness of its sense: for a term=x there corresponds one and only one universal term or a single type of universal, an alterity of a single genre. Philosophical multiplicities remain unitary or included each time in one genre of universal alone. The opposition or transcendence to a term=x contains the possibility of a multiplicity of singular opposites, but each time they belong to a single plane. Let us call *plane-of-transcendence* this single universal which is opposed each time (by each singular decision) to a term=x and which unilaterally contains a virtual multiplicity, if not of philosophies, then at least of the modes of a single philosophy. That there be a single plane-of-transcendence for a whatever phenomenon=x, i.e. one philosophical interpretation alone: this is the Heraclitean postulate that gives its coherence to philosophical decision but also limits it internally.

Perhaps there will be objections that a single philosophy should not be considered, but the historical manifold of the

---

13 In this description, we shall simplify the problem by simply supposing two non-thetic *a prioris* (Transcendence or the Other or the Universal—thus identifying NTT and NTP—and NTU with its extension in Totality).

decisions which have sprung from this postulate or which it has not prevented from being born. From this point of view, there are as many planes-of-transcendence as decisions. Each of these has its practice of metaphysical articulation, its experience of the Other, its energy put into transcendence and its conception of the universal. If for a moment one considers the diversity of decisions in history and is given the right to posit them as indifferent to one another, one could imagine that the most concrete philosophy is that which posits this diversity of qualitative types of universal. Whereas Spinoza and Nietzsche use an infinity of attributes, but which are univocal and thus manifest the same type of opposition or transcendence to a term=x, the consideration of the whole sphere of the history of philosophy *as a single philosophical decision* could give us the feeling of a super-Spinozism or über-Nietzsche-anism: for whichever phenomenon to be interpreted there would ultimately correspond an infinity of planes-of-transcendence or qualitatively heterogeneous attributes, not simply in their genre but in their mode of transcendence in relation to this phenom-enon. Instead of the univocity of Being or of the Attribute which is said in a single sense of the given, there would thus be a radi-cal plurivocity of sense itself, of the universal or of the attribute as such. The Greek limitation (to each thing there corresponds a single type of universal, a single plane-of-transcendence) and even the ultimate Spinozist and Nietzschean limitation (to each thing there corresponds an infinity of planes-of-transcendence or attributes of the same type) would finally be lifted. This would not simply posit *all philosophies* as a single philosophy, but would posit them as particular cases of a super-philosophy which would con-tain them all as possibilities. Since these possibilities are founded on the idea that there is a single type of attribute or opposition, they would only see their own type and, through it, would mutu-ally wage an unconscious war against one another. But there would also be a possible philosophical generalization of philosophical decision. So it is that Heraclitus, Plato, Aristotle, Kant, Hegel, Nietzsche, Heidegger, etc., each have in common the fact that for the same ontic point=x of reality, they make one and only one type of universal or attribute correspond with it; and even if they wind up in a plurality, it remains the same type; Dialectic, real Opposition, Difference, etc., this is always the univocity of syntax. Here on the contrary, we ultimately lift the Greek postulate of the unicity of syntax or of sense. For every real point possible, there would be an infinite multiplicity of universal-type syntaxes or heterogeneous oppositions. Each term would neither be provided with one type of universal, nor one plane, but with a universal of universal planes, a radical multiplicity of philosophical decisions.

However, is this multiplicity of planes-of-transcendence really more valid than that of the singular points in each plane? One fact alone suffices to indicate the contrary: these various planes-of-transcendence are not in fact equivalent or indifferent to one another, as we pretended to believe for a moment, but are immediately in conflict. And if *a* philosophy (a plane-of-transcendence) involves philosophy [*la* philosophie] as a whole every time to the fullest extent, it is impossible to really ward off contradiction and war. War once again signifies a unitary reduction of the planes-of-transcendence themselves. *It is impossible for unitary or sufficient decision to accept* de jure *an indifferent multiplicity of decisions, i.e. planes-of-transcendence.* It is impossible for it to make a term=x correspond with a radical infinity of equivalent interpretations rather than one alone, which implies the war among all and between the others and itself. Or instead all philosophical decisions are specifically considered as a single decision, and the multiplicity of attributes for the same phenomenon is no longer indifferent but reduced to a unique interpretation and turns toward war; or instead this opposition among planes takes into account this multiplicity of interpretations, but it remains limited because it is a multiplicity of attributes within a single super-attribute. Philosophical decision oscillates from the One (-multiple) to the Multiple (-One) and cannot manage to *recognize an indifferent infinity or an equivalence of decisions for a whatever phenomenon=x.*

The real introduction of a multiplicity of equivalent planes or attributes for the same phenomenon to be interpreted will imply—this is now obvious—a transformation of the essence of transcendence, particularly its freedom from the unitary yoke. The modes of transcendence can become really infinite and equivalent only if transcendence itself is unleashed from scission and the type of unity attached to it. An intrinsically multiple transcendence must have something besides *divided Unity* or the *unitary Dyad* for its essence, which are the ultimate requirement of philosophical systems. How do we free transcendence and the Other?

The philosophical passage to the *a priori* is always founded on the Other, for it is the motor and motive of the operation: the *a priori* is the Other of the empirical. But this Other is aligned with the universal, or instead is blended with it and is thetic and therefore unitary. It is not simply aligned with Unity, which will come to take hold of it again in the second operation—transcendent unity—but is inserted between two positions. The solution thus cannot simply consist in proceeding like the contemporary deconstructions of metaphysics *by reversing the hierarchy of Unity and of the Other, but also by putting the Other outside-Unity*; by affecting the latter by the former as Other simultaneously aligned with it and outside it. This solution is so interesting because it desperately conserves the system of the thetic Other, of transcendence as undecidably combining with position. On the contrary, *the Other from the start should be a multiplicity of non-thetic transcendences or of universal but non-positional attributes, equivalent from this angle and corresponding to a term=x*. This is the whole difference between a restrained deconstruction of metaphysics and a radical opening of it, between a philosophical opening, or a decision, and a real or scientific opening.

We know the solution from vision-in-One. It consists in no longer thinking at all within the matrix of the unitary Dyad or of the coupling of contraries that requires one and only one contrary for every term=x. *But it first consists in liberating, paradoxically before the Other itself, the term x from its latent relativity to the term that will be opposed to it.* To think in terms rather than relations, and on the basis of an absolute or real term=x—the One itself, which has no need to have a contrary opposed to it so as to itself be determined; to already be given it, determined in itself, before it is put in relation with other terms. Philosophy cannot commence in this way, it commences by definition *in* a coupling or *in* an in-between, and it is condemned—this is the limitative postulate itself—to only give one universal to x alone. On the other hand, the problem of transcendence can be posed in a radically open way on this new basis of the ante-dyadic One.

If from the start the term=x is autonomous and in itself like the real itself (the One non-thetic (of) self), what in effect does the Other become, what must transcendence become in order to continue to "correspond" in a certain way to x, all while freeing an indifferent multiplicity within it, the equivalence of an infinity of really heterogeneous universals? *The supposed autonomy, now radical, of the term=x renders not only philosophical decisions but also all the modes of the Other contingent and thus equivalent in their mutual contingency.* Their contingency in relation to the One signifies that their radical multiplicity is valid *de facto*. But it also implies that the essence of the Other or of the attribute/universal be in turn the same as that of the One-term, that it be extracted from scission and relation (relativity), from decision and not simply from position, that it be, as for the term=x or the real One, being-immanent. Transcendence or the universal therefore stops having the form of the mixed *plane* or of *position* and stops being limited to a type which is determined each time and which defines a particular philosophical decision. In this way, a multiplicity of interpretations—of descriptions—rather than one alone can be given to a term=x only on condition of first changing our experience of the essence of the term=x, and then solely our experience of the essence of the Other (and of what vision-in-One has demonstrated to be the non-thetic *a priori* in general); on condition, therefore, of radically leaving behind the Greek terrain of thought. On this terrain, the aporias of Unity and of the Multiple, their mutual inhibition, continue to limit thought internally and constrict it to remain in the form of philosophical decision. Since it is a question of the first articulation of the *logos*, that of "metaphysics," the solution can be formulated in yet another way. One can free the *meta*-(physics) from its metaphysical limitation, or the Other from its unitary constraints, and multiply ad infinitum the possible equivalent "metaphysics" and the corresponding *a priori* as descriptions of the same phenomenon, only if this phenomenon is sufficiently real so as to no longer be relative to the Other itself and only if it in turn receives a "unary" essence—a being-immanent—rather than a "planar" essence.

Meta-physics in the Greek regime is always unique, more exactly unique-as-multiple and multiple-as-unique, which is not very different from saying: for whichever phenomenon, only one plane and only one philosophy can be made to correspond with it each time. There is thus no permanent escape from the Greek paradigm, no internal transitions or adjustments: the essence of philosophical decision itself must be grasped if one wants to be able to be given an infinity of equivalent interpretations or possibles (*descriptions*) for the same real phenomenon.

Vision-in-One as generalization of the transcendental operation: the foundation of the radical opening of philosophical decision as "non-philosophy"

Philosophical decision, as we said, is the *Logos* as double articulation. The second articulation distinguishes and unites, but mainly unites transcendence and immanence, the Other and Unity.

It is the Unity and, hence, the superior Totality that recovers transcendence at work in a dominant way in the first articulation and re-unites it with itself in an ultimate identification. This is the becoming-Unity, becoming-immanent or becoming-transcendental of transcendence (of scission, of the *a priori* still relative to experience), the passage from the determined universal or from the general to the total. This mechanism is that of philosophical decision in the superior stage of its process. This superior Unity which is united with scission, which is reconciled with the Other or the universal, a Unity of which we shall say that it is unitary, is now what acts explicitly.

In virtue of its unity with the Other, it will be concluded that: there are as many modes of the thetic or philosophical Other as there are of this Unity. Here the unitary aporia is simply taken up a notch: concerning these superior Unities or Totalities in which "complete" philosophical decisions are condensed, it will also be said that they are each unique-as-multiple and multiple-as-unique. Here Unity and Multiplicity still double cross each other and cannot be rigorously identical or freed from one another. For any phenomenon whatsoever, one and only one complete decision or Totality will be capable of corresponding with it. And if one wants to make a multiplicity of decisions of Totality correspond with it, they will be understood unitarily as its modes, parts, degrees, etc. but never as an unlimited number of *de jure* equivalent Totalities.

If, on the contrary, one now departs from the result obtained in the generalization of the first operation and if one is given a non-thetic Transcendence, rather than a decisional and positional Transcendence like that of philosophical decision, what type of Unity, and then what type of Totality, can be obtained? Obviously it cannot be the same type as this scission-Unity, this Other-Unity that forms the Greek regime of thought or philosophical decision. The latter envelops in itself the restrained multiplicity of the Dyad of contraries, which is of aporetic and slightly positive origin; it remains bound by its tenants and supporters to the blending of decision (transcendence) and position (Greek inseparability of Being and Unity). Here the solution, which would still consist in positing all philosophical decisions of Totality as a single decision or even as its modes, would remain desperate and would be content with renewing the internal limitation which the Heraclitean postulate represents. This would be to pass from a Unity to a Super-unity, from a Totality to a Super-totality, in an effort that would be unable to shatter the unitary contraries. That task would not be possible except by *the foundation of Unity as such, then of Totality, as radical opening, qualitatively infinite due to its non-mixed character*. This is obviously what we have called, in relation to vision-in-One, the *a priori* of non-thetic Unity (NTU) and the *non-thetic Uni-verse*. The One itself will not be conflated with this Totality-Unity that we are seeking as the ultimate effect of a "non-Heraclitean" generalization of thought. There is definitely the real One, that of vision-in-One. It founds a multiplicity of heterogeneous but equivalent Transcendences. There is also now NTU as the other *a priori* of representation or mode of the (non-) One. The One—as the description of vision-in-One has shown—also founds it as the last *a priori* and unifies the *a prioris* in the form of multiple and equivalent Totalities which no longer manifest any restrictive or unitary efficacy upon non-thetic Transcendences (*a prioris* are no longer mutually inhibited by their blending).

Vision-in-one as equivalence of philosophical decisions and a prioris of decision

Each point of the real=One *de jure* must be able to correspond—in virtue of the One itself and its indifference—with an infinite and heterogeneous multiplicity of equivalent Transcendences, Universals, Unities and Totalities, and not with only one instantiation of these *a prioris* in conflict with the others. There is a radical positivity of Transcendences and Totalities, an essential multiplicity of Others and Unities (of which the ones-as-multiples Other and Unity of philosophical decision are merely particular cases). They are no longer intelligible within the Greco-occidental framework: in effect, this multiplicity of types of Transcendences, Universals, Unities and Totalities can no longer be explained by transcendence understood unitarily as decision (and thus being partly bound to a position). Indeed, in philosophy there is a multiplicity-by-division and a unity-by-totalization, but these are merely unitary phenomena that no philosophical decision can surpass. On the contrary we have, on the basis of the One, a non-decisional multiplicity of Transcendences, Universals, Unities and Totalities that have not been obtained by scission and totalization, i.e. by procedures that return to unitary Unity. This is possible only if we have an immediate givenness (to) self of Transcendences, Others, Unities or Totalities: a being-immanent that does not itself need to be affected by the Other, i.e. here, by a scission or even by a Unity reflected in itself, i.e. here, by a totalization.

As radical aprioritic multiplicity that is not empirical or empirico-rationalist, it cannot derive from the plurality of the thetic *a prioris* or universals of philosophy. It is obvious that we shall not seek the absolute opening of possibles beyond decisions in the empirical consideration of the decisions existing in history, which are always precisely supposed to be positional-decisional couplings. It is thought's very nature, its very experience that must "change" in order to break the reign of "Heraclitean" thought and to attain this *de jure* multiplicity and equivalence of aprioritic possibles, and therefore an equivalence of the real's descriptions.

The Greeks have put two terms—and only two—in an overly restrained, i.e. reversible, relation: immanence and transcendence, unity and scission. This type of simplification of thought's givens can only lead to infinite complications and rearrangements. So as to generalize the problem of a "non-Greek" experience of thought, it will be necessary that, rather than making a term=x correspond each time to a single other term (for example: a type of transcendence) in unitary, reciprocal or simultaneous relations of the One and the Dyad, a term=x or immanence will be made to correspond with a multiplicity of Transcendences, Universals, Unities and Totalities ultimately given as equivalent, *which is possible only if immanence is sufficiently real to render all these terms not merely equivalent by their essence in the One but contingent, and thus equivalent once again but this time with regard to the One. This is no longer a unitary coupling like the Greek, because Transcendences, Universals, Unities and Totalities will ultimately suppose immanence but without reciprocity.* The solution consists in "dualyzing" or in principle breaking the Greek axis of the One/Multiple that supports onto-theology but which receives a completely different sense here. Whereas in onto-theo-logy it was enclosed in or knotted with itself and supposed unique (the discourse on the One-as-Multiple is supposed unique-as-multiple, thus always unitary), here this circle is broken in the most definitive way. It is more than opened: replaced by a multiplicity-without-scission of non-decisional Transcendences, non-positional Positions and non-totalizing Totalities. They are all founded in a "One" which does not constrain them, which is no longer this ideal immanence that philosophy knows, but a real immanence that fully leaves-be this multiplicity of non-thetic *a prioris* and of scientific representation.

Furthermore, this multiplicity in turn and without return[14] must precede philosophical decisions in order to be able to open them in such a primitive fashion and to render them equivalent, something they have always refused of themselves.

A "non-" philosophical thought is certainly the same thing as a "non-" thetic or "non-" mixed thought. These two "non-s" have the same phenomenal or real content, and the latter, the (non-) One, stems, rather than from decision or from Being which does not know it, from an instance of reality that bears witness to another experience of thought: the One non-thetic (of) self.

So as to ground this indifference of a multiplicity of equivalent *a prioris*, it will be necessary to have access to an experience, for example, of the Other as without-scission or "cracking," or of Totality without "totalization"—and thus without "unitary" unity; all of which are no longer what they are in philosophy, i.e. an Other-of-the-Other ad infinitum and blended with Unity, or an auto-enveloping Totality-of-Totality. This "simplified" multiplicity of *a prioris* in turn supposes a radical being-immanent for its essence, which precisely is not blended with them and which can be, for example, the Other's essence without itself forming a blending with the Other.

We call it the One qua unreflected transcendental experience or qua vision-in-One: it forms the absolute foundation of scientific thought and the ultimate being-immanent of non-philosophical generalization.

Lastly, the necessary condition to augment the number of dimensions of thought in an unlimited way, beyond the single dimension of alterity and totality that comprises decision, does not reside in the addition of dimensions of the same type or of the same essence, but in another experience, non-thetic (of) self, another essence of thought. If in this way one finds the positive reason which defines the Other or Totality and the *a priori* of philosophical decision in general in a multiplicity more heterogeneous than that of decision itself, but which is equivalent and no longer corresponds with a scission and a totalization but with a being-immanent, then one gains access to an experience of the multiplicity and heterogeneity of possibles that offers an opening to thought which its Greek constriction would have prohibited

---

14 French "à son tour et sans retour." This playful turn of phrase indicates a wide variety of non-philosophical themes, including uni-laterality, uni-versality ('one-turnedness'), determination-in-the-last-instance, non-reversibility, impossibility of (Copernican, philosophical) re-volution, non-auto-position, etc. [TN]

from the start. Thought has its "headquarters" outside philosophy and is therefore no longer negotiable by it. Thought's headquarters is science, insofar as its essence and its "transcendental truth" is restored to it. The veritable opening "of" philosophy therefore consists in founding it on a pre-unitary experience of thought's being-immanent. *Science alone as grounded in vision-in-One can radically open philosophical decision and make it leave behind its spontaneous practice. Science alone can make philosophy acknowledge that it is practiced naively as a particular case of a more expansive system of thought that legitimizes a* de jure *unlimited multiplicity of possibles: non-philosophy.*

The non-philosophical style, this equivalent infinity of decisions and of *a prioris* of decision for the same phenomenon, is the concrete content of the *Principle of equivalence of all philosophical decisions.* Later we shall pursue its description by exemplifying it vis-à-vis the case of "deconstructions." At this time, we shall end this chapter by examining the case of spontaneous non-philosophical practices that already exist in history, their insufficiency and the necessary condition for giving them a scientific foundation.

The spontaneous non-philosophical practices of philosophy and their scientific foundation

There have always been non-philosophical practices of philosophy. In order to grasp their scope, which remains limited, several preliminary distinctions should be made:

1. In spontaneous philosophical practice, where unitary thought is willed as such, the philosophical and the non?philosophical[15] are already and in every way mixed up. There has always been the non-philosophical: a point of view, a perspective, a material, a given, etc. left to its empirical blindness or its gregarious, quotidian, vulgar non-sense, etc. But this is the not-yet-philosophical, it will have to-become-philosophical, to be re-internalized, signified, verified, sublated, critiqued, deconstructed, etc. To such an extent that this non-philosophical is only postulated or tolerated because it is submitted in the last instance to the authority and second coming of the becoming- or finally-philosophical. It does

---

15 The original text reads: "non?philosophique." Laruelle's use of the question mark indicates the variable and unstable status of the orientation of what binds the "non(-)" to the "philosophical," including the different ways in which the "non(-)" is understood depending on the particular philosophy considered. [TN]

not work for its own account but for philosophy's re-affirmation as such, it responds without ever really disappointing the call of the Principle of sufficient philosophy. In the state of a tendency, there is thus an absolute idealism proper to philosophy, which is an invariant that each thinker can diversify and realize in his or her own way. This modern usage of the non-philosophical tolerates two variants: the one superior, the other inferior to it.

2. The superior variant of this tendency is recent: between the philosophical and the non-philosophical, there would be almost a duality, a quasi-dualism. The non-philosophical receives a special positivity that renders it a little more autonomous than it was in relation to its last re-affirmation. Nevertheless, what is never destroyed or absent is the limited character of this project. No doubt the non-philosophical is not entirely internalizable or negotiable by it and resists it to the point of practically transforming it within certain limits. But these attempts, after a bit of delay or stoppage time that seems sufficient for them, succumb to the Principle of philosophical sufficiency. Philosophical faith is always active: to defer it is not yet to carry out its real critique. This is why from the start there is a certain weakness in really and rigorously determining the phenomenal content proper to the "non-" of the non-philosophical. On the one hand, this alterity, this experience-of-the-Other, is still impregnated by ontological negativity and has not acquired its most positive form. It no doubt receives a positive content that expresses a certain alterity or is its symptom: *the* political for example, the "party takeover" or "class struggle" being its non-empirical essence. In general sometimes it receives an empiricist, unique and particular mask that *blocks* the alterity of "struggle," while sometimes it receives an unlimited multiplicity of masks or guises that *generalizes* the symptom philosophically— Withdrawal, Unthought, Un-said, Difference, Outside-closure, Remainder, etc.; empiricity is then excluded from the positivity of the Other, but the latter remains all the more undetermined. On the other hand, because these two form a system, a circle—even broken and deferred—subsists between the *non-* and the philosophical which are still reciprocally determined. The PSP will have been unsettled, it will not have been destroyed.

3. The general tendency to the philosophical submission of the non-philosophical also tolerates an inferior variant: all the empiricist and technical uses of philosophy by specialists (doctors, theologians, scientists, poets, writers, etc.), but also by the history of philosophy, by its linguistic or textual reduction, are reified modes

of this unitary experience of the non-philosophical. They push decision toward its breaking point even less than the preceding types. They remain aligned with it in the last resort due to the fact that decision is stronger than they are. These are still (extreme) *possibilities* of philosophy and are beholden to its sufficiency.

Most of the usages of this type remain under the obedience of the philosophical Authorities and only breaches them with their consent or their hinter-thought. These solutions must be eliminated, namely: 1) that which leaves the *non-* undetermined or believes to determine it by diminishing it to the historico-empirical manifold of the aborted or repressed attempts at "popular philosophy," at "philosophy for the use of …"; 2) that which believes to determine it by the idea of political practice—political and thus "non"-philosophical practice of philosophy—and which does nothing but under/over-determine it by a philosophy of importation or contraband that does not at all manage to give it a real and positive essence; 3) that which identifies this project with a deconstruction of philosophical decision—the *non-* then being an Other-which-*is*-not, a capacity of absolute (-relative) alterity which affects the closure of philosophical mastery but which continues to suppose it as fundamentally unavoidable. This is also to say that it leaves the Other or the *non-* undetermined, refusing it any positive essence and receiving this transcendence in turn in the mode of transcendence, i.e. in a vicious and redoubled manner. These three types of non-philosophical usage of philosophy are programmed by it. Such as they are regularly practiced, they arise from unitary faith or from unitary spontaneity. Indeed, the scientific principle of the equivalence of philosophical decisions will also be applied to these usages: they have as much value, at least for the subject (of) science, as the "hard" usages of philosophy or the usages "in view of" it *as such*. But they will no longer have more truth than philosophy "as such" or, for example, than its historicizing and academic usage. It will be necessary to unlock a fourth and completely different type of non-philosophical practice in order to be able to grant it a scientific value.

All these solutions are philosophical in various modes because they attribute to the *non-* and to critique a priority and a primitiveness of the metaphysical or "first philosophy" type. Every philosophical critique (of philosophy) is *first critique* and, as a result, can only be founded upon a non-being or an Other which it *supposes given*, which it leaves undetermined in its real essence and which dooms it to concentrate all its activity into the resistance against this non-being that originarily undermines it. Philosophy is a faith: as such, it is the continual drive to survive despite its intimate inessentiality. Philosophical authority tolerates certain usages of this type, but on condition of already unitarily compromising the notion of *usage* which it begins by dividing: an extra-philosophical usage, a still philosophical usage. It even accepts being divided between an authority which is inferior, "metaphysical," "gregarious," "logocentric," etc. and which must be unsettled, and an intact superior authority that continues to supervise and partially govern the operation. In this way philosophy is always exerted through the non-philosophical of this type, but this is no longer what is in question. The problem of philosophical Authorities no longer has any interest from the moment that it is treated with philosophy, with its operations and the claim that it attaches to them, such that it does not end up as a radical duality submitting philosophy to science, a duality which no longer derives from a supposed given Other—which is moreover unintelligible and inessential—but from the real or from the One. If philosophy always and everywhere requires the non-philosophical, the problem lies elsewhere: what matters is neither the empirical content of this alterity, *nor even the latter as such*, because philosophy still decides, in a superior gesture, on it. What counts is the real origin of this alterity, its provenance in the One's being-immanent or merely in the transcendence of the World. If it remains first and undetermined, then it forms a system with philosophical mastery, and all the nuances concerning this coefficient of alterity have no *real* importance.

The non-philosophical usages of philosophy only have some chance of being multiplied and rendered positive, of no longer being the traces of an auto-tortured-to-death body, if they stop ensuing from philosophy's critique so as to first ensue from science. Before expressing an auto-critical or even hetero-critical capacity—the whole inter-philosophical war—the *non-* must express the (non-) One, the real's indifference to decisions, the equivalence of all decisions in the *chôra* instead of their hierarchical conflict. And the equivalence of philosophies must be extended to the equivalence of their usages.

What is it that makes the plurality of these usages—in opposition to the unique philosophical usage, despite everything, of philosophy—communicate with the *non-* of the "non-philosophical?" This *non-* must immediately receive a positive or immanent phenomenal content. This rigorous phenomenal content is the (non-) One, Determination in the last instance. As a result, the *non-* ultimately stops being a maker of war and indetermination, which is the case when philosophy posits it as "nothingness," "annihilation," "non-being," etc. still in accordance with Being or the philosophical will, rather than in accordance with the One. Therefore this *non-* no longer corresponds with these different forms of non-being, nothingness or annihilation (whatever their forms may be) but with the *chôra* and all the non-mixed *a prioris*. They are directly founded in the One without co-determining it in return, thus definitively escaping from philosophical circularity. The *non-*(philosophical) can then affect the philosophical in irreversible exteriority or in a regime of heteronomy. Between the real and philosophy, there is no longer this equation, this more or less off target identity which philosophy posited as being itself or the superior form of itself. Henceforth, without still being a "side" or a term in a coupling, the real remains inherent (to) self without being alienated and, as a result, the equation of philosophy passes from the other side, more exactly "from the side," from the possible side *alone*; it is inscribed in the (non-) One as in the Uni-side of things that ensues from the One. All the philosophical syntaxes and games to which they give rise are expulsed and liberate free "terms," terms henceforth without *reciprocal* or *unitary* relation to the real. It is in this way that non-philosophical usages of decision can be founded in this duality.

We can then generalize the idea of *non-philosophical usages of philosophy* on condition of founding it as rigorously as possible. It will no longer be an accidental empirical trait: neither a historical diversity or a spatio-temporal continuum of philosophy, nor a program for philosophy's deconstruction, but a systematic project founded in the precedence of science over philosophy. *A field of new pragmatic possibilities, founded in the positivity of the Determination in the last instance, is opened and frees a perhaps infinite multiplicity of new non-philosophical practices of philosophy.* These are not new philosophical varieties, new systems obtained by variation, grafts, intercessions, etc. on the invariants of decision. Under the codes of science, these are new *usages* of philosophies, whether they exist yet or not. In the name of vision-in-One and its structures, it will be necessary to shed light upon the ultimate phenomenal givens of the non-philosophical, those that the subject (of) science lives in an immanent way, so that it becomes possible to found upon them all these usages, albeit scanty and timid, and so that they will henceforth no longer be re-internalizable or sublatable by the *logos*, so that they will no longer even form a system with it within philosophical faith.

We call "universal" or "ordinary" pragmatics that which, no longer being a byproduct or subset of decision, is founded upon science, derives from it alone and leaves-be as its object—a scientific type of object—philosophy as such. Rather than generalizing pragmatics philosophically and ad hoc (pragmatics could not in fact be extended to philosophy lest it claim in an illusory way to constitute a meta-philosophy), in this way it is put back on the real base of its phenomenal givens or on the infrastructure of science. This is to open up the dimension of a radical future for it, a future-without-logos or without-horizon, a representation without positional constriction. Hence *a radically experimental practice of philosophy that is foreign to its circle or its philocentrism.* The human consequences are obvious: only a science of philosophy can really vanquish its illusory claims, and if there is in turn a means to render philosophy subject non-thetic (of) self, to procure for it the usages of this nature and to put it back in the limits of the most radical human finitude, it is here. This is a renaissance of philosophy in the spirit of science.

Example of the archive: the illegalities of philosophical practice

As an example—but this is merely an example—one can take the case of the archive and trace the trajectory that goes from the archive in philosophy to philosophy as archive.

1. The history of philosophy in all its forms—even the most normalized—is still a manner of practicing philosophy and can be fully re-interpreted and engendered as a possibility of philosophical decision. If one wants the latter to "work," it is in every way possible to do this work on the archive.

2. The archive is a material that bears witness to several ways of philosophizing. Not merely by the texts, inscriptions or documents that convey them and serve as their support, but in itself, in its materiality of support, which allows it to be treated as *monument* and not solely as *document* (Foucault). Yet its materiality is not a neutral or inert property: each philosophy has its way of "deciding" on its type of materiality. The latter always runs the risk of appearing within a philosophy as the *non-philosophical* (as objectivity, the reified, the degraded, the deficient, the archaeological, etc.). But every decision is precisely capable of including

this non-philosophical moment that it internalizes, sublates, deconstructs, etc. and whose genealogy it simultaneously constructs. This is why the archive truly has a place in philosophy: it suffices to be given the means to do a "philosophy of the archive."

Then what is the place of the archive in this project that strictly treats philosophy as a material and, at the limit, as a new type of "archive?" Two points of view will be distinguished.

3. Archives primarily interest us because of what they bear witness to and what they relate (either by inscription or by themselves) of the eventual practices of philosophy that are peripheral, marginal, popular, delirious, etc. From this point of view, they are a necessary material, and their practice is included in the most general project toward an experimental treatment of philosophy. They are necessary for the inventory of "illegal" non-normative forms of the production, distribution and consumption of philosophical statements; forms (let's say in an indicative way) that cannot immediately fall into the historicizing auto-reference proper to the practices of the universities. The archive can provide suggestions and can function as the reservoir for "non-conforming" practical models of philosophy. Theoretical and practical indications can be obtained from the labor of the exhumation of peripheral, minoritarian or repressed usages of philosophy.

4. The second usage is more difficult to employ but more innovative. It consists in taking the results of the first as *material for a certain labor* (on the content of the archive and also perhaps on the archive as such, if it is possible—this is not certain—to distinguish the two) and in maximally augmenting the non-objectifying distance or non-thetic indifference at the end of which these non-normal usages could be treated as an absolutely and indefinitely transformable whatever material outside any reference or obedience to philosophy's own codes and rigor. This distance already exists in what the archives present, where philosophy is often treated in a heteronomous or heterodoxical way. Yet here what is attempted is to radicalize this gap: *to definitively found in reality and in positivity the* de jure *possibility of the most heterophilosophical treatments of philosophy,* where its homophilosophical practice would be nothing more than a particular case of its heterophilosophical practice....

To "accentuate the gap," to "found" it "in reality and positivity," means that philosophical decision—under the archive or not—would in any case no longer be treated in an "objectifying" way, i.e. still on the basis of itself and under its ultimate authority, since objectification is a structural function of decision. If science, unlike philosophy, does not principally or essentially utilize objectification, if on the contrary it can "leave-be" decision, then it alone can found a new, non-objectifying (non-reified, non-degraded) status of philosophy-as-archive and of its most heterodoxical treatment; but with the certainty from the very beginning that it is possible to do this, that this right can be founded and that in this way the accusations of deviance brought to bear against these usages will be dismissed.

Here it is not a question of *afterwards* deconstructing the dominant university usage, the "Great philosophers" style, of philosophy by way of its marginal usages to which it would be opened. Indeed, there is also an effect of this type. But, on the one hand, here one no longer proceeds afterwards except by first postulating the full validity and reality of these usages (they are thus no longer "marginal") of which the philosophers' "normalized" philosophy is then nothing but a particular case without special validity. On the other hand, one radicalizes the "deconstructive" effects brought onto the official philosophical body by plunging all of these practices into the equivalence of the *chôra*. One not only justifies that there is a "recognized" multiplicity of philosophical positions and interpretations for the same phenomenon to be interpreted, but that there is also and *de jure* a multiplicity of reformulations, reuses and variations that can be carried out on *philosophy* ["*la*" *philosophie*] or "a" philosophy. For example, on a paradigmatic or emblematic statement like "I think therefore I am," it must be possible by right to carry out a series of variations that will give rise to as many philosophies and above all non-philosophies as possible. What does such a statement become—not merely from the point of view of its sense, but in its very formulation—the moment that the practices operating on it stop being coded and normalized by the "philocentric" usages and the authority of the Principle of sufficient philosophy?

Science of philosophy, non-philosophy, pragmatics

A science of philosophy in this way allows for the *founding of the right of the non-philosophical usages of philosophy*. As we said, there are already non-orthodox or non-normalized usages of philosophy which are sort of its *illegalities*. But these *de facto* non-philosophical usages, which also remain more or less under the authority of philosophical sufficiency, must be founded in rigor and in reality, science (in its transcendental sense) alone being able to radicalize such a non-philosophical *usage* as real. What can be exerted from science and in particular from the *non-thetic a prioris* upon the material of philosophy, but also all their results, are therefore called operations. This is what establishes the concepts of "experimental philosophy," "philo-fiction," "generalized deconstruction," etc. of which it is the systematization and foundation.

Non-philosophy is a discipline that combines science and philosophy in an unprecedented way. It derives from the posture-in-One of science, that upon which it is founded, but it has philosophy for its object. Non-philosophy is thus the extreme point or the global effect of a science of philosophy and that which can renew philosophy's traditional practices. Whereas philosophy's spontaneous practices relate it to itself and turn it into an auto-exercise or an automatism of repetition, a science relates philosophy to itself instead and represents a change of base in our relation to it. The "non-philosophical" category is therefore scientific instead of philosophical; it is the category of an absolute phenomenal positivity and represents a generalization—a scientific, here "Lobachevskian," type of generalization—*of philosophical decision beyond its auto-referential or restrained usages*. It does not relay one philosophy through another by continuing to honor the PSP, for it brings philosophy to its rigorous form, *in the sense, however, in which it inserts the latter in a science as its object*. This mutation of philosophy implies the invention of new expressions, practices, writings, possibilities of this special way of thinking. It is a global change of perspective on its finalities and functions, the abandonment of its spontaneous auto-exercise for its insertion into a scientific representation. This is what will also be called, but from another point of view that will be specified, "hyper-speculation."

Obviously, this is possible only if this real instance of science immanently implies, as we have shown concerning vision-in-One, another specific usage of language in general and of philosophical language in particular. This usage of the *logos* will itself no longer be a *usage-of-logos*, an auto-logical usage of philosophical discourse and of philosophical statements (but not only of them). If this instance brings with itself, whether *a priori* or immanently, the reality of a positively non-philosophical usage of the logos, a usage which is descriptive in the last instance rather than constitutive, then the reality of a non-philosophical pragmatics is acquired once and for all.

This scientific usage of language is the sole means of radically breaking the PSP. Instead of language's literary usage or even its deconstruction, this is the supreme "experimentation," namely its insertion into the transcendental structures of science that eliminate its authority. For the usage of language in view of science is the most primitive: it is a usage from the point of view of the real rather than of effectivity. If it is science that lifts the PSP, then it can also make another usage of philosophy: this and this alone is the true content of the idea of philosophical experimentation. The Other (transcendence), which establishes fiction in the *logos*, is then generalized and can give rise, for example, to a generalized and positive deconstruction.

Due to their origin, non-philosophy's rules are themselves absolutely universal: the "grammar" of non-philosophy envelops that of philosophy as a particular case, but in the sense in which a science can comprehend these relations of the "generalized" and of the "restrained." It founds the distinction between philosophical decision reduced to the state of simple material and the PSP, which is instead lifted. And it can be clarified or manifested by its labor upon philosophical language without, from this angle, falling back under the authority and fantasy of the omnipotence of the *logos*. Thus the scientific experimentation of philosophy, its pragmatics and ultimately its critique are inseparable: they are exactly the same thing. This very generalization is the sole real content of what can be understood by "philosophical experimentation." It results in drawing out the consequences of the (strictly "real") genealogy of decision from the non-thetic *a prioris*, a genealogy which, here still, has no philosophical sense but only a scientific sense.

The true splitting is no longer *inside* the philosophical decision between the Other and representation, but between philosophy and science. This is therefore no longer a delimitation; it is a generalized deconstruction that finds other procedures than those of limitation. The constitution of a science of philosophical decision is identically the manifestation of philosophical resistance as such and therefore its founded denunciation in which philosophy finally advenes[16] as immanent lived experience of man or of the subject (of) science. Philosophy must advene onto the positions

___

16   The verb "advenir" refers to something that "befalls" or "happens" accidentally, but also more literally as meaning "to come (to)." It also resonates strongly and etymologically with the word "avenir," which is used in the following paragraph and is translated as "future," although it has the sense of "the to-come." [TN]

of science, and its resistance must be manifested and emplaced in this way. This means that the texts produced no longer have philosophical value, but they have a value for the subject (of) science. This is the only way in which man as such or as "ordinary man" can practice and accept philosophical decision. In other words, if it has no meaning for the philosopher insofar as he submits to the PSP, the discourse produced in this way has one for every man, *and thus also for the philosopher as subject (of) science.*

This program is reminiscent of others: it makes certain Kantian, Marxian, Husserlian, Wittgensteinian, etc., appearances emerge, but on condition of disentangling them, as Husserl required vis-à-vis Descartes, from all the philosophical (decisional and positional, and not merely doctrinal and dogmatic) content of these philosophies, or on condition of conserving only their residue through their vision-in-One. Science is something like the real base or infrastructure of philosophical decision, that which simultaneously founds, emplaces, displaces and ultimately qualitatively differentiates *logos* games, unbinding philosophy from its interminable stalemate in these games, opening up a future for it that is really unlimited because it is non-"horizontal." This real infra-structure cannot be acquired—we know it from the thing itself—by a Revolution, a Conversion or a Reversion, a Withdrawal or a Deconstruction, since these all remain operations managed and promoted by the philosophical Authorities. Despite its idealist delirium concerning the real, philosophy does not need to be put back on its feet: it remains what it is. It is man on the other hand and he alone, the subject of universal pragmatics, who must be placed back in himself as in his own basis, disenchanted or unshackled in order to be able to use philosophy in accordance with himself. The scientific invention of philosophy is in front of us, we who have never been included in it nor concluded from it.

Chapter IV:
The procedures of non-philosophical pragmatics

The six basic procedures of non-philosophical practice

A rigorous description, i.e. here an "empirical" science in general, whether it be that of one philosophical decision or another, consists of three intimately intertwined aspects which appear as such only when its transcendental, rather than simply empirical, scope (valid for the real itself) is recognized: a theoretical and descriptive or "scientific" aspect properly speaking; a critical aspect (analysis of a resistance to the name of the real); a practical or "pragmatic" aspect of real or non-philosophical transformation. Here the focus will be on the first and third points: the inventory of theoretical or descriptive procedures, the rules of non-philosophy in general.

The non-philosophical style requires a precise or regulated labor upon philosophical material. Far from being arbitrary and signifying a confusion of genres, it has its own procedures like every process of production of knowledges. Six stages, which are successive *de jure*, are distinguished but—save for technical difficulty—can perhaps be carried out simultaneously in the non-philosophical re-writing of the material. To clarify what the rules work upon, it is necessary to remember that, within philosophical practice and even on its margins, language and thought are no longer reduced to linguistic sense supposed common. They are overdetermined and receive a supplementary sense, truth and value that make them enter under the laws and into the kingdom of philosophical discursivity. A supplement: not only of rational sense, but also of ontologico-categorial, existential or positive-dialectical sense, etc.—specifically according to the philosophical decision that takes hold of them and subjugates them. A veritable *exploitation*—in every sense of the word, both technological and capitalist—of language and thought by philosophical decision: this is the enterprise that is concealed beneath the "reason" *Logos*. It proceeds by continual redistributions of this supplement according to the philosophical syntaxes, experiences and problematics that are grafted onto the supposed spontaneous grammatical and significative organizations with which, moreover, they form a system.

Thus what is replaced and at least inhibited (precisely in the *chôra*) by non-philosophy's new "syntaxes" is the ensemble of these syntaxes and philosophical decisions, those conferring authority onto "common" language and its already philosophically structured section. The problem is not of knowing whether or not there is a layer of spontaneous and pre-philosophical linguistic significa-tion—this is still perhaps a philosophical thesis—but of engaging, as "material" or "occasion," all possible significations and all us-ages of language (insofar as they are potentially interpretable by a philosophical decision) in a process defined by non-philosophical rules of usage. Since these rules solely have an immanent source, they impose upon language and thought an "abstract" usage that is completely distinct from its transcendent or "figurative" usage.

List of the rules of procedures

Preliminary rule.—Of the choice and enrichment of philosophi-cal material. It formulates a certain number of procedures labeled "empirical" or "naive," i.e. intra-philosophical or still expressing philosophy's authority over itself.

Then, the procedures properly speaking of this reformulation or re-writing, which consists in treating the chosen utterance or statement as material, as that in which the structures of vision-in-One are formulated. Thus, each time these are modes of the (non-) One or static dualities that are characteristic of the *repre-sentation* (of) the One.

Rule 1.—Reciprocal redescription of the One and of the mate-rial, the latter before being identified, but only in the last instance, with the One or with radical subjective Identity; it is therefore identified with non-thetic-Unity=NTU, because, for it to be radical, this becoming-subject of the material remains within the limits of the (non-) One or of the representation (of) the One.

Rule 2.—Radical suspension of the authority of decision over itself and of the codes transcendent to science and to the real essence of the decision through which this authority is exerted. This is the rule of the *a priori* constitution of philosophical material as philosophically inert, where philosophy's claim is now included as transcendental Illusion. It guarantees the "passage" to the real equivalence of decisions and therefore proceeds to what is called the "defactualization" and "defetishization" of philosophy. Since this rule is still said of the *chôra* or of the chaos of philosophical decisions, it consists in describing, in accordance with the *chôra* or with the uni-lateralizing em-place, the transcendent philosophical given that is reduced in this way and that appears as such qua material. On the other hand, the *a priori* of the *chôra* must itself be redescribed through this material.

Rule 3.—Reciprocal redescription of the *a priori* of non-thetic Transcendence=NTT in the philosophical material's language and of this material in NTT-form. Like all the rules, it prescribes a double labor: here on the decisional aspects or aspects of transcendence which are those of the material and which must be suspended so as to unleash or manifest the NTT that corresponds with it; but also a labor upon NTT, which must be reformulated in the material's specific language.

Rule 4.—Reciprocal redescription of the *a priori* of non-thetic Position=NTP in the material's language and of the material in NTP-form. This is the same rule as the preceding, but it prescribes suspending the positional and universal aspects of the material and redescribing NTP in accordance with the latter.

Rule 5.—Reciprocal redescription of the "support" function, which the *chôra*'s material will assume as non-thetic *a priori*=S(F), and of the material's language. But from the start it prescribes reformulating this material's function, rather than the material itself, as being in turn a non-thetic *a priori,* and then prescribes inserting this support function into the NTU function that programmed the first rule. Rule 5 in reality is the immediate unity of rules 1 and 5 and can only be clarified by the first rule. NTU includes a necessary relation to a support supplied by philosophy as material.

Rule 6.—Redescription of the results of rules 2, 3 and 4 in accordance with rules 1 and 5, which now form a system in the same way in which the support-function (rule 5) was previously described in terms of rule 1. The result is what can be called the *non-mixed* or *non-thetic Totality* or *Universe*. Or instead: knowledge as *non-thetic Reflection*. Since this rule registers all the preceding rules without exception in a synthesis where even the material is included, the non-thetic Universe and the material are reciprocally redescribed automatically.

All of these procedures together form the process of a non-philosophical science of philosophy.

With rules 1 through 5, we have all the *a priori* structures of vision-in-One, properly speaking, and therefore of non-philosophy: *chôra*, NTT, NTP, NTU and S(F). This is non-philosophy's first side, which consists in a dualysis of philosophical decision, i.e. in the description of the *a priori* dualities that vision-in-One contains, one of the poles of which is real or immanent, the other outside-the-real or transcendent. Rule 1 is the most important because it describes the pivot of the whole operation; it guides this analysis of resistance and already begins the other operation, which is that of relating these non-thetic *a priori* structures to philosophy and making them function within the limits of the latter: no longer the limits of its sufficiency or its claim, but of its state of philosophically inert material or language (the *chôra*). In a certain way, these two operations are already simultaneously carried out from the moment that it is recommended at each step—here for example—to describe the *a priori* and the material *reciprocally*. But, to be fully rigorous, the operation is only carried out fully with rule 6.

Since non-philosophy takes place in the representation (of the) real, and not in the real where it solely has its being-immanent, and because it has its place in the originary Dyad or in the (non-) One rather than in the One itself, a certain circularity, albeit a minimum of circularity, is inevitable. But it is reduced to support-function, i.e. a duality-without-scission between the *a prioris* and the material which are "reciprocally" redescribed. This is why rule 1, which describes the reciprocal reformulation of the *a priori* of the (non-) One as NTU or subject of representation and of the reduced philosophical material, in a sense directs all the other rules (we have kept it in mind) but, at the same time, could strictly appear only after the *a prioris* of the *chôra*, of NTT and of NTP and prior to the non-thetic Universe.

One last terminological specification: what we elsewhere already called *non-thetic Transcendence* (NTT) designated the sum of the *a prioris* of vision-in-One without differentiating between them yet. This simplification resulted from an insufficient analysis and evinced a certain influence of philosophy. It is therefore necessary to reserve the term and acronym NTT for one of the real *a prioris* of objectivity.

Preliminary rule: on the constitution of philosophical material in its specificity

This is the rule of the choice of material or of the "occasion"-given and of its "enrichment" in view of its future transformation.

1. It first prescribes choosing a particular philosophical decision and constituting it (some of its statements, its objects, its problems, etc.) into "material" functions by elaborating and exhibiting, in a still naive or intra-philosophical way, the specific decisional and positional structures of these statements (etc.). Any statement, problematics or problem can always be "worked" in view of reducing it to the invariants that form a philosophical decision (Decision and Position, Reversal and Displacement, etc.). These invariants are by definition capable of singular variations, and the whole problem is then to formulate them in the particular language at hand: for example, to formulate in Cartesian language the structures of decision that appear more or less disguised in Descartes by an external material, but which *must* be made to appear explicitly. It is a question of making the invariant structures of decision manifest themselves within the particular language of the philosophy being considered.

This is still a necessary but preparatory empirical procedure, not yet a specifically scientific and transcendental procedure. It is the stage of the *preparation* of philosophical material. Perhaps it can be utilized in a brute or immediate way; but then one runs the risk of not perceiving how a decision acts here and what the specific structures are that distinguish it from every other object in the World and in History. Decision must be foregrounded as such, because this is a science of decision rather than of philosophy "in general." A science cannot take as its object an immediate given or the illusory *representations* of this given; what is still necessary is an elaboration of its specific object, a definition of what one wants to explicate or describe, etc. Here this object will not be such and such a singular and historical variation, or even the logical and systematic structure of a philosophy, which is merely one of these variations. The description of philosophies in terms of logic or of mathematics, for example, the exhibition of their body of rules accessible to a formal or even material logic is undoubtedly possible, but this would be to stop the analysis too soon and is not what we call a "decision." Such a system of rules precisely supposes an implicit decision and a position which then are themselves ignored or denied as such. One must first exhibit what is more fundamental in a philosophy and from its point of view: this is not the logic to which it can refer itself and which it can always internalize, but the manner in which it is appropriated, the completely original "transcendental" operations through which it internalizes philosophy. The intra-philosophical theory consecrated to the invariants of decision could be called the "naive theory of philosophical decision" and could serve to prepare the transcendental science of decision; nothing further will be said about it here.

Nevertheless, it seems important not to abandon the particular language and treatment of these invariants and to explicitly formulate them in the idiom of a certain decision, even when they themselves seem to deny that, for example, such invariants exist and that something like a decision exists.

2. The rule then prescribes the material's enrichment, an operation that still remains under the authority of the PSP like the first rule. It consists in experimentally enriching the production and reproduction of philosophical mixtures. The philosophical contemporaries, those of Difference and Deconstruction, have known to vary the invariants of decision but still without exhausting all the procedures of possible variation.

It is not absolutely necessary for non-philosophy itself to proceed to these variations, but it is interesting to supply it with a complex material which will have undergone the maximum amount of deformation and enrichment that it is capable of supporting, without being destroyed, within the constraints pertaining to its nature of decision and within the limits of its "resistance." The constraints imposed by the resistance of philosophical material are those of decision as a *mixture* of transcendence and immanence, but this mixture can itself be complicated in a structural or essential way, as for example Heidegger and the restrained forms of Deconstruction have done recently, by a couple or a new structure that has come to overdetermine it and combine itself with it: the distinction of the (real-) ideal and of the real, for example, in the form of the distinction of a (real-) ideal transcendence and of a real transcendence (finitude, withdrawal, standing-reserve, *différance*, etc.); of a logos wanting to be master of itself and of a real alterity outside-logos, etc. Philosophical space is thus no longer simply in two coordinates, but in four dimensions so to speak, ideal transcendence extending itself by a real transcendence and ideal immanence extending itself by a real immanence. The philosophical reduction of whatever information is a quasi-necessity for facilitating the work of the following phase, but it does not exclude the "experimental" enrichment of the invariants.

3. It is possible to combine several philosophical decisions that are exerted, for example, on a single statement of which they are the interpretations; these intra-philosophical variations will then determine as many corresponding variations in each of the following stages—in which they are conserved as "support"—as there are non-philosophical variations. Conversely, a single decision can be used on heterogeneous statements that it will re-interpret univocally: but then, so as to assure the most diversifying economy and distribution of the material, the whole interest would be to utilize a "serializing" type of decision (the contemporary thoughts that have introduced serialism into philosophy).

4. Concerning the introduction of techniques which are other than philosophical into the philosophical material, techniques of creation that would be pictorial, poetic, musical, architectural, informational, etc., several possibilities can now be unleashed:

a) the philosophical material can be worked by these techniques on condition that they are not transferred to philosophy naively, like a savage transference of technology, but pre-adapted to its ultimate laws, i.e. submitted to the auto-affecting circularity that is the essence of every decision, or submitted to the simultaneity of the One and of the Dyad;

b) these techniques can both be used naively as presentation or inscription support of the philosophical material and of the finished "non-philosophical" product. But then they remain in their original naivety and will not undergo any transformation, whether philosophical or non-philosophical;

c) they can also be transformed with the aid of decisions, then in turn treated as an other-than-philosophical-material with the aid of the rules that would be for this material the equivalent of what non-philosophy is for philosophy. It would be a question of imagining in this way a "non-informatics" or a "non-poetry," etc. and thus of capitalizing on the maximum effects of the type: poetry-fiction, logic-fiction, religion-fiction, etc., which are all symmetrical with the aspect of philo-fiction that non-philosophy primarily produces. In order for there to be a veritable "philosophical creation" like the creation in the arts and the sciences, all the technical procedures of these domains can be introduced *de jure* into the philosophical material, but on condition of their treatment by decision, by its "auto-affection" or "auto-reference" and by the non-thetic *a prioris* of non-philosophy which, due to their universality, are valid for every material.

This rule is ultimately complex:

a) choice of philosophical (or respectively: other-than-philosophical) material;

b) choice of its type of enrichment by other materials or other technologies on condition of their "affection" by a philosophical decision;

c) choice of one or several organizational, equivalent and simply juxtaposed decisions that impose a first transformation on the material.

To sum up the sense of this preliminary moment:

1. A whatever material, capable of affecting the non-philosophical *a prioris*, is necessary in general: it responds to an "occasion" function, then to a "support" function (which is itself *a priori*) of non-philosophy's process.

2. The philosophical content of this *a priori* of the material is contingent; it can be whatever, but it is more interesting to choose the most complex philosophical material that will be enriched with respect to the constraints of the decision's coherence.

3. All material not of philosophical origin has every interest in undergoing a primary reduction to the decisional and positional structures (transcendence and immanence) that comprise decision, a procedure which does not exclude, on the contrary, reciprocal, i.e. still philosophical, "deconstruction"; for example, that of philosophy's statements and of literary texts.

4. If this first rule is empirical and naive due to the type of work it programs, and if it remains within the PSP because it elaborates the material from the sole point of view of its philosophical sense and authority, it is already scientific-and-transcendental by its origin because it authorizes a philosophically indifferent choice of decisions. An "occasional" material of empirical philosophical givens is necessary because it is required by science or vision-in-One, but it can be whatever philosophically or can no longer be guided by "positions," which would, on the contrary, require that one and only one decision be chosen to the exclusion of others and that it be taken as an absolute "factum". Some reasons of frequency or salience can guide the choice, but it is free from all philosophical constraint or authority.

136

5. However, if decisions are already supposed equivalent from the outset of this rule, they still conserve their respective identity. It will be necessary to reach Rule 1 to admit or render *transcendentally acceptable* an authentic "chaos" of philosophies, the radical dissolution of the PSP alone being able to lift definitively all of philosophy's authority over itself, to leave behind the sphere of self-representations that the material itself gives and to render the non-philosophical process possible in this way.

Rule 1: on the reciprocal description of NTU and of the material

The six elementary rules form a "quasi-system," and all of them must be progressively mobilized together in principle. However, the first is symbolically more important than the others and immediately distinguishes the non-philosophical style from the philosophical style. It condenses them all or renders them real in the order of representation, just as the One on its side renders the *a prioris* real. It registers their hyper-philosophical or hyper-speculative universality. It is useful to posit it clearly at the threshold of non-philosophical practice (even though rule 2 is the most important from the point of view of the material or object).

It states that *an utterance can and must first be described, but in line with the last instance, as an immanent lived experience or as a mode of the One—more concretely: as a radical human subject*, even if this is solely and necessarily in the mode of a subject in the element of the real's representation, rather than in the real. A text of non-philosophy is constructed around a word, a statement, a philosophical text: this guiding-term must stop functioning as a hierarchizing and ontological unity and not merely as a pole of thematic unification. This is only possible if it is described first as identical, only in the last instance, to a human essence or to a radical lived experience, as a being-immanent *extracted* from the World and even anterior to it. The sense of this first rule is the following: the representation (of the) real subject or of the One must itself be treated as integrally subjective, even though it be nothing but the *representation* (of the) real; the Dyad of the (non-) One is as subjective as the One itself, but it is so in the mode of the (non-) One.

That is the condition for this utterance to pass through the complete cycle of phases, each of which impresses a different status onto it from the "transcendental" point of view or in accordance

137

with the real. The destruction of the thematism, objectivism and even more profoundly of the auto-factualization and ontological auto-referentiality of language, is acquired or given without return after the first phase, but it cannot yet appear or be manifested such as it is (this will happen in the following phase). This first rule, which sums up the entirety of non-philosophy without still explicitly manifesting it, is conserved and explained by the following rules. To commence through the "radical subjectification" of the utterance, more exactly through its description as immanent subjectivity albeit in the mode of the (non-) One, to describe it or reformulate it as if it were already a One-subject without requiring a supplementary subjectification, is to avoid the transcendent operation of a unitary "reversal" of hierarchy and is the condition so that it can pass through new reformulations and descriptions and receive a usage without philosophical limitations or hindrances. Everything is knotted together here: the powerlessness of language to constitute the One, and yet its unary or subjective essence but as representation, this freedom of invention, the possibility of an unlimited multiplicity of descriptions without effect on their "object" but which this object determines without reciprocity. It suffices to respect the order of Determination in the last instance between the One and the (non-) One throughout non-philosophy's six rules for it to be nothing but the description in the last instance of the One or of the real states of affairs which are at the basis of philosophical decision and, in particular, of what is exerted in the statements taken as material.

Given the powerlessness of language as for the real, this rule then specifies that *any utterance whatsoever by right can be treated in this way* (and thus can also be reduced to the state of inert material). This goes for any term or decision whatsoever that is taken hold of: due to the equivalence of philosophical decisions, which the (non-) One implies and which it takes from the One itself—and sometimes in approximation with the technical difficulties of treating certain terms in this way which would have grammatical structures that would make them rebels to their preliminary philosophical exploitation and too removed from the name and the attribute. An utterance like that of "substance," for example, can be inserted under the rules of non-philosophical usage, and nothing, from the One's point of view, prevents that it be described as a mode in the last instance of radical lived experience, which is the One's essence; nothing prevents that a being-immanent be recognized from this angle, and nothing prevents that it then be treatable also as an inert material, then as a mode of the other real *a prioris* and of non-thetic Reflection—thus detached from its fetishizing "concept" or "category" usage, which is its own usage in a philosophical regime. Instead of being elaborated on an already factual and transcendent basis, an empirical and *a priori* or ontological basis, such an utterance is immediately related to the conditions of its immanent lived appearance in the (non-) One and in the One. In this way and as (non-) One or representation, it ultimately receives a phenomenal content of indivision, a real state of affairs that will describe its other usages in the last instance in accordance with the subsequent phases.

This possibility of treating all language as non-philosophical material, i.e. as real but only in the last instance, signifies, without still manifesting it as such, that the philosophical closures, demarcations, decisions which specialize a certain vocabulary and which unitarily hierarchize the usages of language in the functions of "concepts," "categories," "transcendentals," "existentials," etc., are broken. The placing outside-the-real of decisions and the *placing-in-chôra* of language and of the philosophical formation cut out from it, and even of textuality or of writing where language and philosophical decision are supposed to belong together, is still the implicit inevitable consequence of this first rule. Utterances will be freed from the hallucinatory task, not of representing the real but, instead, of believing to constitute it by this representation itself. Radically subjective or realized, they will not, however, be able to be referred to the real except in the last instance alone. Freed from all objective reference or intentionality, they will be available for adventures not programmed by the norm of philosophical norms, namely the belief in reality restricted to the linguistic constitution of the real. The moment it is a question of the One functioning as last instance, even before the real or non-mixed *a prioris* intervene, their traditional usage of *logos,* their decisional and positional function is implicitly lifted and replaced by a function of description "in the last instance" alone.

Rule 2: on the chaos of philosophical decisions and the reduction of material to support functions

1. This is the first rule to manifest the suspending effect of the (non-) One as such, i.e. to describe the immanent, thus already achieved, suspension of the PSP and of the authority of decision

over itself. This is a rule that stipulates the indifference of decisions in regard to the One or their equivalence for science. It is equivalent with a veritable defetishization or defactualization of philosophy.

As we suggested, philosophy in effect continually identifies every decision with an *objective philosophical Appearance*; it is perceived and received spontaneously in the form of an unavoidable *a priori fact*. Not merely of a transcendent given, but of a rational and necessary fact for itself, of a "metaphysical" or "logocentric fact," or of a "Tradition," an "infinite Telos," a "Destiny" or "Dispatch" through which it is supposed "unavoidable," despite all the breaches or incisions that it tries to reveal: due to its *de facto* existence, both its necessity and its future, its past and its repetition are already designed and programmed in the virtual state. It is a question of a veritable "auto-factualization" or "auto-fetishization" from which it does not separate its exercise, whether it be critical or dogmatic, massively logocentric or instead deconstructive. It cannot not presuppose itself—more profoundly than any "presupposition" that it can critique or demonstrate—as real; it inevitably concludes from its effectivity to its reality and, this is a necessary consequence, to its right to legislate on the real. This secret resource of "philosophical faith" is the same thing as its transcendental fetishism. This spontaneous belief, this transcendental hallucination is more "resistant," more profound and more extensive than that of the "natural attitude" or that of "logocentrism," because these beliefs and the idea itself of "logocentrism," for example, are still posited by decisions inside auto-factualization or the belief-in-itself-as-in-the-real. However, it is this extreme resistance that the (non-) One has already suspended by manifesting it as such and by rejecting it as transcendence, all while keeping decision as "material" by making philosophy "pass again" from the state of "factum" to that of simple "datum," but of a *given* which henceforth no longer has the form or one of the forms of the "fact." How does one conceive this state of "radical given" or of "material" where decision is reduced?

2. This first, negative and positive, effect of the (non-) One, this structure of representation—here founded by the posture of science—we have called it by the old name of the *chôra* as the uni-lateralizing em-place of decision. As transcendental, already achieved suspension, the (non-) One neither denies nor destroys what decision is; it merely suspends the PSP. The residue, still transcendent or outside-the-One yet transcendentally unleashed,

is precisely what we call the "radical given" or "whatever material." This slogan—to treat philosophy as a whatever material—discovers its origin here, in this suspension that makes the philosophical ultimately appear "such as it is" or the material as "whatever" in the sense that it is deprived of all signification or of all explicit or virtual philosophical function. The *chôra* is what reduces philosophy to being simple material for a representation (of the) real. All decisions float undetermined in it as philosophically equivalent or inert. This space is a chaos of decisions in a very precise sense, a non-thetic juxtaposition far (from the) real, in the faraway as such, non-thetic faraway (of the) real. This chaos is that which, without reversing philosophy and displacing it from the claimed place that it would be for itself, finally gives philosophy its first real place, the primitive Emplacement that comes after its absence of place and responds to what we have elsewhere called unilateralization. Philosophy, which spontaneously believes that it is its own place and a place for the sciences, can be brought out of this illusion or this auto-fetishization only by being thrown into the first place that is destined to it, into the *chôra* which ultimately uni-lateralizes it "far" (from the) real. Thus non-philosophy supposes the transcendental chaos of philosophical decisions that have become indifferent to the One, but only from the point of view of their philosophical pretension rather than that of their effectivity itself which is implicated by science as simple material that is destined, and thus stripped bare or sterilized, to serve as support or signal for the unleashing of the subsequent *a prioris* and to be transplanted into knowledge-form or into Universe-form.

3. Insofar as it ensues from the One in which it has its being-immanent and in which it loses its mythical aspect in order to be grounded in the scientific posture, the *chôra* is the abyssal depths, the untapped reservoir where what governs, rather than the mixture which is always regulated by a superior blending or coupling of the One and the Dyad, is the ante-dyadic chaos of a manifold which has lost the superior law of the blending, including that of the coupling. Whereas philosophy (Plato, Descartes, Kant, Nietzsche, Husserl) only deals with chaos as a strategic argument, without having elucidated it in its essence of the last instance—a chaos by simple deprivation of reason or of philosophy—and as an argument of intimidation so that its claim to legislate be granted and so that one recognize its authority, science instead sees "in-One" its transcendental necessity and its transcendental origin as (non-) One. This is why it is prohibited from

141

philosophically blending with the Cosmos—the unlimited amphibology of "chaosmos"—because it is instead what engulfs or unilateralizes the World, the cosmo-philosophical authority over things and not merely the "cosmic concept" (Kant) of philosophy.

The scope of a rigorous transcendental foundation of chaos is grasped better if one knows that it "corresponds" with that which, within decision, functions as *Other* (more or less re-marked) and as operation of *Reversal* of dual hierarchies or of dyads. Philosophical chaos is precisely this still transcendent operation of reversal of a certain limited local order, by and on behalf of a new hierarchy reconstituting the philosophical order, as can be seen in deconstructions. In opposition to this Other, which is always held between decision and position, the (non-) One does not result from a decision, for it is a dyad-without-scission that can therefore suspend every possible hierarchy, every decision and position, without reconstituting another one. This is only possible if it has renounced reversing, if it instead has suspended Reversal itself and the Displacement that ensues from it. The (non-) One conjugates the minimum abasement of philosophical decision with the maximum suspension of its claims. It represents the scientific or real universalization of philosophical Reversal, since the latter is always tied to a scission and to a hierarchy—to the blending of the One and of the Dyad. A science does not do as philosophy does: it does not reverse hierarchies, something that would come back to ratify them, multiply them and affirm them. Instead, it suspends the spirit of decision or of hierarchy, which is nothing but this auto-factualization or auto-fetishization by which a decision is self-assured. The *chôra* seen-in-One is therefore distinguished from Greek chaos, or relative (-absolute) reversal, as well as from Judaic creation or absolute inversion.

It is also absolutely necessary, so as not to conflate this concept of chaos—which is descriptive and scientific (whatever material or material such as it is)—with its philosophical concept and so as not to experience a feeling of unintelligibility, to put chaos back in the immanence of vision-in-One from which, and only from which, it draws its pertinence. It will not be forgotten that vision-in-One is the opaque or ultra-realist side of scientific thought, but the side which assures it its own rigor and which must not be conflated with an absence of consciousness or of reflection, or a deprivation of "world" and of "Logos," etc.

4. On what exactly, on which moment of philosophy, does the (non-) One bear? On the phenomena that manifest

auto-fetishization and the PSP. Since science requires an external given or an "object," not everything in decision will be destroyed; only its mixture-form, combining from itself Immanence and Transcendence, Position and Decision, is lifted. The suspension of this form (the One-Dyad circular correlation), since it is what organizes these two "terms" and imposes reciprocal relations of identity and of difference upon them (which are themselves variable according to the decision), unleashes a matter of statements, of operations or of problematics, a whole materiality of philosophy that accepts being together within the *chôra*. This manifold is not indifferent to itself from the syntactic and semantic point of view, but solely from the point of view in which it was previously differentiated and distributed in accordance with the laws of mixture-form. The suspension of this form, contrary to what philosophers suggest, does not suppress the syntactico-semantic organization, but procures another experience of it which is, rather than that of "common sense" or "common consciousness," what we call science and "ordinary" thought. What is essential is the lifting, not of the goals, finalities and objects foreign to decision but, instead, of decision itself as theoretical point of view on itself. For decision, the mixture-form is not destroyed properly speaking, but suspended as point of view or "theoretical" authority and conserved as a whatever material henceforth alongside the "terms" within the *chôra*.

Mixture-form is the same thing as the phenomena of unitary reciprocity and circularity, of auto-reference, of reciprocal determination and repetition, of fold and scission, of doublet and redoubling, etc. Consequently, the minimal philosophical syntaxes and hierarchies are arranged among them (like the Deleuzian partialization of the object and serialization), and not merely the most dogmatic and most substantialist forms of synthesis or of "identitarian" liaison: generally all the philosophical economies of common experience and of philosophy. The (non-) One unilateralizes them and definitively returns them to their transcendence beyond the *radical given* necessary for science. In other words, here it is still their authority of theoretical point of view that is suspended; they subsist within the *chôra* as a whatever material whose laws we seek, and, toward this end, they are destined to serve as signal for the unleashing of the *a prioris* of objectivity (rules 3 and 4). In effect, the *chôra* is a non-thetic *a priori* but which supplies the material or object; it will be followed by the non-thetic *a prioris* that give objectivity-form to this material.

Any philosophical statement whatsoever, however simple it may appear, can be treated as a philosophically inert manifold of "givens" or can itself be treated as such a given. On the other hand, several statements of heterogeneous philosophical origins can be treated together and combined in a single text: only from the point of view, however, of their reduction to the state of material for a science. For if the chaos of material is an immanent scientific requirement (even if it goes unnoticed by scientists in their everyday practice, it is a transcendental postulation of their practice) which furthermore only concerns the acquisition of material—obviously not the "laws" that will describe it—and has the limited sense of a suspension of the representations that accompany it, it can always be felt by philosophical resistance to be a simple hodgepodge. The necessary placing-in-chaos of decisions by science must be distinguished from philosophical resistance, which will see in this rule nothing but a contradictory attempt at subversion and provocation.

5. The suspension of mixture-form (object-form/fact-form, etc.), the defactualization of decision, therefore frees a manifold of material. This is a manifold of transcendental origin, even if it is that of the transcendent phenomenon, and it is required by science, rather than imposed upon it by philosophy or by the World. This moment of skepticism is radical, in the sense that it derives its origin from the One itself. This is an immanent skepticism, rather than worldly or tied to a transcendent exercise of reason or of sensibility; this is a skepticism of the last instance and is scientific rather than philosophical. It takes on the form of the exhibition of an ante-factual or ante-empirical manifold that is no longer the correlate of an ideality: a manifold of a Transcendence or of a uni-lateralizing Faraway which "leaps" outside the empirico-rationalist decision, in general outside the couplings of contraries, and which is more opaque than the "empirical," which is still *de jure* intelligible. The contraries of which philosophy is stitched henceforth float in a pure dispersive state in the *chôra,* and this dispersivity is no longer itself a contrary—the One already is without contrary. Before the manifold of non-thetic *a prioris*, there is the specific "multiplicity" of the One and the *chôra*'s own dispersivity, that which arises from the suspension of philosophical unity-forms alone and which reduces them, even the most partializing and most differentiating, to the state of radical givens for vision-in-One.

The effect of rule 2 is what we call *the transcendental dis-location of philosophical decision.* In the sphere of philosophy and under the authority of the PSP, several attempts at dislocation have taken place via a systematic introduction of a supplement of alterity to what belongs to every decision "naturally" insofar as it is an unstable and forced amphibology. However, philosophical dislocation is first like the decision itself and thus limited, it is an *auto*-dislocation that confirms its unity and its resistance by its distension, which is affirmed on the edge of the greatest danger and which it imposes upon itself and whose influence and ulti-mate mastery it keeps. If a science postulates the dislocation of decision, it does so with the means and intentions of another bear-ing. On the one hand, this is an authentic dis-location: decision is driven from its claimed place and even from its topology. On the other hand, it finally receives a real place, that of the *chôra,* which has the structure of the most radical dispersivity, that which is not obtained by a simple dis-tension of contraries but by a reduction of every "contrary" to the state of solitary or ante-dyadic manifold, identical to the emplacement by uni-lateralizing transcendence. Ultimately this dislocation of decision has effect only because it is no longer "first" but second and because it ensues from the real itself as an effect of the One. Rather than a discordance or an in-coherence that would form a system with coherence, or a dissemi-nation that could not "happen" in the stability of the logos and of presence, the *chôra* imposes a heteronomous dis-location (but of transcendental origin) upon decision that manages to reduce it to the functions of "whatever material".

6. Reduced in this way, the philosophical text is henceforth "manipulable," at least in accordance with the *a priori* rules of science rather than with an unspecified technology. This can be repeated within these rules and on condition of its chaotic disloca-tion—rather than under philosophical conditions. It is necessary to invent a repetition that registers and confirms the destruction of the philosophical style of the repetition, development and lin-earity of the philosophical "story" (all the phenomena that express auto-factualization/fetishization). If deconstructions already re-duced the metaphysical fact to a textual factum or an archi-writ-ing that would partially defactualize it into a sort of textual mate-rial, it is advisable to pursue this reduction further and to treat the "textual" fact itself as a sterile material alongside the "metaphysi-cal" fact in compliance with the equivalence of decisions. This last principle therefore signifies more generally that all philosophical

techniques of indifferentiation, of skepticism and of reduction are usable in an equivalent way, provided that they are also in turn treated as simple material reduced to and aligned with the *chôra*. A very partial list of these philosophical instruments of the non-philosophical *chôra* can be sketched out: 1. the techniques of nihilism (flattening, equalization, indifference, equivalence, etc.); 2. the techniques and arguments of skepticism (contradictions and deformations, doubt, suspension, reduction, etc.); 3. the descriptive techniques of the *chôra* and of place (topos, topology, depths, abyss, etc.); 4. the procedures of tautology, accumulation, hodge-podge and exacerbated repetition, etc.

These techniques, and others well known by philosophers, are thus destined to dislocate the philosophical material, i.e. to first suspend all the forms of auto-reference and circularity (and not merely of centrality and presence). But they are not naively usable: they must still in turn be "reformed" in accordance with the *chôra,* deprived of their decisional and their positional ins and outs, including every transcendent form of position, exteriority and stability.

Rules 3 and 4: on the reciprocal redescription of the a prioris of objectivity and of the material

1. With these two symmetrical rules, the elaboration of non-philosophy's properly "objective" sense begins, for which rule 2 will have supplied the material. This was already beyond philosophy's labor on itself, since it is a labor that corresponds with the theoretico-technico-experimental layer of the sciences. One of the theses of the non-epistemological description of the sciences is that this "epistemological" or "empirical" layer does not exhaust science's essence—vision-in-One, which alone interests us—and that it must receive its sense from this essence and from it alone. What we describe with the name "non-philosophy" is this scientific sense into which philosophy's labor on itself must be inserted as simple material. This description began with the suspension of the philosophical sense of this labor and was pursued by its insertion into objectivity's aprioritic structures.

We thus know these aprioritic structures, which are also called, like the *chôra,* "non-thetic" in a general way. These are exteriority-form or NTT and stability-form, "being"-form or NTP, the Other and the universal Base in their non-mixed form.

As we already noted, unlike the *chôra* as the *a priori* of material that impresses a stronger contingency on transcendence from which it only requires an "occasion," the notion of the *a prioris* of objectivity supposes a necessary given as signal—signal rather than occasion—so that the *a priori* form of its objectivity can be "extracted" or "separated" from it, which will furthermore be related to its essence of the last instance in the One. In other words—this is one of the One's effects as essence—instead of the *a priori* being a sort of redoubling or vicious and still specular duplication of the transcendence of "perceived" material, here it still appears as its simplification. The philosophical or mixture-form of transcendence supposes that the latter is redoubled, divided in itself, duplicated or folded; this is the doublet of the transcendent and of transcendence through which philosophy "does" transcendence with transcendent things. On the contrary, NTT is nothing-but-transcendent, non-decisional or non-positional (of) self, without a transcendent thing so as to be reflected in the latter and to reflect the latter in itself. The same remarks must be made for NTP. Philosophy does not really have a simple and "economic" concept of position or of the thetic but a doublet of position and of the posited and makes position with the posited. On the contrary, science "economizes" or simplifies position, prevents it from being divided by a transcendence or prevents it from being redoubled, self-reflected or specular, like decision also always is on its side.

What rules 3 and 4 stipulate is this labor of extraction and of simplification, this placing outside-the-real of circularity and of mixture, no longer in general as in rule 2, but on the precise cases of decision and position. This extraction of the *a prioris* is completely different (as will be shown) from the rationalist and "analytic" abstraction of a universal form outside a given of experience (a method that remains within the mixture and under philosophy's authority). Rather than an always unitary abstraction, this is what we call a method of *dualysis* or of *dualyzation* of decision and position: between the mixture-form of a given=X and its simplified, non-thetic or more exactly non-mixed form, it necessarily makes something pass besides a critical line or a line of demarcation—always mixed or unitary—i.e. something besides a decision. Precisely: the static duality, without scission, of essence (*a priori* included) and of contingent material, the (non-) One as immanent pole (and) as transcendent or outside-real pole.

Rules 3 and 4 also program this "extraction" of the *a prioris* of objectivity, i.e. of the non-mixed form of transcendence and of position. NTT is unleashed as the real state of affairs that is at the basis of the philosophical form or mixture-form of transcendence. Since it no longer itself has this mixture-form, it is not merely a non-positional transcendence, but from the start non-decisional; more exactly, it is deprived of its *blending* or of its coupling with position. Symmetrically, the same thing will be said of NTP, which is not merely non-decisional, but from the start non-positional, or more exactly: deprived of its blending with decision and of the limited and transcendent form that this mixture gives it. Here as before, it is not at all a question of claiming to destroy or deny the material itself but only its aspects of mixture-form. But the suspension of mixture-form is not necessarily equivalent—we shall return to this point in relation to rule 5 and the support—to the placing out-of-play of the ingredients of philosophical decision, i.e. of transcendence and immanence, of decision and position, and also of unity. These ingredients not only subsist in the state of whatever material to be described in a scientific way, i.e. in their reality of the last instance, but we know moreover that they serve as a completely necessary signal for the unleashing of these *a prioris* of objectivity.

2. After having isolated the forms, objects or functions in the material that represent the instance of the Other or of transcendence (whatever their mode may be), on the one hand that of position, on the other hand that of the attribute or universal, the procedure concretely consists in reciprocally redescribing the *a prioris* in question in the language of these instances and the latter in accordance with the *a prioris*; it consists in working on the decisional and positional aspects of the material and in suspending them, more exactly in suspending the form that they have in their philosophical blending. The non-thetic aprioritic functions serve as the immanent guide for this labor, but the thematics and conceptuality, the systematicity and regime of the decision's statements which serve as material must be taken into account in the reformulation of these functions themselves. The material is redescribed by keeping its ingredients of transcendence and immanence, of decision and position, but by "denying," or rather by suspending the redoubled or circular aspect of these functions, in short their mixture-form. Let us repeat that the placing outside-real of mixture-form, unlike in the sense of rule 2 to which they seem to "return" but by in fact remaining inside its suspending sphere of efficacy, is here not the placing out-of-play of every transcendence and of every immanence possible, but on the

contrary the condition for their unleashing or their manifestation as *a priori*.

The result or effect of this production, the *a prioris* of objectivity, is in some sense a transcendent and universal but non-thetic image (of the) material. The point of view and the object are indeed NTT/NTP, but they are described as if they were reflected in the material and its particularities. In the following phase, it is the material that will be the point of view or the object, and it will be redescribed from the immanence of NTT/NTP. However, from the moment of this phase itself, one can consider that the philosophical material already indirectly undergoes a non-thetic idealization and a non-thetic universalization. The primary philosophical text is re-written or "rectified" in the language of the "non-thetic," which eliminates all references to a decisionality (break, leap, transcendence, nothingness, annihilation, will, etc.) and to a positionality (project, opening, horizon, reference, world, plane of immanence, totality, etc.). It is neutralized, for example, in the discourse of the pure or non- "doubled/folded" event, in the discourse of exteriority non-redivided in itself and non-inserted into a position or a universal; and it is also treated, with all possible procedures, including rhetorical and literary procedures, as henceforth being such an event. Even position or Being can be described, once their auto-reference is suspended, as the fulguration of possibles non-thetic (of) self. In other words, this treatment is already "non-philosophical" and itself supposes a usage of language that is no longer a unitary usage of "logos." This is why it is possible, at least by right, to describe, for example, position as a non-positional event by utilizing the philosophical language of position; it is rigorous and legitimate to describe Being as a non-ontological or non-thetic event by resorting to ontological language.

In this way, everywhere the structure of a decision will be revealed, its reduction by NTT/NTP will follow; with the aid of its particular language, what will be described is its phenomenal essence, i.e. that through which it is experience of an Other-without-horizon, of an Exteriority-without-position and of a Position-without-decision, of a "simplified" position. The element of variation is here constituted by the material's particular thematics, conceptuality and syntactic modes utilized in view of describing the means of production that is also particular to it. Only the contingent material's language can offer a chance of variation. For example, the essence of "place" is "atopic," that of "position" is "apositional," but all of this must give rise each time to the variations made possible by the material. In this way, what is combined is a continual rectification of discourse of scientific origin and a variation of languages, objects and syntaxes of empirical origin. It is possible to speak uniformly of "NTP," but this expression is already the usage of a certain particular vocabulary. "Exteriority non-positional (of) self," "non-ecstatic Transcendence," etc. are formulations such that they strictly suppose quite different philosophical materials of departure, even if they designate the same phenomenal experience that the subject (of) science has of the object. What changes vastly from one object to another is the "language" that is now used to describe (without constituting) *the real object* itself.

Rule 5: on the "signal" or "support"
function of the material and its transcendental sense

1. The material is a thing—the rules of its usage by the *a prioris* and of its transformation will be stated—its function qua material as such is another thing and requires being examined in and of itself. There is an internal and "scientific" history of the material, but there is also its support function (abbreviated S(f)).

Let us recapitulate the first point. In rule 2, the mixture-form or philosophy-form, which is precisely the direct material of a science of philosophy, sees its theoretical authority placed out-of-play by a first intervention of the (non-) One. But philosophy-form subsists in its effectivity as mixture-form "such as it is," as "whatever material" of a science of philosophy. Reduced to the state of "sterile" material by the *chôra,* it is *that from which* science again departs, in the midst of the *chôra* itself which, in a sense, it will never leave. But it only departs from it again in order to unleash the real phenomenal givens or givens of the last instance of the objectivity that is at the basis of this mixture-form. As we know, these phenomenal givens are those of the aprioritic structures that condition decision. The extraction in question is therefore that of transcendence and of the base, of the Other and of Universality here reduced to the state of simple *a prioris* of science no longer functioning in a philosophical regime. This extraction consists in separating them via their "simplification," as we said, outside the mixture-form which is therefore *this time placed out-of-play no longer merely as theoretical point of view, but as the effectivity of the material—the latter passing from the state of inert material to that of signal.* This extraction or manifestation of the *a prioris* is indeed a "reduction," but in a sense this is a reduction weaker than the *chôra,* for it places mixture-form outside-the-real or outside-immanence no longer in its pseudo-scientific auto-reference or auto-position (rule 2), but in its effectivity of inert material. This is why it is indeed a suspension in which, far from denying the material, it assigns the latter a necessary, albeit limited, function within science. There is no science that is not obligated to take an "object" and its internal properties into account: this is what we call taking back the World, not as point of view or authority in general, but in the authority that it no longer possesses except as object henceforth reduced to the state of "given." This authority of the reduced object is obviously no longer that of its spontaneous representations or of its auto-position, and if the World, i.e. philosophy-form re-intervenes, it is in completely different functions, those which are required of it and tolerated by science.

Which functions? Precisely, after those of occasion, the functions of *signal* for the operation of the dualyzing abstraction of the *a prioris* of objectivity (NTU included). "Signal" means that a whatever given has been necessary for the experience and descriptive elaboration of the *a prioris*; that they, unlike the One itself, i.e. unlike their essence, cannot be manifested without reference to a transcendent given. This is a thesis that does nothing but describe a necessity onto which Kantianism, for example, has had to be folded: the *a prioris* are always and completely in view of experience and for it. Their degree of dependence with regard to the empirical remains to be specified, and, on this point, it is doubtful whether Kantianism is of the nature of a philosophical decision, whether it has also proceeded not so much as an extraction but as an empirico-rationalist, unitary and circular, even profoundly empiricist abstraction of the *a prioris* on the basis of experience (in its psycho-anthropo-epistemo-logical occurrence). This is the second point: *the signal-function, after that of occasion, also signifies a radical limitation of the function of transcendent experience in the manifestation of the* a priori. *If it states that a "reference" is necessary, this is in order to reduce it to the state of simple signal of the operation of dualysis, which extracts the new* a prioris *outside the mixture-form in which they are included and by which they are informed.*

We know the result of rules 3 and 4: it is a new description of NTT and NTP themselves, i.e. of that which takes the place of "means-of-production." This procedure of non-philosophy strictly corresponds with the means-of-production and not with the material as point of view. The means is no doubt already given or *a priori*, but it is concretely reformulated in accordance with the material

151

upon which it works. By non-thetically idealizing the material, it is reformulated or re-written by using its language: if NTT and NTP are, in a sense, always-already-there from the point of view of their reality or their transcendental "possibility," since they ensue from the One which is their essence, they also have their "signal" or their "negative" condition of existence—which is nevertheless not circular—in effectivity and are actualized only if there is a transcendent material to claim to affect the One. *The signal-function does not reintroduce a circle, because all the non-thetic experiences in general—the One above all—but also the a prioris in their own weaker way precede, in a mode which is no longer that of the logico-historical or ontological mode, the material of effectivity, here decision and its language, even if they resort to this philosophical language.*

2. Nevertheless, the occasion and then signal are local functions of the material. When dualysis in reality reaches what it is part of, the (non-) One qua subject (NTU) which represents the One itself in the last instance, it can only describe the inclusion, in this *(non-) One subject*, of the necessary, albeit limited, relation that this subject and the *a prioris* involve with the material: the aprioritic dimension of this relation or the dimension included in NTU is called S(f). S(f) signifies the possible minimum of intervention or of experience's role in the operation that unleashes a non-thetic type of *a priori*. The minimum, i.e. a necessary intervention, but which is not at all equivalent with a reciprocal determination or a unitary division (a mode of which is abstraction) of the two "sides" at hand, namely those of transcendent experience and of the *a priori*. This dualysis does not free the *a priori* from its reference to experience, from its validity for the latter and limited to it, but from the danger of unitary amphibology, from the "fall back" into the empirical, which is inevitable in philosophy. This is only possible because it is a second operation; because it ensues from real essence or from the One; because it comes after the manifestation of transcendental immanence instead of—as is the case in Kant and in every decision—preceding it. Since the manifestation of the scientific *a priori* and its transcendental deduction are rigorously the same thing here and arise from the same operation, the *a priori* from the outset is "saved" from its fall back into the empirical, into unitary division-confusion; but experience's own causality is also therefore reduced to functions of simple signal—of "support."

Concretely, the material, what it becomes through its reformulation from the *a prioris* or its usages in the S(f) that it fulfills, will not be conflated with the S(f) itself which is an aprioritic structure of science. The role fulfilled by the material as support receives a transcendental function afterwards, and the function that it represents is itself reformulated or redescribed while the material is recognized and described as assuming this function. This function is necessary in general, whatever its content may be: it is an *a priori*, and this support function qua function is not itself effective and transcendent but receives the non-thetic form or is lived in the "recurrence" of the latter. It is therefore no longer an empirical function, but an "objective" and transcendental function that sees to assigning philosophical material and that partially legitimizes this material's existence.

There is no philosophical type of circle here. Such as it has been described in its essence alone, science supposes the radical contingency of its material (of its "object" in the sense of a given): it "leaves-be" its material but at the same time renders it contingent. However, it requires this contingency: there is no science without a particular material, since the transcendental structures would then remain virtual and empty, and a "transcendental" science must also be "empirical." The difference, the play between this radical contingency and this necessity of the object, makes it fulfill this function of support which is required or determined by science transcendentally. This function eliminates, for example—and this is merely an example—that of "shock" or "impulse from without," which was formulated by Kant and Fichte in the particular, still transcendent rather than rigorously transcendental, context of mechanics and dynamics as general interpretation of science and in the context of reciprocal Determination, i.e. of a philosophical decision.

After the description of the *a prioris* as "means-of-production," a description which would utilize the language of decision but under new non-philosophical conditions, what will now be described is the support-function that the material in question assumes in the language acquired in the preceding procedure, which had as its object the description of NTT/NTP "in situation." But this rule 5, where it is S(f) itself that is phenomenally exposited, object of a non-thetic exhibition or exhibition of the last instance, will not be conflated with rules 1, 3 and 4 where the *a prioris* are exposited on the basis of the support-material, but whose support-function then has still not been elaborated as such.

Rule 6: on the non-thetic Universe or non-thetic Reflection (of the) real

1. We have definitively acquired the *real object* (RO), philosophical decision as scientific object. But the journey of the non-philosophical process is not finished yet. It is now necessary to pass from the

real object to the *object of knowledge* (OK) and to inscribe the preceding result in the element of "non-thetic-Reflection" (=NTR), which is the complete scientific representation of the real. This is when the usage of philosophy as science's object and no longer as logos is carried out, the ultimate pinnacle, whose foundation is science and whose material is decision, that arises from non-philosophy.

In the preceding steps, every decision had been suspended in some way: the decisional, positional and unitary aspects had been "reduced," at least insofar as they were given on the basis of the indissoluble mixture that they formed. Nevertheless, this was precisely the reduction or dualysis side: the description of a residual or immanent side and of a reduced or transcendent side. But at present, science sets off again from the (non-) One as non-thetic subject (of) representation, and with it, with NTU/S(f), what enters the scene is the reality of knowledge. NTU is conflated with the *a prioris* of objectivity, but also with the "object of knowledge" (OK) which is distinguished from the real object. Science requires a real object or a certain type of objectivity, but it also requires a representation that has the particularity of not being a part of this real object. This is why the object of knowledge is obtained by a "synthesis" of all the *a prioris* and by the efficacy, over the *a prioris* themselves, of a power of suspension superior even to that of the *a prioris*: this is obviously still the (non-) One, but as representation's own non-thetic subject.

2. The OK corresponds with the ultimate transformation of the real object (RO=the unity of the two aprioritic forms of objectivity and of the material in its theoretico-technico-experimental content in general). This is a discontinuous transformation, for if the RO and OK have the same "empirical" content to the point of being indiscernible from this point of view, and even if this content contains the RO itself from the angle of the *a prioris'* efficacy on the material, they nevertheless still have an absolutely different transcendental status. Both of these, like all things, no doubt have their essence in the One in the sense of what determines them in the last instance. But while the RO is acquired on the basis of a relative dependence on transcendent experience, thus containing if not the mixture- or decision-form then at least still its real aprioritic ingredients in the form of an NTT and an NTP, the OK, which certainly still depends on the material of mixture-form, instead no longer depends on it naively and externally, but *a priori*: this is the S(f). Whatever remains of empirical naivety in dualysis is lifted or suspended in the OK. The status and authority of the *a prioris* as such or spontaneously unleashed are placed out-of-play by the OK, and furthermore they are also conserved in it but under another transcendental state.

Which state? Precisely that of non-thetic representation or non-thetic Reflection (of the) real.

This state of "simple" representation, more simplified even than the *a prioris* themselves, corresponds with a radical sterilization of the RO itself, of its ingredients of transcendence and position, exteriority and stability. These ingredients no longer subsist except in the state of non-thetic or non-mixed representations (of the) real. They have not lost their function of *a priori* for experience or their relation to it, but experience now finds itself grounded in the (non-) One as subject which includes the S(f). What we call the OK does not at all, as we said, correspond with the concept, with the abstract, with the rational, with the idea, etc. of epistemologies, whether dialectical or not. RO and OK above all are not distinguished like the concrete and the abstract, experience and the concept, etc.—that which would arise from a new decision. But they are instead distinguished as what still has not undergone the most radical suspension and which is still tied to transcendence, i.e. the *a priori* simply exposited or exhibited—and what has undergone this ordeal and which is definitively purged of every merely contingent or supposed given reference to transcendence or to the auto-position of philosophical decision or of the PSP.

Whereas the RO, due to its *a priori* ingredient, has its essence of the last instance in the One or the real, but an occasional and specific cause (although not circularly determining) in the material, the OK is the simple correlate of the One itself, the ultimate essence of science or its "real" and "veritative" bearing. No longer is it related empirically (although not circularly) to experience or its mixture-form as occasion—as is the case with the RO—but indirectly and aprioristically, through the RO which henceforth constitutes its content or representational manifold. The OK is itself sterilized as reflection deprived of all specularity and reflexivity, such that the final complete structure of science is Determination in the last instance along with its correlate, non-thetic Reflection, and its means, the non-thetic subject (of) representation or (of the) (non-) One and the S(f). This parallelity of the World and of the Transcendental for which Husserl sought in vain is realized in an ultimately non-circular way with the OK. It is realized in the form of a parallelity of content between the RO and the OK, but such that now the OK is no longer still a mixed realization of the real's representation, but its strictly pure transcendental representation and no longer *also* aprioritic or dependent on effective experience. NTR, as correlate of the One, no longer depends on the *a priori*, for it is not its unitary division or its transcendental redoubling. One therefore passes from the real object to the object of knowledge through a sort of impoverishment, not in reality but in effectivity or in reality supposed given. If the latter has the same "empirical" content as the former, it has a different "transcendental" status, since the representation of the real object is definitively "un-realized" by the One which transforms it and also transforms the whole (non-) One into simple "non-thetic Reflection" or into the correlate of a Determination in the last instance.

3. What then is the special instance which this parallelity, founded in the One and without circularity, realizes? Which so radically separates the OK from the RO? Which places the latter out-of-play as *a priori* and conserves it as simple non-positional and non-decisional reflection (of the) real? This is obviously the (non-) One, since it alone can produce this effect. This is not the first time that it is required, because with non-philosophy it is a question of what happens in its sphere and only in it. But here, with the OK, the (non-) One accomplishes, so to speak, being reduced or "(non-) unarized."

Let us recapitulate its successive interventions. It intervened first to lift the authority of the PSP or of decision over itself, i.e. as point of view, leaving the transcendental residue of the material as the only inhabitant of the *chôra*, to the point that the following phases (rules 3, 4) again depart from this material. It intervened a second time to place outside-immanence no longer merely this theoretical authority but the material itself, the sterile given of mixture-form, thereby leaving as transcendental residue no longer the material, but science's own *a prioris* of non-thetic objectivity. It intervenes a third time, even more radically, to place the *a prioris* themselves outside-immanence as obtained by the dualysis of philosophical resistance, leaving as transcendental residue only the representative subject or NTU and what the latter reunifies: the OK or NTR as correlate-of-representation (of) the One or (of) the real; as (non-) One accomplished. There corresponds an immanent pole specific to each of its interventions that is also an effect or a mode of suspension. The receptive instance of the whatever material, or of the material such as it is, is what we have called *chôra*, which is where what is realized is the placing outside-the-real of philosophical authority and the return to the immanence of non-thetic representation. We have called non-thetic objectivity that in which is realized the placing outside-immanence of the authority of the material or of mixture-form in its effectivity. NTU is that in which the placing outside-immanence of the *a prioris* of non-thetic objectivity is realized and which is conflated with the new residue.

But NTU begins, through the S(f) which it includes, a regulated "return" to the philosophical given: this is what we can no longer call the World but, properly speaking, the *Universe*. If the

156

expression of "NTR" is reserved for generally describing the effect of Determination in the last instance and the essence of scientific representation, then the ultimate and total effect of non-philosophical science, the space of thought and of representation which is specific to it and whose essence is that of being NTR, will be called *non-thetic Universe*. Like the World, it is a transcendental, and not physical, concept. Whereas philosophy has the World as correlate or can be called its most general form, science has the Universe as correlate and can be called its most general form.

It will be noted that the intervention of the (non-) One is differentiated and specified by what is presented as resisting the One or as denying the real. If the (non-) One has drawn all its effects at the level of the constitution of the OK which signifies the accomplishment of science (this accomplishment is neither systematic nor historical, it is structural and realized each instant from the moment there is scientific "knowledge"), its intervention is graduated in accordance with the nature of the material and of the instruments of resistance which the auto-representation and the very existence of the material convey. In a sense, the *chôra* is the most powerful effect of the (non-) One because it suspends the PSP or places philosophy outside-the-real, i.e. the source and maximum degree of resistance, and because it is established in representation's own reality or immanence. But this is also its most limited intervention, because science requires the conservation of a transcendent residue that plays the role of a radical given. It therefore imposes a sort of restart if not in the World, at least *from* the World or mixture-form both reduced to the state of whatever material. Not only must philosophy's global resistance be overcome from the start, *i.e. manifested within the chôra itself*, so that science can be recognized in its essence and so that a non-philosophical science of philosophy can be possible, but also the "external" and "worldly" transcendence of the material itself, the very existence of the scientific "object" must at a certain moment be reabsorbed, i.e. posited *a priori* as a necessary reference required by representation's own immanence so that science can be recognized in its autonomy. It is necessary that its employment as simple occasion and signal for the extraction/manifestation of the *a priori* be relayed by its constitution as necessary *support* to the manifestation of the OK. This diversity of phases and effects in the intimate transcendental architecture of science is necessitated by science's reference to the World or to philosophy, an obligated reference when one passes from the description of science's essence to its application as effective science.

4. A more precise and above all better founded description of the OK or of the Universe belongs to a systematic theory of science—this is not our object, which is more "practical." The employment of this rule requires a labor of suspension of all the elements of (even non-mixed) decision and position and the redescription of the RO, support-material included, in accordance with this placing outside-immanence which therefore does not *deny* them. The ingredients of the RO are then redistributed under the law of the OK as elements of the simple scientific representation of the real states of affairs which are the *base* of the last instance of what was given as material and even of its auto-representation, here philosophical decision and the PSP. In this way all the progressively acquired theoretical material is reduced or "(non-) unarized" one last time and reverted to the state of ultimate transcendental residue, of the real's simple description which "was" the base of the last instance of decision and which the latter postulated while denying it. This redescription will utilize, for example, the terminology of indifference, of the abyss or abyssal reflection, etc.; all of the content in the "real object" will be redescribed as un-real, i.e. itself deprived of all transcendence but as enjoying an absolutely unlimited opening. NTR is therefore neither an exteriority, nor an immanence, but something even stranger than non-thetic exteriority and can only be said in terms of disinvestment, indifference, distancing, absolute loss, collapse (of the World and, consequently, of the logos), but also in terms of an already given uni-versal opening, etc.

These six rules of a non-philosophical science of philosophy only make sense due to an absolute descriptive fidelity to the specific language, codes and objects of a particular decision, and all of the latter must be transformed according to these new rules. Scientific knowledge does not transform philosophy in its effectivity—the latter would not be the object of science but that of philosophy itself. This knowledge is satisfied with *manifesting* its *reality* (that which is the labor of science) through the production of representations or knowledges. Spontaneous philosophical practice represses its real essence; the latter is what science uniquely elucidates and, by elucidating it, transforms this practice in its own "non-philosophical" way. As for decision's effective structures, they are the object of an intra-philosophical or "naive theory" that only intervenes in the "preliminary" rule. The science of philosophy does not work for philosophers, it thinks for man and in him.

Chapter V: Universe-languages and universal or non-philosophical pragmatics

Treating language as a whatever material

1. Non-philosophy is the practice of language no longer as Logos but as simple procedure of a scientific type of representation restored to its essence as such. Instead of treating language as determining the One, thus as partially being the One or the real, it transforms language into a mode of the (non-) One, it confines language in the sphere of "simple" representation. But which language is required to "fulfill" the non-philosophical Appearance or the Universe, always grasped in an indivisible whole? Which language to embody non-thetic Reflection? That of the material, the material as language—there can be no others. The principle of this pragmatics is the reciprocal reformulation of non-philosophy's structures and of the material's content; of the transcendental and aprioritic structures of vision-in-One and of the particular language offered by philosophy's "occasion." To avoid a misunderstanding, it should be recalled that the *reciprocity* of this reformulation is no longer that which governs the philosophical and which we have excluded. Rather than between the real-of-philosophy and the philosophy-of-the-real or in this infinitely monotonous circle, everything happens between the absolute real of vision-in-One and philosophy reduced to the state of indifferent given. The process begins through dualysis, through the description of the *a priori* dualities—and this word dualysis indeed indicates a labor of transformation. But if a description implies a labor, it is not on the *a prioris* in their essence—nor, moreover, on the very effectivity of philosophical decision—but on and in their anterior representations which are inadequate (philosophical or transcendent). The whole process of transformation happens

159

within language alone or rather within representation alone—(non-) One or Appearance—between an unsatisfying first description of the One and of its *a prioris* and a second description that rectifies the first. The labor of reformulating the One's descriptions and of its structures affects the descriptions themselves but does not reevaluate the real. It remains content with reworking old descriptions, on the one hand "reduced" in their old transcendent claim, on the other rectified according to the body of immanent rules which express the formally already-there structures of vision-in-One.

2. What does "language" mean here, i.e. "language of the material?"

Philosophy-form (decision or mixture-form) is inseparable from the empirical givens that it invests according to a circular process of identification and critique. Science and philosophy in a certain way have this material in common. But the various sciences have the objective of knowing it by inserting it into an anti-idealist scientific posture in the last instance, and, consequently, they unleash it from its mixture-form by struggling against its philosophical appropriation. The science of philosophy, such that it is programmed by vision-in-One, is specific and takes the mixture-form itself as theoretico-experimental material and given. The non-thetic *a prioris* belong to the essence of every science without exhausting it, but they are nevertheless only able to be manifested as such on the basis of the philosophical material because philosophy is what resists science par excellence and what it must "critique" (this, however, does not mean that philosophical decision in general conditions the very essence of science). But philosophy-form is inseparable from an empirical manifold which, if it is not the direct object of the science of philosophy, cannot fail to be taken into consideration. In all rigor and contrary to what certain, for example, rationalist doctrines may implicitly believe, philosophy-form has no language defined once and for all—language "deprived" of reason—but invests all language and is invested by it. What will be the consequences of this?

a) The non-thetic *a prioris* corresponding with decision (precisely because it is a question of the essence of science and not of any particular science) in turn will not be able to be formulated outside their reference to the decision's particular material. It is inevitable that their description borrows from the particular language of a certain decision which must serve as occasion, then as signal, for their unleashing. This constraint no doubt only signifies that a decision as such, without particular specification, is required as support. But since any decision whatsoever is always particularized because it is so universal, the same particular (-universal) language is utilized first as material fulfilling the signal-function, then as support-element of description of the *a prioris* themselves.

b) Let us reiterate: one cannot conclude from the empirical frequency of such a language (for example, the ontological) in a decision to the determination of science's *essence* by it and by this language. However insistent or unavoidable it may be, language is not in the determination of the real but in the determination of the knowledge of this real: it is from the start reduced by science to the state of descriptive, and not constitutive, procedure via the non-thetic Reflection (of the) real.

c) These two remarks are obviously not contradictory. The un-leashing of the *a prioris* into their specific content is not that of the essence of the last instance (the One): this content is *de jure* inseparable from a particular language that meshes with such and such decision, just as much as the description of essence can be elaborated indifferently on the basis of any language whatsoever, provided that it be "emplaced" in the *chôra* or reduced. The *a prioris' essence* of the last instance is not determined by the language of such decision; instead, what is specific in each of them must have the same origin. This is why there are two *a prioris* correlated by a decision in general, i.e. in total, four *a prioris* (*chôra*, NTT, NTP, NTU). This mutual cause must be sought in the material's nature—here, that of the philosophical material whose *a prioris* are being elaborated. Vision-in-One necessarily utilizes whichever material and whichever particular language, and if that language neither de-termines the essence of the real nor, consequently, the essence of the *a prioris*, it instead determines what is particular or more exactly specific in each of them: for example, an immanent experience or immanent lived experience in the last instance (of) "simplified" or non-positional transcendence ("non-mixed" to be more precise); an immanent experience or immanent lived experience in the last in-stance (of) universality or of simplified or non-decisional position ("non-mixed"). It is for the specific side of the *a prioris*, not for their essence, that there is a material and that it enjoys the necessary role of support or of occasion. However, this must be even more precise, for the description of the One-essence also requires a language that is by definition always as particular as it is universal. But it requires language merely in view of description as element of the represen-tation (of the) real rather than the constitutive element of the real itself. On the other hand, what is specific (decision and position) to the *a prioris* requires a particular language and decision not solely as an element of description or of knowledge, but as occasion, signal and support of their specific reality: it is not a question of the real in itself—essence or One—but only of the specific reality of the

161

a prioris; and, similarly, the particular languages and decisions are not, properly speaking, constitutive of this specific side of the *a prioris* but are only necessary as occasion or support for their extraction, rather than for their "abstraction."

In this way, the following will be distinguished: language as constitutive of the real itself (philosophy); language as merely descriptive in the last instance (science's *essence*, the One-real); and finally, language as support of the specific reality of the *a prioris*, i.e. of the (non-) One's dyad, since support is more than the simple description or reflection in the last instance (of) the One and less than the real's function of constitution. The description of the *a prioris* therefore requires language in two ways: for the description of their essence of the last instance, and as occasion then signal for the unleashing of their specific diversity, which is their contingent side, that which depends on the World or philosophy-form. Concerning this last point, it is necessary to add that the specific side of the *a prioris* is determined first by the support function, which is not a particular language or decision, but the necessity that there be a decision in general or philosophy-form so that the extraction of the *a prioris* can become possible; and that it then be determined only by the particular language of the support-decision.

A "particular" (regional, specific) language is always universal, and not solely from the moment that it is considered explicitly from the angle of a decision. Speaking of particular language, we have wanted to designate that which aims, more or less precisely and hindered by more or less of philosophy, for a domain of objects or radical givens in the scientific sense such as we have determined it. In other words, these particular "languages" themselves veritably have their respective sciences. Here it would be a question of this particular language (in the scientific sense) that a or the decision represents for a science of philosophy; and a question, this time in the philosophical sense, of the particular language—which the matter of philosophy or the content, called "empirical" by philosophy, represents—that philosophy-form necessarily invests and from which it cannot be separated, because it depends on this language in a constitutive way and not merely for its description or its auto-description, not merely as a support or occasion.

This fidelity to the idiom of departure allows us: a) to respect the specificity, the idiomaticity of decisions, which are both invariant and singular and which are the manner in which the object "philosophy" is presented, the enacted synthesis of the invariant transcendental operations and of the singular variations; b) to treat this particular language as a representation or a knowledge of the decision of which it is the description, but able to be transformed and rectified under conditions which are now those of science and no longer of philosophy; c) to produce "literary" or quasi-aesthetic effects.

3. Non-philosophy is therefore always a double operation, even though neither this reciprocity nor this duality again gives rise to a circular or unitary practice since it is a question of the static duality of the (non-) One as dyad-without-scission. Such dualities can only be described: their description on the basis of the material is equivalent with their extraction by the One; it accompanies their extraction at least as its simple non-thetic reflection, as a manifestation that neither makes it come about nor transforms it but remains content with exhibiting it. However, the description itself or the representation contains a certain labor, and this description therefore has a double aspect. In effect, it exhibits these *a prioris* on the basis of the material such as we have seen; it does not produce them in their essence, because it remains content with manifesting them as always-already-there and as having no need of this operation; instead, it indeed extracts them from the material from the point of view of their specific content, and the latter is always the same: philosophical decision and its invariants. But since it is always at the same time particularized by a determined language from which it is indissociable, this extraction is accompanied by a labor of transformation on the material-language, now in accordance with these non-thetic *a prioris* extracted-as-already-there. Because the language (the variations of syntax, of experience, of conceptuality that form a particular philosophical decision) is contingent, it is transformed in this very extraction. Conversely, it is impossible to consider the descriptions of the *a prioris*—if not their being-immanent, at least the descriptions of this essence and now those of the *a prioris* (as if they were not determined) as representations and only in this way—by the models-of-language supplied by the material.

This last constraint is equivalent to a beginning of the transcendental deduction of the *a prioris*. It already shows that they do not have validity outside the material-language that they serve to transform in view of non-philosophy. In effect, non-philosophy is from the start an analysis, a dualysis rather, descriptive and gathered in the unique representation of the dualities or dualitary *a prioris*, all of which are equally operations of transcendental reduction that end by eradicating philosophical resistance and rejecting it, insofar as it is transcendent, as a transcendental Illusion or as outside-the-real. On the other hand, it is the equivalent of a transcendental deduction, of a justification of the *a prioris* and also those of objectivity, probably all of them in accordance with the material and within its limits: therefore in accordance with the philosophical resistance

163

whose degree of reality they structure and which in some way can be their own. In general the support-function registers the necessity of this relation of NTT and NTP to the idiom of the material and to the *chôra,* the latter of which perhaps having no need of a deduction, even though it receives a deduction from the dual itself in a sense (the One and philosophical resistance which is the occasion of the dual). Non-philosophy is the ensemble of these two operations.

The concept of "universe-language" and of "universal pragmatics"

Non-philosophy apparently resembles other contemporary attempts: from afar, it evokes a certain psychoanalysis of philosophy; a certain therapeutic critique of metaphysics; a certain deconstruction of logocentrism. We know why it is not conflated with any of these practices. They all suppose philosophy valid for the real, when this is not the case. On the other hand, at the end of the process, there is the problem of the last eventual philosophical appearance of non-philosophy. As such, by its essence if not its material, it cannot give this appearance. This is because it is the vision or ordeal in-One of the most radical opening, the non-thetic Universe, which *precedes* the old Greco-philosophical cosmo-logos and suspends its principle—namely that the real would be a mixture of immanence and of transcendence—as outside-the-real due to this very transcendence. The Uni-verse is the place where language must advene.

To understand this new type of language, it is necessary to remember that Determination in the last instance is not a transcendent causality, i.e. effective or worldly. It is not manifested by an action *on* non-thetic Reflection *supposed given* in an external way but "by" the very existence of this immanent reflection, of this universal quasi-space of representation that will be language's obligatory "objective" dimension and of its descriptions, and by the rules of non-philosophical labor that structure these decisions and progressively lead them back into this dimension. The non-thetic Reflection, *non-philosophical Appearance or Universe*, such as it is seen in the One and by it, no longer acts on the One and thus manages to render inoperable language's so-called auto- or hetero-referentiality to the real, its ground of intentionality, that which is mixed or circular. The non-philosophical usage of language substitutes for the logos and the linguistic tautologies in which it is carried out an opening that is *de jure* infinite, the immediately given-in-One limitlessness in which the One's descriptions will necessarily come to be deposed.

In effect, the non-thetic Universe or Reflection is the static result of the "process," that as which the non-philosophical and the new pragmatics of language are manifested. The process began by dualysis, the description of the dualities of the *a priori*, with the effects of suspension of philosophical resistance that they produce. The process continues with a synthesis—a non-unitary, non-circular synthesis—by which the non-thetic subject (of) representation or of the (non-) One, the representation-subject (of the) real— NTU—unites all the preceding *a prioris* and relates them (through the necessary support-function that it contains and to which it is submitted) to the *chôra*, i.e. to the material and therefore to the resistance through which these *a prioris* structure the kernel of reality that forms its real base. Non-philosophy, as we said, is not merely a continual dualysis of resistance, it is also an ongoing "transcendental deduction" that limits the validity of the *a prioris* to philosophical decision or to its "language" in the broad sense (the syntactic and conceptual content of such philosophy).

The language dualyzed in this way is also that to which is related, that in which is formulated, all the *a priori* structures of vision-in-One. Every mode or every occurrence of this process, i.e. ultimately the usage of (virtually philosophical) language under the aprioritic and transcendental conditions of vision-in-One, is called *Universe-of-language*. The finished product of pragmatics can no longer be called "statements," "language games," "phrase regimes," "textual forces"—still distant avatars of the cosmo-logos—but, in all terminological rigor, "universe-languages." Universe here is taken in the sense of this transcendental and non-empirical (transcendent or cosmological) entity that forms the unlimited quasi-space of non-thetic Reflection.

Here non-philosophy no longer produces the Universe in its essence; it only makes it manifest its being-immanent without transforming it. Yet, under these conditions of immanence, it *extracts* the specific content of the *a priori* of the Universe. On the one hand, it re-describes this *a priori* on the basis of the corresponding ingredients of philosophy and of their particular language (totality, mixture-form, etc.); on the other hand, it re-inscribes all the products of this type that correspond with the previous rules in the quasi-space of this Universe such as it will be re-described. The *Universes-of-language*, or better yet, the *universe-languages* are this "final" product which is always subject to infinite reformulation or rectification.

The non-thetic Universe is not the total "dimension," but that of strictly non-decisional totality—which is already opened *for* language and can alone free it from the mutual prevention and inhibition that philosophy introduces into its usage. The Universe-form, correlate of the representation (of) the One, is in effect no longer limited internally by its division and its refolding. Since it is simpler than philosophy's Cosmos-form, than the cosmo-logical concept of thought, it is also richer and freer, immediately "extended" or infinitely "flattened." The Universe-form of language eliminates the latter's old auto-inhibiting principle of necessary philosophical repetition, *the transcendent principle of repetition*. Philosophy is an experience of thought founded on the folding of the real, of thought, of the thought of the real—it belongs to the occidental pathos of catastrophes. From the point of view of the Universe in this radical sense, *folding is an inhibition, catastrophe and complexity are still transcendent suppositions that appear natural but are useless*. This is an artificial nature of thought which we are beginning to discover is a transcendent hypothesis and a contingent postulate. *Non-philosophy is profoundly contrary to the contemporary, "postmodern" or "super-philosophical" spirit of the "Complexity-Whole."*

Unlike the Cosmos, the Uni-verse is a given, and not supposed given, opening; it is already open, and its space is no longer folded or curved because it does not simultaneously co-belong to the real. The specific space of science-thought must not be conflated with a determined representation of physical space, which is something quite different. Such a philosophical amphibology is dissolved by universe-languages. If the non-thetic Universe consummates the experience of a thought absolutely without fold, deprived of cosmo-logical fold, it will clearly be seen how the universes (of) language are distinguished (due to their really and nothing-but-infinite opening) from "textual forces," "phrase regimes" and even "language games," which are practices intrinsically limited or mutually prevented by the divided and folded space, the curved and catastrophic space that they still suppose in order merely to half open it or re-divide it a little more or a little otherwise.

More than ever, the radical ante-philosophical "simplification" of the usage of language, which makes its philosophical economy seem like a contingent hypothesis and a simple occasional material, signifies a return "to the things themselves," a departure rather in the "state of affairs" that is the state of extreme determination. This is a departure in the rigor of the thoroughly determined and sufficient phenomenon: because the phenomenon does not require language, is not logos, it can manifest language as phenomenon and therefore determine it. Immanent phenomenality, i.e. determination, does not require the appearance of objectivity or of presence; no more than the *determined*, which precedes determination, requires complementary operations of under- and over-determination; no more than a really universal pragmatics requires being founded

166

upon transcendent, restrictive and purely ad hoc hypotheses of a "decisional *a priori*" of communication, or a "consensus" with multiple avatars, or even an "archi-writing" also not founded but simply supposed given. All these hypotheses are those of *exploitation*—the exploitation of the undivided force (of) thought by the transcendence of philosophical decision. The liberation of language in relation to itself, i.e. to its usage of logos, passes through the refusal or suspension of this philosophical resistance that confronts hypothesis with hypothesis, decision with decision so as to better occupy a scene that it created. The basis of a truly universal pragmatics in the being-immanent-of-man is necessary from the start.

The performativity of description

A thoroughly immanent pragmatics allows posing in a more rigorous manner the problem of the mode of intelligibility, of receivability or non-receivability, of the texts of non-philosophy. As we know, the problem is that the One and the non-thetic *a prioris* are fully manifested and received as such, not solely by the One, but by the (non-) One, i.e. *also* by the philosopher himself and, one could say, by his resistance. A block of resistance—its manifestation *such as it is*—must be produced, the philosophical interpretation and re-appropriation must be really and absolutely inhibited without possible equivocation. It does not suffice to say: here's philosophy, put yourself back in the One and describe what you see…. The suspension—the manifestation as suspended—of the philosophical gaze and the manifestation of the non-philosophical itself must both be undeniable, i.e. practical or "performative."

The reciprocal reformulation of the One, then of the *a prioris*—which are already given in a description—and of the material-language, requires us not to be content with thematically stating, as in a classical treatise, that this reformulation is necessary without then effectively putting it to work. Not only is non-philosophy accomplished exclusively in the works or exercises that imply a "passage to the act," but also its nature of immanent pragmatics obliges it to produce statements that could be called performative strictly in descriptive passivity; statements that manifest by their very existence what they must describe in the last instance—statements identically descriptive and performative: this is the very sense of "non-thetic Reflection." This point requires further explanation.

The main "procedures" of subjective modalization (NTU) of the material, of its reduction, of its progressive uni-lateralization as non-mixed *a priori* and then as non-mixed reflection, destroys the philosophical illusion of any constitutive role of language whatsoever at the root, but also every philosophical type of decision bearing on this language.

In this sense, non-philosophical pragmatics can be defined by saying, for example, that *all language becomes performative in it but in the form of a performativity of description*. On the one hand, the One is not active or does not act in the mode of a transcendent causality; it is as thoroughly passive as the real can be, i.e. intrinsically rather than extrinsically. This passivity therefore must fully penetrate the new usage of language, which is description (of) description. Language can no longer be half-active, half-passive, for it no longer tolerates this decision; but it is thoroughly descriptive of passivities, and passive in this task. On the other hand, it no longer describes transcendent actions or objects supposed given in the World, because it does not exert itself effectively as action: it also falls outside this decision. But it is instead "performative," if one can still call it that, in the sense that it is exerted without remainder and thoroughly manifested as its operation (of description): it is what it does, it does what it says by saying it. It is no longer constative, at least in the sense that it would designate and describe objects present in transcendence. But furthermore, it is thoroughly descriptive or constative—yet only in the last instance. Language's vision-in-One therefore implies a strictly performative (and) constative usage, the identity which is neither analytic nor synthetic of these two functions, their lived or real identity *before* their scission. This identity of the performative and of the constative is realized in the form of the usage of language as thoroughly passive description of the One's essence-of-passivity. Language, in its non-philosophical usage, is the One's absolute *presentation* or its absolute reflection as dyad of the (non-) One and only in the last instance.

This is therefore a practice that only exists in the immanence of its exercise. Whence the necessity of inventing each time formulations which are not satisfied with thematically describing what is in question—lest they again give rise, as this treatise risks doing at each moment, to the transcendent and fetishistic illusion of philosophy and of its discursivity—but which *de facto* reveal for the One-subject the new functions assigned to the material. The combination of the two styles, the ultra-descriptive style and the ultra-performative style, is here necessary so as to avoid the reconstitution of the philosophical disjunctions of the theoretical and the literary, of the scientific and the poetic, of the rational and the non-rational, of the philosophical and the extra-philosophical, etc. Hence the quasi-poetic, quasi-scientific, quasi-religious effects that not only ensue from the material utilized, but also from the immanent, more than

168

"conciliatory" and "totalizing," nature of this pragmatics founded on the radical Identity that precedes the "future" contraries themselves.

Immanent and mystical pragmatics

Its immanent or practical employment within the very core of language clarifies that non-philosophy is not in its essence—other than from philosophy's point of view—an ascesis and a mystical identification with the One, a hyper-philosophical hallucination; that vision-in-One is a "scientific" method of the description and production of texts (or of events that are other than textual when the material is no longer philosophy) rather than a method of transcendent psychological or psycho-philosophical labor; that everything happens, if not "in language" (in the sense of a "textualism" that would be the dead fruit of this *originary linguistic turn*, of this usage-of-the-turn of language, which is called "philosophy"), then at least in the non-thetic Reflection or *universal Appearance*; that this activity no longer depends on external motivations and finalities taken from the World; that it does not have the form of the psycho-mystical and philosophical processes of identification, but that it is founded in an immanent being-identical which excludes mystical identification much better than philosophy can, but which we do not hesitate to call "the" mystical necessary for every rigorous thought. This is why vision-in-One must be manifest or "legible"—albeit in its immanent mode—in the very language insofar as the latter develops into the element of universal Appearance.

The grand structures of non-philosophy—the One, the non-thetic *a prioris*, universal Appearance, the support-function—are indeed *lived experiences*, but in the most rigorous, nothing-but-transcendental sense. They are no longer in any way mystical experiences of ekstasis or transcendence with which the subject would have to identify. Parallel with this substitution of *immanent vision* for *always transcendent intuition* (because it gives the object itself), the language, philosophically understood as correlate of objective intuition, is reduced and inscribed in non-thetic Reflection. This double mutation signifies that vision-in-One and non-philosophy generally do not once again consist in abandoning "language" for "intuition" and in entering into an effective or transcendent process: it is solely a question of the real. Non-philosophy is condemned—this is its finitude and its solitude—on the one hand to be identically the One without being able to abandon it or return to it, to live an Identity rather than an identification; on the other hand and furthermore, to manifest by non-thetic Reflection (and language in philosophy's case) the lived experiences of this Identity; to move, not in the "signifier" and "textuality" supposed auto-posing and auto-factualizing by philosophy, but onto non-thetic Reflection or "in" the open-without-limits of the Universe, where language is reduced and de-posed, de-fetishized, i.e. no longer referred except *in the last instance alone* to the One-real. We remain One, and as One we *directly* see this actual, non-horizontal opening globally given-as-undivided, where we *directly* work on a language which has lost its status and its usage of logos and which has become in turn a phenomenal content of vision-in-One.

The fact that we remain "in language" therefore no longer has any philosophical sense and not only liquidates textual fetishism but also the aporias that its usage of logos puts between it and *intuition*. Instead, the finitude of what we are as One obligates us to limit ourselves to the contingent material—but transcendentally necessary as contingent—and to the language that it offers us in order to rectify the first descriptions of the phenomenal structures of vision-in-One. Non-philosophy is nothing but the unlimited re-description—unlimited due to its finitude—of vision-in-One itself. The description or manifestation of the One and of the *a prioris* is not necessary, it remains contingent in relation to them. But *if* it must be carried out, *then* it can only be done in and from the non-thetic Appearance and by language.

The suspension of philosophical "rationality"

Concretely, the main "negative" task (not just rule 2, all the rules have a similar side) is to detect, manifest and suspend the grand structural rule in all its aspects and without remainder, the invariant of invariants of the philosophical style: the rule of Unity-of-contraries, of unitary-dyadic coupling or of reciprocal determination, namely what we have usually called philosophy-form or mixture-form. The transcendental residue of this reduction, as we know, is philosophical decision itself and its isomorphic ingredients, but all reduced to the state of inert material. However, this ongoing reduction is but the "negative" aspect of the rules which furthermore prescribe each time a positive description of the residues present in each level or defined by each rule.

These rules are those which the auto-description of vision-in-One has exhibited in the form of the universal dualitary structures that compose the real or phenomenal content of this vision. For that, there is a whole immanent structure of vision-in-One as

170

scientific posture which will now structure and define the new usage of language insofar as it has been explicitly or potentially supposed philosophical. Rather than a "syntax"—this term too immediately expresses decision and reciprocal articulation—there is a non-philosophical *order* that imposes an irreversible succession of dualities or distinct usages of the same utterance, of the same notion, of the same statement, etc. These are the six successive phases of the material's redescription or reformulation.

Together all these rules suspend the philosophical economy of language, the logos, and are substituted for it. Speaking of the *chôra* in terms of principle, it implies neither anarchy nor chaos in the vulgar-empirical sense of the "no matter what." The *chôra* implies "all"; it conserves "all," except philosophical faith, except the law of the All/Whole. This is ultimately the positive suspension not only of the "rational" usage of language—of this philosophical decision that hides in the so-called "rational" norms which philosophy sometimes supposes given as absolute—but also of the ensemble of the arbitrary decisions and limitations imposed on language, of the transcendent divisions and bifurcations of "intelligibility," of the restrictive norms and codes of philosophical receptivity. Placing philosophical syntaxes outside-the-real, for example those of predication and its logico-transcendental internalizations, also those of substantiality, dialectic, structure, difference, etc.—clears the way for the investment of the material by a body of *a priori* dualitary structures whose being-immanent assures us that they are receivable by every man and that they are authentically universal, valid for every decision, more universal than these ready-made, restrictive and normalizing norms and codes which were inherited from the Greeks with the logos and which prohibited thought from being replaced in its most radical opening.

Perhaps, so as to oppose it to the philosophical or to the *restrained* which is carried out via the presupposition of philosophy's real or essential existence, it can be understood why that which suspends, beyond its existence qua occasion and material, philosophy's belief in its reality and makes it appear as illusion would be called, for example, *generalized deconstruction*. Generalized deconstruction has the force—that of the One—of affecting the invariants of philosophical decision itself—decision and position, the whole in their state-of-mixture—and not merely certain so-called "logocentric" forms or forms of "representation" of these invariants. Vision-in-One reduces these invariants structuring philosophical faith themselves, and not merely the theoretical, speculative and legislative effect-of-faith in the real that they produce. The consequence of this reduction is the possibility of carrying out a more universal usage (i.e. not limited by these mixtures) of whatever utterances or whatever statements. Their philosophical usage (pragmatics in the currently understood, unitary sense) is no longer the unavoidable horizon of proper thinking or that of the pleasure of speaking. Unitary determination or the Greek closure is proved useless and abusive.

The non-philosophical usage of language therefore defines a new universal pragmatics that is valid for ordinary language as well as for philosophy. As an "abstract" and descriptive rather than "figurative" and constitutive pragmatics, it procures a new freedom in the usage of words or statements outside their philosophical codes of origin, their rational norms of receptivity and their operative program (decision/position; reversal/displacement). This freedom can only incite the resistance of conservatism that philosophy secretes. But it becomes "acceptable" or pertinent, albeit always in its own way, if it is described—as we are doing here—as seen-in-One and if the traditional auto-factualization of language, with the philosophical auto-fetishization to which it gives rise, is suspended without remainder.

The main argument of philosophical resistance against this ultimate freedom is that of "bad chaos," the precariousness of the arbitrary, the insane anarchy of whatever conceptual aggregations. As an objection stemming from resistance alone, it has no theoretical relevance. The "chaos" that philosophers manipulate as a straw man—even those who call for its Nietzschean "chance" and who would already therefore refuse to be intimidated by the rationalist objection of the "no matter what"—is never as pure or radical as they imagine, but always somewhat imaginary, simultaneously fantastical and empirical. This is still a philosophical decision, and thus it is auto-contradictory or auto-limited and is resolved in affirmation. Instead, the One, since it is not acquired by a decision, can found a chaos as immanent transcendental experience on the one hand, as one of the aprioritic structures of vision-in-One without being denied by it or reconverted into an affirmation or unitary synthesis; on the other hand, as absolutely determined and bearing upon philosophical decision alone or the mixture-form, rather than undetermined and doomed to the "no matter what."

If one commits the confusion of specifically identifying the *a priori* of the *chôra* with a more or less anarchic conceptual dispersion, ultimately obeying the empirical norms of the dispersion and dismantling of unity, it becomes impossible to indivisibly suspend the philosophical decision that inevitably returns with this chaos, which is simultaneously too limited and too vague. Whatever degree of disorganization of philosophical form there might be, it will always be unequal to the *chôra,* which is necessary to suspend the

172

validity of decision itself. Transcendental reduction must be integral or undivided; it does not have its essence in a simple operation of auto-scission, auto-alteration or difference, ultimately re-identifying and unitary. It cannot be partial and have the nature of a *krisis*, or it is then an originarily dual or dualitary *krisis*, a dyad that will have never been engendered on the basis of the One by a scission. Since the transcendental *chôra* has its essence in the One itself but does not continually derive from it via scission, procession, etc., it cannot be measured against empirical or even rational forms of critique and no longer against a decision-of-anarchy, which all operate on the ground of their memory and suppose the validity of their old economy. By indivisibly lifting philosophy's authority over itself-as-material, it unlocks non-philosophy from its last bonds, its last effects and its ultimate "tribunal" in the fact-of-philosophy or in its sufficiency. Since it is not exhausted in a simple anarchy of conceptual aggregations (which would, furthermore, never be radical), it makes possible another "economy" of thought outside the norms of philosophical "rationality" and founded upon the immanent rules that provide the efficacy proper to Determination in the last instance.

Non-philosophy is not a negative henology

Can non-philosophy, which is the developed concept of the thought of the One, be interpreted as a "negative henology?" This is impossible for two reasons.

The first reason is because its simultaneously "critical" and positive instrument, that which the *non-* precisely expresses and of which it bears witness, is not in any way one of the forms of negation or nothingness that we find in philosophy. It is a question of the originary dyad of the (non-) One. But the latter cannot, since it has its essence and its being-nothing-but-immanent in the One, have the same effect and above all the same essence as nothingness in all its forms (non-being, annihilation, the negative, negation, destruction, scission, etc.) which suppose the element of Being rather than of the One, of philosophical decision rather than of vision-in-One. *The (non-) One, in relation to the One and taken in its complete concept, is instead like a "superstructure" in relation to an "infrastructure."* This is why it and the "negative" no longer have the same real or phenomenal constitution at all. They are even strictly incomparable. Precisely because it is founded on the (non-) One rather than on non-being, on an experience of suspension simultaneously milder than nothingness and more universal than it

173

(since it suspends Being itself insofar as the latter still arises from a form of transcendence), non-philosophy cannot be called a negative henology: at most, it is "suspenseful," a static suspension or reduction—the state of superstructure—rather than a negation. And it is not at all a negative philosophy, because the *non-* here no longer derives from philosophy, is no longer dominated and legislated by it, but finds its essence in the One alone and is brought to bear on philosophy when the latter is manifested. It suspends philosophy in an undivided way, including all the ontological functions of the "non." Here philosophy is no longer master over its destiny, for it is no longer what acts upon itself: neither auto- nor hetero-critique, because *the (non-) One emanates from the One alone and affects the philosophical in a "dualitary" way, i.e. in a way even more heteronomous than the Other of deconstructions.* Non-philosophy is a real process; a negative henology would be an effective process.

The second reason is because the (non-) One with its different modes, from the *chôra* to the non-thetic Universe, is not at all a first and unitary instance that would affect the One itself. It is nothing but an irreversible, static *effect* of the One, a unilateralized dyad. It is no longer even, like non-being, nothingness, annihilation, the negative, etc. co-constitutive of the One's essence like they are of the essence of Being. Also, the effect of "negation"—of simple suspension, rather—is strictly second to it, non-constitutive of the One and only effective in its descriptions. This powerlessness to constitute the One, i.e. immanence, therefore no longer has the same sense as the ontological powerlessness to "categorialize" Being or the One insofar as it is thought in the extension of Being, i.e. in transcendence. The (non-) One is first drawn from the One's reality and sufficiency, thus—since the One determines it—from language's radical insufficiency (which is nevertheless positive in its own way) to constitute the One, for language does not describe it except in the last instance. It is not drawn negatively from the sufficiency of Being, from the height of transcendence, but from the positivity of immanence.

Here still, the great theoretical maxim is to dualyze the problem, to think in a dualitary, rather than unitary, way. A negative theology or even a negative henology are unitary, and they postulate—for this reason—the commensurable incommensurability of the real and of language, or the fable[17] of the ineffable (what the word *heno-logos* sufficiently indicates); these are still decisions, but of auto-negation. Instead, non-philosophy is dualitary from the start. On the one

---

17 It should be noted that this word not only means "story" in a conventional sense but also stems from the Latin "*for*" meaning "to speak" as well as "*fas*" for "divine speech." Henology refers to the discourse/logos of the One or of unity, particularly relating to Plotinus and the neo-Platonists. [TN]

hand, the One is vision-in-One, positive and immanent phenomenal content, but not ineffable—it is described in its positivity. *What is no longer posed is the problem of having to speak the One in the sense of constituting it and then of discovering that this would be an impossible task.* On the other hand, language is fully capable of *describing* the One and of doing so in a non-illusory way within this function of description in the last instance, which the One requires of it, and within the limits and contingency that it imposes on it in this function. Language is not incapable or insufficient (unitary prejudice), it is thoroughly contingent or determined in the last instance, which is completely different. That it proceed by suspension, which is itself repeated, is not at all an incapacity unitarily measurable by a height or a transcendence. The One of vision-in-One is not, like some of its onto-theological forms, transcendent to language, its ineffable Other; it is instead language that is the One's contingent Other and is thus constrained to describe it, but only to describe it in the last instance. There is decidedly no reason to see in it a form of "negative henology" developed in terms of a "negative theology."

Chapter VI: On non-philosophy as post-deconstruction or "non-Heideggerian" deconstruction

The concept of "post-deconstruction"

Earlier we treated the non-unitary generalization of philosophical decision in general without taking a particular decision as an example. We intend to reiterate the operation on the case of "deconstructions" and situate non-philosophy in relation to them. In American parlance, this perhaps could be called: *Post-deconstructionism.* But is it a question of borrowing some sort of *American way of thinking?*[18] It is foreseeable—this is an essential law—that a post-deconstruction will hastily relay the primitive forms (Heidegger and Derrida) of deconstruction. As one can already imagine, it will be a question of the "ideological" generation of a supplementary variant of contemporary deconstruction, to which will be added a pragmatic, semiological, technological or political index or into which will be injected an analytic, Marxist, Wittgensteinian component, etc. Since this history is inevitable, let us occupy this place in our own way; let us imagine for a moment what an authentic deconstruction or "post-deconstruction" would be, that which would not be acquired by a supplementary variation but would bear witness to a theoretical emergence. Certainly terms in *post-* are stupid in general and serve as the banner for gathering those who refuse to think further than their present and what they know. But it suffices to rigorously describe in a spirit of positivity the phenomenal content of this posteriority, which certainly has a more theoretical than historical sense here, for it to be no more stupid than any other word of philosophy, whose compulsive recourse to prepositions is quite readily acknowledged. This word—post-deconstruction—must be

---

18   Italicized and English in the original. [TN]

understood as the indication of a problem: that of a scientific, rigorous and real foundation of deconstruction. Can it be transformed into a non-philosophy in accordance with a new experience of thought where philosophy, which is no longer master of itself or of man, is rendered contingent by an experience that is even more primitive in which science as vision-in-One will have been ultimately recognized? What does it become in its principle and its procedures when one passes from its philosophical forms, which function under the authority of the PSP, to the new forms that it acquires on this scientific foundation?

A post-deconstructive thought is no longer a task having priority and once again motivated by arguments of weariness and repetition. In relation to science, this can no longer be nothing more than a second or derivative task. It cannot result from the simple extension of existing deconstruction to new objects or of its enrichment by new procedures, or of a supplementary twist, turn or revolution, *but must express the real change of base that science contributes in our relation to philosophy*. Post-deconstruction is indeed a new stage of philosophy's critique, but it is the stage that corresponds with the discovery of the precedence of science over philosophy and the consequences that ensue from this: the constitution of philosophy into a new scientific continent.

The term *post*-deconstruction will therefore be read in the sense that deconstruction stops being first, like the metaphysics that it critiqued, in order to become … *posterior*. Rather than the form of deconstruction that would come after its "classical" or orthodox form, it will be understood as what is itself determined by the *post* of that which comes after science. Not as one form of deconstruction after another—which is a way of assuring continuity—but as the second rank that comes after science which alone determines it as second. Therefore, what we will proceed to is deconstruction's displacement—its emplacement, rather, for a displacement would still be a supplementary philosophical operation tied to a preliminary reversal. It is a question of describing it in its *real state of affairs*. And in light of its real conditions, it can only attain the second rank.

In a general way, a science of philosophy does not at all found the same deconstruction as that which is restrained by the PSP, because here it merely serves as material.

How non-philosophy is distinguished from deconstruction

Non-philosophy makes use of the Other—but even so it is not a mode of "textual" deconstruction. This holds for two reasons:

1. On the one hand, from the very beginning it works on philosophy in accordance with the One, then with the (non-) One, rather than with the Other. Without vision-in-One—of which it is nothing but a second aprioritic structure and in which it has its essence—the Other remains what it is in deconstruction, a circular entity, supposed given without any proof and therefore is itself transcendent. The Other cannot found a science of philosophy, but at best an appropriation of the latter through a religious tradition or a compromise with it. Moreover, since it is not founded in the One's essence and its being-immanent is not elucidated, it remains of the order of a unitary dyad, of a scission at worst and of a positive distance at best, or of a supplement of absolute alterity with which one attempts by artifice to make "do" with a relative or ontological Other. The substitution of the breach for scission, of *différance* for difference, of dissemination for dispersion, incoherence for coherence, etc. does not radically modify the unitary situation, i.e. the fact that the Other is always *supposed-given* here, like Being and with Being, as an alteration of decision and with decision, and in a way that is no more rigorously founded than Being and decision are. Everything holds together: only an elucidation of the radical being-immanent of the Other can detach it from its context of unitary scission (which is enclosed in an identity that is contemporaneous with it) and give it as an Other absolutely non-decisional and non-positional (of) self.

2. On the other hand, it does not suppose philosophy valid or given so as to deconstruct it afterwards in its most massive and most apparent unitary forms. Deconstruction believes to be able to distinguish between philosophy's supposed real essence, its postulated validity, and some of its "inferior" forms, of its most logocentric or gregarious modes, etc. From the outset non-philosophy prohibits this facility and this decision which is made in order to forevermore save the essence of philosophy and in order to protect it from a radical critique as well as from a science, placing it on the "good side," on the side of the real. For it turns out that the real is not a "side" and does not tolerate decision—this is what founds non-philosophy and requires the global suspension of the undivided essence of philosophical decision, its complete reduction to the state of material or simple given.

In this way, while non-philosophy does not *suppose given* (in transcendence) but effectively is given the real or the One, philosophy *supposes given* the real or only approaches it in exteriority and in the mode of transcendence. The real, i.e. consequently, not so much the One, but Being and the Other, *the precedence of the Other over Being at the same time as Being*. Deconstructions in general, whether "textual" or not, resume the Greek paradigm of the unitary simultaneity of the One and of the Dyad and satisfy themselves with modifying its content, with putting the Other as such, either relative (-absolute) or absolute (-relative), in the place of one of its terms. The unitary matrix is only on guard against incoherence and dislocation, but its validity for the real is always affirmed. Deconstructions augment the arbitrariness of philosophical decision instead of suspending it: they cannot critique the dogmatism, centrality or gregariousness of metaphysics except by adding to the postulate of decision or of the real supposed given the equally unfounded postulate of the Other destined to affect decision or identity. These are unitary quasi-dualisms where all the pieces of the machine are simultaneously supposed given and supposed to function.

Nevertheless, a coherent functionality is not a rigorous and founded thought, a machine is not a true thought. The effort of injecting supplements of incoherence or threats of dislocation into this functionality does not diminish the unreal character of this construction but augments and confirms it. If the real is in no way a construction, then no deconstruction will be capable of giving it again. Every philosophy engages in the infinite multiplication of circles, scissions and doublings and in the proliferation of doublets. Not only the empirical and the transcendental, position and decision, etc. but Being and Other-than-Being; and now the Other-who-is and the Other-who-is-not, the Other-in-Being or relative (-absolute) and the Other-outside-Being or absolute (-relative); an Other disguised by and in "logocentrism" or masked by "metaphysical" representation, and an Other supposed unrepresentable, even by a mask, but which requires being identical with the former, despite everything. Philosophical illusion believes it is capable of self-limitation: it thus proceeds by complexifying itself and (re)doubling itself, while non-philosophy proceeds by simplifying; it deconstructs, while non-philosophy dualyzes; it postulates two transcendences, while non-philosophy is given one alone; it believes to be able to limit Greek transcendence by Judaic transcendence, while non-philosophy de-rives every transcendence possible.

This *forcing* is the destiny of transcendence left to itself, of decision unbound which has lost the sense of its bearing in the immanence (of the) real or lost the sense of its base in the radical posture

180

(of) the One. On the contrary, non-philosophy is the suspension of decision *before* its unbinding, a non-decisional suspension that contrasts with decision's unlimited authority. Rather than supposing philosophy to be valid so as to establish it within a periphery or on the margins that are not its "own" but remain acquired externally and without rigor, non-philosophy is given the One without simply supposing it, from the start it is exerted as vision-in-One and observes whatever comes to philosophy. Rather than opening it and possibilizing it, it includes philosophy as simple occasion of this vision. We know this: an authentic "generalization" does not consist in an opening, in an extension or even in a supplementarity (this would be a Judaic generalization and appropriation of philosophy, which are merely as cultural and non-scientific as its Greek appropriation, even if they are very different from it) but in the insertion of philosophy under its conditions of reality finally established in a rigorous way.

A non-linguistic pragmatics of language

Philosophy ignores the being-immanent of the Other. It thus only knows the Other through the "effects" to which philosophy necessarily reduces it by inscribing it in the milieu of the World or by submitting it to the form of identity. Philosophy manipulates it while being offered to it in this mode: as non-being, as (dialectical) scission, as undivided and positive distance (topology), as breach and supplement (deconstruction), etc. Instead, non-philosophy only knows the Other in accordance with its affect rather than with its effect; non-philosophy experiences the Other, without manipulating it, in its real essence or in the being-immanent that it decants from the One's posture. Non-philosophy does not utilize the Other to breach or unsettle philosophical effectivity. The latter is merely the signal, occasion and support of this non-thetic Other; however they no longer maintain the circular relations that condemn the Other to "function," that commandeer it for tasks of delimitation, fracture, dispersion, dissemination—namely a number of more or less external teleologies that are imposed upon it. In a general way, vision-in-One is *jouissance* (of) the Other, which is also unreflected in its essence rather than reflected and re-divided, and it is also *jouissance* (of the) *a prioris* that follow it: universal Base or attribute, ultimately the non-thetic Uni-verse or non-thetic Total. Instead of, for example, commandeering them for tasks of the *universalization* of the empirical, of the attribution and determination of a subject (here it is already determined by itself), vision-in-One is the transcendental enjoying (of) the universal given in itself integrally or given as undivided before any operation of universalization. And in the same way, rather than using Totality for functions of the totalization of a manifold, it is seen (from) non-thetic Totality as undivided and unreflected before any operation of totalization.

There is an inevitable consequence: while deconstructions work on philosophy through operations which are at least semi-technological (decision or reversal of hierarchies, their position or their dis-placement), non-philosophy includes what is no longer anything but a material in an economy of an origin wholly other than the technological. While the former is semi-technological, semi-transcendental, simultaneously practical and theoretical, the latter is purely transcendental and does not know the distinction between the practical and the theoretical. While the former opens closures, demolishes and reconstructs the edifice of philosophy by transforming it, the latter inserts this edifice—as well as the labor on it—into an ensemble of representations and of thought that neither extends nor prolongs it but forms a possible coming from elsewhere.

In other words, by this account deconstructions appear efficacious, while non-philosophy appears sterile. But they are efficacious only within their illusion to attain the real, an illusion in which they move without noticing it for a moment. Not only is non-philosophy's inefficacy a pure appearance (it disturbs philosophical textuality itself more seriously than deconstructions, which remain submissive to the most insistent Greek prejudices), but it is also permitted to think that a true thought is preferable to a merely "efficacious" decision, as every philosophical decision of "truth" is in the last instance, and that the dissipation of the illusion is more efficacious than the illusion itself.

In a general way, because vision-in-One excludes for itself the philosophical pragmatics of the One, of the Universal and of the Total, it ultimately makes possible a radical pragmatics, a *usage* of language without limits. Because it delivers them in their essence from their transcendent conditions of exercise in it, vision-in-One can take them as the basis of a usage (which is itself universal) of language. Non-philosophy is a non-linguistic pragmatics of language. Since there is vision which is immanent in-One, in effect it is legitimized of itself as a usage of language that is no longer limited by language, at least insofar as it is potentially logos. We accede (to) the One, (to the) (non-) One, (to) Exteriority, (to) Universality, (to) the Universe without language, and it is through these structures, which we are integrally given without remainder as undivided and unreflected, that we in turn see language. We accede (to) them without dividing or refolding them on themselves, without partializing

182

or doubling them, without subtracting anything from them and adding any supplement to them. This is why, from them, we also accede (to the) heart of language and can create, under the name of non-philosophy, the most universal usage of language that can possibly be imagined.

A whole chain is unlocked from philosophical decision and the philosophical fold: from the One to the universal pragmatics of language, which corresponds with the other end of the process, by passing through the concrete phenomenal content of vision-in-One when it is vision-of-language-in-One. Rather than supposing it given (in transcendence), from the moment that an undivided phenomenality of the One (the transcendental) and of Being (the non-thetic aprioritic structures) is really given, and from the moment that thought, rather than in their "milieu," sees them in the One itself or as direct modes of its concrete being-undivided, it becomes necessary to abandon the transcendent processes of scission and identification and of decision and position, which are techno-philosophical artifacts.

It is the absolute finitude, without remainder, of vision-in-One which therefore places us in the in-itself of things, that of language in particular. The "in-itself" or the in-One here no longer signifies the blending of the finite and the infinite, but merely that reality and radical finitude are the same thing. A non-philosophical pragmatics stops surveying or transcending language through language, it works "on the ground" or more exactly from the inalienable immanence of language's phenomenality. Rather than supposing language simultaneously under- and overdetermined and sometimes imposing a refold and sometimes an overfold onto it—in any case, the supplementary fold which comprises the minimum of the philosophical operation—thus leading language to its own phenomenality in accordance with that of the real; a non-philosophical pragmatics determines language in the last instance by the One so as to say it differently, but on condition of rectifying these concepts which are simple indications; it transforms language into the "superstructure" of the One, which is its "infrastructure." Instead of making reference to the text in general and to a particular text of the Tradition, an essential or constitutive reference like deconstructions make and, in reality, to various degrees, like all philosophies that work on it toward or from its margins—non-philosophical pragmatics treats language as an inert material in terms of its properties of *logos* and simultaneously as that "upon" which the One is directly acting without the mediation of philosophy's operations—as that in relation to which it is determining in the last instance. Since its criteria are no longer textual-and-philosophical, it no longer judges the usage of language and of the labor upon it on the basis of its auto-position or its auto-factualization of "text-to-be-deconstructed," of "fact to be analyzed," etc.

The unitary presupposition of restrained deconstruction

What is more deeply embedded in deconstructions and in particular those of the "textual" sort? In its contemporary forms, has deconstruction drawn out all its consequences? Has it attained the extreme limit of its power, i.e. the abandonment of its power offered to the efficacy of the Other? Undoubtedly it has, insofar as it remains an operation guided by philosophy. But we know that the fact of being led by philosophical authority ultimately establishes its limitation.

In its restrained form, it remains locked *into philosophical presuppositions which are unperceived as such, even when they are claimed to be inevitable constraints*. These presuppositions are not indifferent: they limit its efficacy over philosophical decision because they postulate that the operation is still guided by the authority of the PSP; such presuppositions restrain its scope by maintaining one last residue outside the operation, that of philosophy's authority and sufficiency. They are no longer simple intra-philosophical prejudices which a superior degree of critical vigilance could eliminate and which decision of itself could isolate in itself. It is doubtful that it is any longer a question of judging deconstruction restrained from the point of view of its objects and from its point of view by procuring new objects for it, new arrangements and extensions, or a new internal, differentiated and more refined economy. It is instead a question of these presuppositions that coincide with philosophical decision, precisely a question of *de-cision*, whether it be auto-positional (metaphysics) or, here for example, inhibited by an undecidable (the deconstruction of metaphysics). What is now in question is less decision than its authority over itself and its ultimate reference to itself (albeit through the Other), its so-called unavoidable necessity. The ultimate presupposition of Heidegger and Derrida, what they do not see as such because they lay claim to it as inevitable in a nevertheless still philosophical form ("one cannot surpass metaphysics"), is precisely the motor of their thought. It is the more-than-representative, more-than-logocentric sufficiency, assurance and security that *philosophical decision even as illusion is necessary or belongs to the real*. This is philosophy's auto-sufficiency, i.e. its sufficiency for the real, and thus for itself. The Principle of sufficiency is purified of its most encumbering forms by decon-structions, but afterwards it subsists in a minimal and incompress-ible form: one can deconstruct metaphysics, but on the foundation of its necessity, of the *interest in* ... Being or Logos; one can vary the most massive forms of this identification, but only to better ac-cept the ultimate identification of the deconstructive subject with philosophy. Therefore the subject of deconstruction simultaneously assumes the *Logos,* its authority and the blindness to the nature of the simple pre-supposition of this *supposed given* authority. This is the foundation of the belief in the necessary or destinal nature of metaphysics, a belief that is perhaps merely the oldest hallucination upon which the Greco-occidental Continent has seized. The PSP's restrained deconstruction thus only affects an experience which is itself restrained by logocentrism and representation, i.e. its most external and massive forms. It is the auto-destruction, tending to-ward itself as though toward a limit, of philosophical decision, the subtlest way in which it can conserve itself and grasp itself again *in extremis* as the necessity of an invariant.

Deconstructions undoubtedly represent a mutation of the old philosophical critique. But it is precisely still a metaphysical type of mutation because it proceeds via the traditional operations of Reversal and Displacement that it aggravates. The *logos* is prevented from constituting itself qua metaphysical auto-position by a real Other who inverts the hierarchy and keeps it displaced; it is there-fore no longer truth, but illusion. And the Other is no longer a least-truth or a nothingness of truth and being; it has become the real or that which divides the *logos* and representation. But this re-versal-and-displacement is the work of the unitary Dyad; it remains under the global authority of the PSP, because the ensemble of this new coupling is conflated with the real. In effect, decision is now "coupled" with a real=Other, but together they are still supposed to exhaust the real. Thus restrained deconstruction is held captive *between the autoreference of metaphysics and an Other which are, to-gether, two unfounded presuppositions, accepted without a supplemen-tary examination as real or valid by themselves.* Sufficiency is now redivided into two equally unthought presuppositions instead of being held within one alone. Restrained deconstructions do not rid themselves of the unthought; they multiply it by two, and a cloven PSP remains what it is from the point of view of science and its subject. One remains content with making the dissimilar parts of the Same function together, thus allowing philosophical decision to culminate in the latter's authority. From Identity to the Same, a supplement of breaking the difference of the Identical has been enclosed, but the true duality which would have rendered decision

185

contingent has not been reached. *Restrained deconstruction is a unitary dualism, it is not a dualitary thought.*

What is called "restrained deconstruction" is that which intrigues metaphysics without having the power to render it contingent; which haunts philosophical decision without succeeding in making it something besides a cumbersome phantom; which only engages the PSP so as to make it stronger, more necessary and the better to submit to. What is called generalized or "non-Heideggerian" deconstruction is that which deconstructs decision itself; which finally deconstructs it without remainder; and which does this on the basis of its radical contingency. It is what confronts the PSP at the root instead of letting it subsist and instead of paying ultimate homage to it.

What is the *a priori* non-philosophical foundation capable of affecting the PSP itself? of positing the equivalence of all decisions within their mutual contingency for the subject? of suspending the authority of the unitary paradigm? of showing that the hetero-critique which conceives the Other as the real is certainly progress in relation to metaphysics where it is decision that is immediately the real, but that it still remains a philosophical prejudice? What is the instance stronger than the Turn, Bend, Reversion and capable of making decision appear as a simple material for another, non-philosophical thought? a material without particular authority over itself, able to be utilized for less "logocentric" endeavors than the restrained forms of deconstruction? This instance is vision-in-One, which is no longer philosophy but instead science. Science, at least comprehended as an absolute transcendental thought is, as we know, the foundation that procures for deconstruction the conditions of its non-philosophical generalization.

Deconstructions and the impossible dislocation of philosophical decision

The intervention of science as transcendental criterion better elucidates the real sense of the belonging of restrained deconstructions to philosophical decision, the truth of their claim to "philosophy."

The Other is the means of placing-metaphysics-in-the-margins. No more than in metaphysics, from one deconstruction to another there is merely a homogenous concept of the Other; on the other hand, there are certain invariant functions that its coupling with Being makes it play out. What matters, therefore, is this articulation which is the absolute and the real unique syntax, and in which each time a thinker is installed without being able to give sufficient reason superior to the arbitrariness of his decision and the will to the circular auto-foundation of his own system. What distinguishes deconstructions from previous forms of philosophy is on this level to which one must go in order to seek it: another syntax articulating metaphysics and its Other, another experience of reality comprehended through the latter, in the name of which one deconstructs the metaphysical illusion conceived as repression of this Other. Hence the functional variations of the terms at hand within the equation that regulates them: thinking=Other; *thought and the Other are the same*—not the identical, in other words, which is instead the metaphysical or the representative deconstructed in this equation. If this equation is the sole invariant, each adversary's new definition (representative identity or metaphysical centrality) will functionally correspond with another definition of the Other. It suffices to know that "dissemination" (Derrida) is rather a multiplicity by transcendence, and that "multiplicities" (Deleuze), for example, are rather multiplicities by immanence, to see that neither one engages the same concept of representation; that, for example, Deleuzian multiplicities could pass for a form of presence-representation, a "transcendental signified" which would have to be deconstructed; that a large number of Heideggerian values (voice of Being; silence; veiling and unveiling) are also breached by Derrida in this way. Everything is heterogeneous at the level of the "terms," and the most serious ambiguities burden the terms themselves with ideological effects: they are "unintelligible," save by metaphysical appearance; what alone is "intelligible" is the coupling or articulation, the invariant matrix or mechanism of deconstruction. And even this is saying too much: as in every philosophy, the only thing that is intelligible is the circular, yet incessantly opened-displaced, movement of this mechanism. Deconstructions remain a machine and a functionality in one of their aspects; in the other, they are an ordeal or endurance of the Other. This is the "real," this makeshift mechanism, this shaky functionality, this poorly balanced equation.

Deconstructions are the response to a seemingly easy problem to define: find an instance of alterity sufficiently strong and non-negotiable to exceed past the experiences of overflow and of multiplicity, of surpassing and of critique that metaphysics has tolerated; define the reality of a non-mastery that can affect philosophical decision in a sufficiently heteronomous way. But it suffices to announce such conditions to make a circle reappear: to know what this instance of the Other of metaphysics will be, it would be necessary to possess its concept from the start. It is completely endemic to philosophical decision to be incapable of extra-territorializing itself or surveying and dominating itself in a meta-(meta)physics that would decide on the fulfilled essence of philosophy ... and of its Other. And deconstructions are obligated—this is the same thing as their unitary foundation—to recognize the reality and omnipotence of metaphysics, its circle as inevitable constraint, even when it is opened and loosened by the Other; they never leave the element of philosophical mastery, even when they affect it with finitude. There are two consequences that follow from this:

1. For lack of being able to elucidate the real or indivi-dual essence of metaphysics and of its Other, this project from the beginning establishes itself each time in a certain functional articulation of the rivals at hand, i.e. in a mode of this invariant. It chooses, yet arbitrarily and contingently, this matrix in general and its modality (such and such concept of metaphysics or representation, such and such complementary concept of the Other). But this matrix itself—which is nothing but decision—is contingent and unfounded: the project of autofoundation and also that of its critique are themselves lacking in a radical originary foundation, or they merely conflate this project with its research. There is an incurable naivety of every philosophical decision, a naivety and a violence. Metaphysics is animated by a "without why" that its *relative* (-absolute) reasons do not exhaust. But its deconstructions are just as incurable, if not more so. These exemplary attempts to undo or delimit mastery and autoposition continue to belong to *the ultimate structure of philosophical decision that is identical with this articulation—in itself contingent— of the logos-to-the-Other, of metaphysics-in-the-margins, etc. and of its auto-position in a more radical sense.* They continue to participate in the violence and the question-begging which belong to philosophical mastery and which they cannot modify. They mitigate, defer and displace decision, but they register it and confirm it in itself more subtly.

2. The Other is both internal to the philosophical circle *and* external to it: it is possible to re-mark it as external or heteronomous by a supplement of intervention. It is simultaneously non-metaphysical and beholden to metaphysical Authority. It can neither be integrally included in this circle nor radically exceed it, it is *qua* circle. What can this discourse signify, this enigma of the "neither ... nor ... at the same time" of the "sometimes ... sometimes" (Derrida), of the difference that makes Being and being (co-) belong together (Heidegger) without synthesis and by simple transcendence? What is therefore announced in the omnipresent motif of Difference, of *Differenz als Differenz* or of the *Austrag* (Heidegger), of *Différance* (Derrida), *is the attempt to bring philosophical decision to its maximum point of dis-location or dehiscence, but which would not remove it and would instead conserve it as de-cision.* Heidegger and Derrida

experiment with a new type of "catastrophe"[19] or discontinuity, but it remains limited by the strophic movement or transcendence of a Turn (*Kehre*, Heidegger). Such a type of catastrophe, which remains internal to philosophical decision and remains content with laying bare the hanging thread or transcendental Unity of metaphysics and of the Other, is thus less efficacious and more unitary than it seems. It can only acquire reality by an interminable labor or progress; it postulates the reality of the infinity of time for becoming real. This is because this catastrophe is merely the desperate mobilization of that which, from another point of view, is an impossible amphibology or synthesis, the Greco-occidental amphibology of ideality (of Being or *logos*) and reality (the Other). Deconstructions are protected by a double refusal: the first emanates from a shameful dualism which refuses to go to the end of its logic; the second emanates from a unity, despite everything, which refuses to be assured by the *logos* in the metaphysical circle but which is still composed *with* it. This ultimate bond, apparently emptied of all *logos*, this transcendental hollowed out by the Other, but which still unites it with logocentrism or representation, signifies the most prodigious effort ever accomplished by philosophical decision toward approaching its point of rupture, i.e. being continued despite the Other and through it. These highly strategic attempts are those of risk or peril, of the greatest danger that philosophy can support *in order to conserve itself*. "Representation" or "logocentrism" designate—in a recurrent way, for these are not facts—some of the effects of this labor, the eliminated part of decision, all or almost all of its voluntary part. The other part remains or resists not only the Other, but the bond of unity between metaphysics and the Other: *the real possibility of an endeavor such as deconstruction*. Philosophy, i.e. the PSP, has never had the best defenses or the subtlest strategies in times of danger: above all when these times close philosophy by opening it to an absolute risk (Derrida) or a "re-commencement" of thought (Heidegger). Such is the real content, the invariant of these attempts, simultaneously their resemblance (despite everything) and their reality: they are the ordeal—and the militant triumph—of philosophy.

Ultimately deconstructions have hunted down and breached ontological and logocentric presuppositions, deformed and displaced the sphere of philosophy, but they have conserved it as sphere of authority and in turn repose on premises that they cannot deconstruct, because such premises condition the project of a restrained deconstruction itself and re-inscribe it in the most general matrix of philosophical decision. If we gather together these premises which

---

19 From "kata" meaning "down or against," and "streph," meaning "I turn." [TN]

form a system, they mark the extreme limits of the philosophical type of critique:

1. One *supposes given* a certain syntax articulating metaphysics and "its" Other, and an experience corresponding with the withdrawal (of) the Other: their coupling is supposed as the ultimate and unavoidable element of every possible thought. This is the matrix of a philosophical decision *enlarged* by the Other or the undecidable but which remains a partial decision in which each thinker establishes himself arbitrarily or without foundation by a begging of the question that therefore no longer defines "metaphysics" alone. This arbitrariness and this ultimate willfulness contaminate all the notions in deconstruction: since they are not elucidated in their ultimate truth, they are partly functionalized and commandeered; their truth still partially falls back on their sense, and their sense falls back on their function. In other words, this arbitrariness of deconstructions and of every philosophical decision in general is perceptible not from their perspective, since they repose on a preliminary identification that is inexplicable to this matrix, but from the perspective of another experience which we have described—an experience of thought and of its essence which is "scientific" yet in the transcendental mode: vision-in-One.

2. The second premise consists in supposing, beyond any reassessment, not only that philosophy *exists*, but that it belongs to the *real* par excellence, at least as what co-determines it. This identification or amphibology of philosophy and reality belongs to the essence of every decision, and deconstructions do not overcome it. It too can only be denounced by another thought that would be autonomous in relation to philosophy and would have a sufficiently radical access to the real so as to unveil a transcendental Illusion in the claim of philosophical decision, extended in this way from metaphysics (Kant) to its critiques and its deconstructions.

3. The third premise reduces the real to the Other or to a transcending received as absolute. It is useless to want to demonstrate how this premise, so as to allow the deconstruction of "onto-theology," is more than theo-logical: it is religious *and reposes on a tradition external to the task of a rigorous or scientific foundation of thought*. This would be a rather obvious thesis, but one which must be foreseen to see it denied. Deconstructions have only been able to exceed Greco-occidental metaphysics (from Heraclitus to Nietzsche) by importing into thought a so-called non-philosophical experience of the real. Everything leads one to think that, far from being its rigorous and liberating experience such as science postulates it, for example, for every man, this is a residue which is quite purified of its religious experience, secularized and transformed into an operation

against metaphysics, a re-marking of its onto-theo-logical dimension, but sufficiently re-elaborated so as to alter it and so as to be turned against its most apparent origins.

The first two of these three premises demonstrate the ultimate belonging of deconstructions to the philosophical decision that they are satisfied with unsettling without destroying; the third premise indicates their belonging to a religious Judaic (Wittgenstein and Derrida) or Judeo-Christian (Heidegger) ground. The only possible "critique" of deconstructions consists in showing that they are the synthesis of these two sources which is moreover untimely[20] and *founded on arbitrariness*. This critique can only be a scientific—in other words, not empiricist—thought capable of elaborating a rigorously immanent theory of philosophical decision.

In what sense non-philosophy "generalizes" deconstruction

In a vague sense, it can be said that non-philosophy generalizes philosophy, for example deconstructions. The limits of this interpretation have already been described. On the one hand, philosophy is universal in its own mode—it is the general-as-total—and non-philosophy on the other hand is not its continuation or one of its variants. It is not given philosophy as the vastest ensemble of thought and representation, save to *open it* a little wider and confront it with the "remainders." It postulates that philosophy's universality is only unsurpassable for the World and within the limits of effectivity, but that it is outside-the-real and thus limited in principle without the possibility of extending this point of view at all. Its task for philosophy is thus not to extend philosophical universality a little further, but to relate it to the real and include it in a qualitatively heterogeneous universality, more primitive and more essential and, in this sense, more "universal" than philosophy because it ensues from the real this time and is not limited by an illusion.

Philosophy's textual and linguistic generalization carried out by deconstructions will have contributed to limiting the unconscious textual fetishism of metaphysics. But it still upholds the old fetishistic postulate itself; it contents itself with the Greco-philosophical idea of language (as signified, as signifier, as identity of the signified and the signifier) as constitutive of the real's essence—albeit

---

20   French *malheureuse*, which more literally means "unhappy," "unfortunate," "miserable," etc. Here, however, Laruelle seems to be emphasizing the etymological sense of the word (in relation to the context of arbitrariness): *heur* meaning fate or fortune, related to *heure* meaning hour or time. Perhaps "misfortunate" would come close to the sense, but then a conventionally negative meaning would prevail. [TN]

partially, here—; of textuality as unavoidable, unsurpassable-as-sur passable, etc., i.e. of a necessary usage of language qua *logos*. Against this language-All or textuality-All, simply unsettled but conserved, we oppose a textual occasionalism, the text or language as minimal material, the only theory capable of ending this era which will have been that of textual Illusion.

For vision-in-One, there is no "general textuality," "family re-semblances" of language games or univocity of the voice of Being— no generalization of the particular. Philosophy proceeds in this way, it passes from being to Being, from experience to the *a priori*, from the particular to the attribute, then from all of that to the One: it generalizes, then totalizes; it universalizes, then unifies. Vision-in-One follows an *apparently* inverse trajectory precisely because it is first founded in the individual given as sufficient. It is an immedi-ately universal and even "total" thought (but in a non-thetic form: the *a priori* of non-thetic Uni-verse) whose universality, which is not qualified empirically and transcendently, reduces the general and the total blended by philosophy to the state of "particular case," i.e. of "material" and "occasion." It returns the philosophy-All, its Tradition, its Destiny, its unavoidable horizon, its closure, etc. to the state of simple support for an experience of thought—which is as absolute in its universality as the individual of which it is the cor-relate—to be absolute in its singularity.

Due to its special structure, Determination in the last instance contains the *a prioris* of the *chôra*, of occasion, of exteriority, of universality and of totality, but delivered from their limitation in their mixture form or from their mutual impediment. Its universal-ity does not result from a construction of hierarchical levels, from a progressive extension, from an operation of supplementarization, for it is not heteroclite like that of philosophical decision. Where-as the latter is a machine made of pieces that function simultane-ously—including their functional, always programmed intervals— vision-in-One contains within the simplicity of its real essence the instance of the non-thetic Uni-verse or the absolute phenomenal conditions of really unavoidable universality, that which is merely the correlate of man-as-One. As always, because philosophy *wants* universality, it does not obtain it and must content itself with a pro-cess of heteroclite accumulation, with a complexification and with a weak dislocation that it believes to be the grandeur of thought. Vision-in-One is no longer guided teleologically by the objective of becoming more universal than philosophy: it is more universal in its "point of departure" precisely because it is already the real and because the individual alone can found the greatest universality or be accompanied by the most radical opening. In turn, philosophy, whether rationalist or not, progressively manifests its nature of arbitrary decision in relation to the real (not grounded in it) and its construction qua related pieces, its complexity qua originary forgetting of the simple or of the One, ultimately its voluntarism, which is the same thing as its impossible synthesis of itself across the hiatus of transcendence. Current deconstructions are the culminations of this process of headlong flight, the admission that philosophizing only consists in attempting to dislocate decision a little more, but nevertheless without breaking it: the attempt to pass off the Greek and the Judaic *coalition* for the model of rigor in thought and the dualistic distension of the unitary paradigm for the only invention possible. No more than previous decisions, deconstructions neither know the real in itself nor the possible in itself, but merely their mixture, the figure of the World of which they are but one of its most desperate mimicries.

The aporias of textual deconstruction

Nevertheless, what makes deconstruction—above all in its Derridean form, which is too hastily called "textual"—theoretically interesting is this matter of a unitary dualism. A deeper analysis of the aporetic mechanism of this deconstruction could contribute to elucidating what philosophy in general is and is condemned to do. The nature of the Derridean mixture is other than that of the simply philosophical, because philosophical decision is nothing but an unequal half, the other half of which—more unequal still—is constituted by a non-Greek affect, a Judaic affect of the Other as absolute. The theoretical problem of this deconstruction is then: how, by what internal unity—and what would such a unity mean here—can this quasi-system, despite everything, function, continue and allow itself to be identified as invariant, in a mismatch but as invariant nonetheless, when this would only be through the capitalization of its effects to which it lays claim? The distension of philosophical decision by the affect of the Other as absolute appears maximal here; it tends toward a point of rupture, where the rupture—as we said—serves to save the "point" itself and its continuity. Somewhere and however it may be willed, the extreme catastrophe continues, makes the rule, continues to make the rule. How is such an "alignment" of the Greek and the Jewish, of the Greco-relative Other and the Judaico-absolute Other, possible despite everything? How does one hop from one foot to the other so quickly by prohibiting oneself from putting both feet on the ground?

This problem is concentrated in the *signifier*, for it alone has the duty to guarantee this ultimate necessary unity, this internal coherence, moreover, within the incoherence of two writings. In effect, the signifier is sometimes interpreted as relative Other (linguistico-metaphysical concept), sometimes as impossible mask of an absolute Other (Judaic concept). This *sometimes ... sometimes* is also expressed in the "relation-without-relation," which is precisely a facile formula of all writing and belies the seriousness of the problem with a stroke of the pen. On what ultimate unity of the "relation" and of the "without relation" does the deconstructive gesture slide? On an apparent unity of the signifier, divided or constituted by two usages, which are furthermore without common measure. What in fact allows the conjunction of these two heterogeneous experiences? What founds the supposed necessary relation in the last instance of the Jewish to the Greek, the reference to the latter in order to think the former?

The incommensurability of the two experiences of the Other is obscured and denied by the appearance of the signifier's unity. It is "the same" signifier that intervenes both times, in two heterogeneous roles: in the last resort, the untranslatable reposes on this elementary translatability of the signifier's identity. But which identity? Precisely the formula: "the same signifier" must be understood without misunderstanding. This cannot be the "same" in the logocentric sense—a sensible and ideal, material and objective identity, since this type of "same," this identity of logos, is only one of the two sides of the story. This can no longer be the same in the sense of the Other's unicity, of the signifier's unicity—the "letter"—that ensues from the Judaic Other, from the unicity of the creature (here, the signifier) which is neither sensible nor ideal, neither material nor objective—for it is also only one side of the ensemble. There must be *at least* an *apparent* identity between these two experiences of the signifier in order for deconstruction, which founds itself upon this identity, to avoid the accusation of simple *collusion*, absolutely arbitrary *slippage* or incoherence in its very foundations. What can these two experiences have in common? Ultimately where are these two heterogeneous identities of the sign articulated in one another, one as idealized materiality, the other as indivision before its disjunction into ideality and the sensible?

Only one answer still seems possible: between the Greek experience of the sign and its Judaic experience, the only common measure is the most empirical perception—or the signified—less the written sign than the perceived and signified sign which is "anterior," by its generality, to the idealized sign of linguistics and to the undivided unicity of the Judaic letter. What founds textual deconstruction's coherence and rigor in the last instance is this: the clandestine recourse to the vaguest perception or signified as the ultimate foundation of the passage or slippage from one of the sign's experiences to the other; the sign supposed given not solely on the grounds of the figure of the World and in transcendence but in the most "empiricist" and "prosaic" form there is. Textual deconstruction does not merely repose in the *supposed given* or transcendence—according to an objection we regularly make about every philosophy—but in the experience and truism of perception: here still—but this is what is now surprising—like every philosophy.

Deconstruction only deconstructs certain forms of metaphysics but conserves everything from it that has the slightest rigor and arbitrariness: fetishism and autoposition. It collapses from within onto this empirical constant: that the sign exists and that the sign is identical to itself before its logocentric interpretation and its Judaic interpretation. In other words, this empirical constant of an identity in the mode of perception signifies what is not elucidated or "deconstructed"—since it founds deconstruction—and because *this transcendent identity of the sign, which is simply supposed given without being elucidated (it thus accommodates all equivocal signs), must be distinguished from the sign's identity of the last instance as grasped by vision-in-One.*

Deconstruction itself falls under the now expanded objection of being founded in a "transcendental signified," in a supposed given transcendence to which it assigns the inevitable transcendental and constitutive function of its operation. It consists in an amphibology of two incompatible experiences of the signifier, an amphibology guaranteed by the vague generality of perception—a blind spot that falls, since it is an untranslatable or an undeconstructible, outside deconstruction because it forms a system with it. It is nothing but the linguistic mode of the same amphibology that reigns in every philosophical decision.

If the deconstructive decision resides in the supposition of the sign's ultimate transcendent identity, then this explains its forgetting or refusal to have to elucidate the essence of Identity before supposing it given in this way and vis-à-vis the figure of language or of a signifier accepted as constitutive of the real. As much as every philosophy, this deconstruction—including those of Heidegger and Wittgenstein no doubt, the latter perhaps under less crude forms—is thrown back toward an empiricism, an external realism of the tradition, toward the respect of Greek authority with which it now joins Judaic authority. This is because it has not abandoned philosophy's founding prejudice, the unitary postulate according to which transcendence (of the World, of the Other, of the Signifier) is constitutive of the real. The sign's alleged identity, whose other side is the refusal to describe its real essence in vision-in-One, is the uncertain and eroded ground upon which the deconstructive will is deployed in order to be assured, despite everything, of a minimum of coherence in dislocation.

The Derridean system of double transcendence cannot be prevented from collapsing on the empirical. Once again, like Kant for example and so many others wanting to strengthen and limit Greek transcendence by Jewish transcendence, it combines two weaknesses that together can give the illusion of a force: the sensible-empiricist weakness of the first, the religious-empiricist weakness of the second. This is to say that not only does double transcendence leave the essence of reality obscure, as much as any other philosophy, but that it gives in further to the illusion of having delivered philosophy from its insufficiencies. Deconstructions are the ordeal of "meta-physics"; they are above all philosophy's salvation and the best guardians of its sufficiency.

How to generalize restrained deconstruction

Restrained deconstruction cannot be generalized on the basis of its own presuppositions, i.e. those of the PSP. All the more so because philosophy is already in its own way the passage from the particular and even singular case to the universal; it is already theory of the restrained and of the generalized. Furthermore, this project then only makes sense if we have access to a more radical and even vaster experience of universality than the philosophical, in relation to which the latter in turn would be nothing but a particular case; consequently, an experience that would be capable of affecting and suspending the Principle of sufficiency itself, and in this way capable of founding an absolutely general deconstruction and of deconstructing decision as such. This Other's power of generalization therefore would have to depend more profoundly on its power of suspension with regard to decision and position, which are invariants of every philosophy; it would have to possess a positively "non-thetic" or non-decisional essence. Only two of the traits of this essence, unknown by philosophy, are relayed here since we have already described them previously. The first is that there exists an instance which draws its validity and its reality from itself without recourse to a transcendence or a decision, the One non-thetic (of) self. There are some absolutely immanent phenomenal givens which are given (to) self without passing through the mediation of decision or the contribution of the *logos* and, for example, through the procedure of a reduction. The transcendental reduction, that which motivates the contingency of philosophical decision, is completed, but this is an effect. The second trait is that this thought of the One, which is no longer philosophy, can only be science, which possesses in itself a transcendental foundation and not an empirical stupidity. A deconstruction which would in this way find its bearing in science, instead of being first as it is in its restrained form, could be generalized to decision as such and could stop simply being valid for its inferior modes ("representation," "presence," "Logos," etc.).

Let us recall that on the basis of vision-in-One there is a radical scientific experience of transcendence or of the Other. Philosophy has always explicitly laid claim to alterity; particularly in the epoch of the second "modernity" (end of the 19th and beginning of the 20th century) where it uncovers the resources for its self-renewal in a Judaic experience of the Other that is finally, so it believes, experienced *as such*. This is why philosophy does not imagine that science, above all when its transcendental structures have still not been explicitly restored to it, can also possess an experience of alterity and which is universal "otherwise" than that of philosophy. This is definitely the case, and it is one of the tasks of a transcendental science to thematize this scientific experience of transcendence: but *non-thetic Transcendence;* of objectivity: but *Objectivity non-thetic (of) self,* which is therefore completely distinct from the philosophical, more primitive than it and its Greco-Judaic forms.

In other words, transcendence and universality always condition one another mutually, for example, as decision and position. Already in philosophy, the Other is what, for example, founds the *Eidos,* the *A priori,* etc. To generalize the Other in a scientific mode as non-thetic *a priori* will therefore be to "generalize" the universal itself and to radicalize the possible, which is still restrained or mixed in its philosophical experience. How have we described this scientific objectivity that is invisible within the horizon of Greek presuppositions, this non-constitutable, absolutely un-decidable Other that is the Archimedean point of the radical forms of deconstruction?

The Other's being-immanent frees it from any simultaneously decisional and positional structure. This is *neither* a decision (break, scission, division), *nor* a position *nor* the synthesis or difference between the two. Science relates its representations to the affect of an "object" whose exteriority, not to mention stability, is immediately given (to the) subject as such without being reflected in itself or positing itself (this is what the philosophical, redoubling and representative experience of the Other is). There is a naive experience (of) alterity even before there is position and opening, and this is an experience that does not need to pass through these procedures.

Before the assistance of a horizon or a project, this transcendence-without-intentionality is lived in the form of a manifold of singular points of transcendence or of affects of universality, experienced as the phenomenal content of what science calls "objectivity." There exists a universality and an ideality, from the start freed from their philosophical positionality. Since this Other is no longer auto-re-ferred, related to itself through itself, i.e. re-divided into the Other-of-the-Other while attached to a position or an open, it forms a multiplicity of real primitive transcendence freed from any external Unity and finality. This transcendence "ensues" from the non-thetic One; it is indivi-dual like the latter and is offered as a multiplicity of radical or individual possibles. These possibles are indeed universals but are deprived of position, of space—whether "pure" or not—and even of intensity. Instead of being infinite attributes in their genre, which would suppose their auto-position and transcendence, they are as absolutely singular as the One-real can be. Thus in science the individual and the universal are radicalized and "generalized" in this way because they are delivered from one another and stop forming mixtures in which they mutually impede one another. When the mixture of the particular/general is broken, science finally accesses a universal freed from its limitation in the particular and also in the "individual." Precisely because the universal now ensues from the *indivi-dual* in the rigorous sense and no longer co-determines it, the latter is beyond its restrained and transcendent forms. The most universal experience of the universal or of the possible is attained when it is no longer condemned to pass through auto-representation or through its states of mixture.

Consequently, even if philosophy often denies it, the Other, which unites with the universal, can be delivered from position or from Being, from auto-position, and can give rise to an experience all the more radical because it will be thought in its own order as de-rived or second after the One, instead of being simultaneously posited with the One in a mixture, which is the element of decon-struction as "first," restrained or philosophical.

Philosophy and epistemology both prevent the recognition that science is a non-thetic experience (of) the Other and that, if it in fact passes incessantly from the "particular" to the "general," it is not at all in the sense in which they both understand this successive passage of theories. Epistemology is the unitary conflation of these two heterogeneous ways of enveloping the particular in the general. Their distinction by science establishes in rigor and in reality a gen-eralized deconstruction of philosophy itself.

The concept of "non-Heideggerian"

Thus with the non-thetic *a prioris* we have the real, more-than-possible, conditions of a generalized deconstruction. We have even acquired the phenomenal reality of the possible as non-thetic (of) self. Such a possible alone from its beyond can "open" decision and its restrained alterity. Two effects must be distinguished here. On the one hand, the immanent essence of the *a prioris*, above all that of the *chôra*, globally suspends philosophical resistance and plunges decision into the abyss of an irrecoverable contingency. This is because the phenomenal content of the real or in general of the "non-thetic," which is more primitive than the Other, contains this *a priori* power of having suspended decision and the World. This power belongs to the (non-) One. It ultimately allows us to give a positive sense and a phenomenal content to the term "non-Heideggerian," for example, or more generally to the term "non-philosophical." It is manifested by the *neither* and the *nor* that suspend decision and position; and by another *nor* that suspends the synthesis or differe(a)nce of the first two negations and therefore decision itself, which can always return and take them up again; and lastly by a final *nor*, the dualitary *nor* that in reality has already preceded the first two, which both remain unitary, as well as the third, which remains that of transcendence as *a priori*, be it non-thetic or not. Here "non-" is no longer acquired in simple opposition to Heideggerian or Derridean deconstruction, *which would once again be supposed given and given as inevitable, just as the PSP would want it to be.* Acquired in an immanent or transcendental way on the basis of the One, as is the case in science, it can affect philosophical decision with a global contingency, suspending its so-called necessity and delivering it—this is the second effect—to the efficacy of the non-thetic *a prioris* that constitute scientific objectivity. "Non-Heideggerian" must also be understood in a way in which "non-Euclidean" is expressed and must include these two effects. If philosophy, not to mention deconstruction, needs a "revolution," or a mutation rather, we have already said that it should be "Lobachevskian" rather than "Copernican." In this form, the "non-," instead of merely procuring for a decision a supplement of alterity masked and given in the symptom, *offers to whichever phenomenon to be interpreted a radical multiplicity of non-thetic attributes or universal points of view*; one would be tempted to say: a radical multiplicity of decisions for the same phenomenon, if decision weren't at the same time "destroyed" as such, on this level at least, in a dispersion of strictly non-decisional transcendences. Decision is not merely de-multiplied,[21] disseminated and dispersed—which are operations that remain unitary—it is "dualyzed."

Thus the concept of a post-deconstruction or of a "non-Heideggerian" deconstruction must be fully grasped in its genesis. It is not acquired through a relative and circular *negation* of Heideggerian, Derridean or other practices that would still be restrained decisions, modes of what remains sufficient in this practice. The *non-* here receives a more positive content than it could have in any philosophy whatsoever. The *non-*'s phenomenal state of affairs, which is that of the possible, is no longer itself and in turn simply possible; it is real or unreflected. This is why it is not co-determined by Heidegger's thought, which would be reflected in it, but derives entirely from the One. If "Heidegger" and philosophy's words intervene here, it is only as material or occasional support, not as a philosophical circle where language would be supposed to constitute reality. This is why the concept of "non-Heideggerian" is irreducible to a new decision and finds its ultimate foundation in science.

The fully and phenomenally positive concept of a "non-philosophical" thought represents a qualitative extension of the possibilities of deconstruction and philosophy. One of the consequences of this radicalization is that the non-thetic Other is no longer necessarily masked and effectuated by the text or the signifier, whose double authority, Judaic and ontological, is abandoned. The text can still serve as support for the non-thetic Other, but it is henceforth contingent along with philosophy itself, its necessity does not surpass the latter's. It is no longer anything but a support of the Other and of its efficacy. In a generalized deconstruction, the Other only and generally requires a support, and the latter, even if it is determined as textual, is precisely nothing but a support. The S(F) destroys "general textuality" and "textualism." Even here, general textuality and language, the index of an internal limitation and arbitrariness of restrained deconstruction, return to their contingency—what falls away is an old limitation. The real foundation of the Other by science renders it autonomous in relation to these Greco-Judaic limitations. Only a non-philosophy is fully and simply human. Non-philosophy is the philosophy of man.

---

21 "Demultiplier" means "to gear/ratchet down"; here, the "de-" is hyphenated in the French. In this context, however, the word better resonates with "dissemination" and "dispersion" if "de-multiplication" is understood in the sense of "differentially multiplied." [TN]

The rigorous foundation of deconstruction as non-unitary

Generalized deconstruction is therefore not a supplementary avatar of philosophical decision but its real transformation. It is scientifically founded by the immanent description of its conditions of reality. The non-epistemological practice of the passage from the (philosophical) particular to the (scientific) general is required in order to bypass the final obstacle to this generalization. By recurrence, decision, the PSP and also restrained deconstruction appear like particular cases of non-philosophical or "non-Heideggerian" deconstruction. The philosophical type of deconstruction will thus acknowledge these types of doctrines or these theories that end up becoming—in a scientific type of context—like particular cases of a more general and open theory. This extra-philosophical opening of deconstruction, but anterior to it, can only be carried out under scientific, albeit transcendental, control. The particular case or the restrained theory has its own logic, which is that of stubbornness or thick-headedness. The only step beyond what a thought can do, a thought which, in the mode of philosophy, seems to reach the final frontiers, is *to change paradigms and ultimately take science as the real base of philosophy*. This paradigm shift does not deny philosophy but frees it from its auto-sufficiency, from its blindness to science and thus to itself; science *leaves-be* philosophy without objectifying it. Already suspended actually by science, philosophy is not denied but offered to a freer, more peaceful and more extensive consideration. It is less decision than its regime or functionality as PSP that is suspended when philosophy's authority over itself is invalidated. In the traditional and naive practices that restrained deconstruction prolongs and reinforces, the PSP authorizes decision's natural auto-reference to extend in an illusory way to the real (man and science). The current forms of deconstruction content themselves with assuming philosophy's finalities and ordinary beliefs by working on them in their own way through a reversal and a displacement. What is opposed to these practices is a "non-Heideggerian" deconstruction, which is not their practical and teleological re-finalization (whether it be disseminated or not), but what is acquired in a transcendental mode vis-à-vis an immanent description of their scientific or real conditions. Rather than affecting deconstruction itself or isolating within it something like Being, Representation or logocentrism, one remains content with describing the real relations of philosophy and of science, and one has discovered the reality of universal deconstruction between the former and the latter, as well as the radical suspension of decision, a suspension which, instead of denying or breaching decision, instead of transforming it by

201

claiming to inter-vene in it, henceforth leaves-be decision as object of science and of unprecedented practices.

As modes of philosophical decision and even of the PSP, unitary deconstructions assume the entirety of the metaphysical tradition, in particular its auto-reference and sufficiency. Instead, a post-deconstruction is founded upon the Tradition's absolute contingency and commences neither by assuming it nor by assuming the existing deconstructions. From the start, it is freed from the restrictions of circularity and is more universal from this point of view. Far from being a perpetual inheritance of the primitive forms of deconstruction or from gathering together and capitalizing on their effects by aggravating them, post-deconstruction instead makes them appear as a simple ingredient of its own universality.

If "non-Heideggerian" deconstruction, being scientifically acquired in the last instance, is no longer philosophical by its foundation, it nevertheless remains so precisely by its object as whatever given. It stops being the entirety of thinking thought, this displaced-displacing substitute of metaphysics or first philosophy that it currently is. It stops being a *first deconstruction* to become an annexed piece in a more expansive edifice that is founded *as thought's science* and in which it represents the critical and pragmatic moment, henceforth second or *unilateralized*. A deconstruction generalized on scientific bases, in the sense that there is a completely original scientific experience of "generalization" or of the "universal," ultimately implies three interconnected tasks:

1. Its foundation in transcendental science, science (of) science or (of) vision-in-One, and thus its de-rivation as second or its unilateralization.

2. Its becoming-real, its reduction to its immanent phenomenal content, that which is lived by the subject (of) science; its generalization by way of an ordeal of the Other or of the possible which is broader than that of philosophy from the start.

3. Its usage as procedure of a scientific type of representation of the real and, on this basis, the "pragmatic" invention of new usages of decision and of restrained deconstruction.

Only a transcendental science can exhibit what in the last instance makes the reality of the Other for man without thereby falling back into its ego-logo-centrism and even less into an idealism. The elaboration and clarification of a generalized deconstruction necessarily engages a radical critique of philosophy. It supposes the discovery of a new paradigm of thought more foundational, real and positive than decision. This new paradigm would be able to transform decision into a contingent event and build a new scientific continent around itself. A deconstruction that is generalized in this way will be a region of this continent. A "post-deconstructionism" belongs to the attempts—on a scientific basis henceforth outside the PSP's authority—of renewing traditional philosophical practices: it belongs to the project of a non-philosophical pragmatics of philosophy.

The non-thetic Other and the critique of Levinas and of Derrida

Insofar as one can judge these "oceanic" matters, the deconstructions of Wittgenstein, Heidegger and Derrida represent the most philosophically advanced point of critical vigilance, the rigorous and sustained effort to put philosophy in relation with its death and perhaps save it with this cure which is still homeopathic despite everything. But as experience of thought and of the real, from the point of view of their rigorous foundation or of their reality, they still suffer from internal limitations which are truly speaking the most general relations of all philosophy when measured against the paradigm of science. We are beginning to recognize these limitations: denegation ("transcendental hallucination") of the real (of science and of man as subject (of) science); principle of the vicious circle (circular auto-constitution); sufficiency (belief in its power to determine the real); auto-referential practices (textual and historicizing auto-fascination), etc. Deconstructions have partially lifted these internal limitations of decision, but they have continued to accept them essentially as unavoidable and to demand the passage of every possible thought through philosophy. This lifting was to respect the PSP and to guarantee it one last survival vis-à-vis the destruction of its most visible and most external forms.

This last obedience to the PSP develops in the form of a massive recourse to the supposed ontological powers of language; it is not known whether the PSP is an illusion of language generated by language's natural exercise, or whether it utilizes language in order to be realized. Deconstructions explicitly correspond with the reintroduction of language, including the signifier, into the horizon of the logos and, from this point of view, no longer fundamentally unsettle the old philosophical sufficiency. Instead, more than the signifier, it is Derrida's introduction of a Judaic supplement of alterity into Heideggerian deconstruction that has elevated this type of philosophy to a new stage and a superior phase of activity. Without this introduction, the signifier would remain a philosophical or semiological object and would not be what it is now: general textuality as constituting-the-subject-in-his-death.

This Judaic hybridization of the Greek body of the logos has taken over Heidegger's efforts to delimit the logos by a quasi-Kantian solution that would extend the solution of the "thing-in-itself." It has had the merit of bringing philosophical decision to its extreme point of dehiscence, fragmentation or dislocation; it has opened philosophy to new possibilities and affects that remained concealed to it. But it will have all the better served to reveal two traits of decision which philosophy has not itself perceived as such because it manifests them without seeing them, albeit in the same proportion rendering them more manifest to another experience of thought more sensible to what is the true "dehiscence,"[22] that of science *to* philosophy. The first of these traits is the survival of philosophical decision, its capacity to continue as the "same," to be prolonged and ultimately to "absorb" the ordeals that recent thinkers have striven to inflict upon it; this is the impossibility of coming to the end of the PSP *by the usage, still philosophical despite everything, of Judaic alterity*. Measured against what the *chôra* inflicts upon it, the heterodislocation of decision is still, and can only be, nothing but an autodislocation. The second trait is the arbitrary, unfounded nature of the philosophical experience of the Other or of transcendence. This would be an "unreal" decision, lacking foundation besides itself; yet, by definition, the foundation is absent prior to decision, which is precisely what has to posit it. Unreal, it thus claims to posit reality and wants to be real in turn through this position. But this reality can only be refused to it, since it will merely have the right to *realization*, i.e. the unitary conflation of the real with its own arbitrariness. More generally than decision, deconstructions, which are also its extreme modes, remain content with *commandeering concepts, like those of the One and the Other, of Identity and Scission, without founding them in themselves or in their reality, without first elucidating the latter, which is fully contained in the One*. Deconstructions treat these concepts as tools and immediately transform them into philosophical machineries that produce so-called experiences and a real servitude. From this point of view, by accentuating the reality of the Other and its non-metaphysical transcendence, deconstructions have not dissipated, but precisely increased the unfounded and external character of this Other, an undetermined experience and factor of indetermination, and thus of war. They are the best conservers of the tradition that they contest and in every way the best conservers of the symptoms of the malaise that philosophical decision *is*. They do nothing but aggravate the Greek decision's unthought character by a double recourse: to a thing "in itself" or a

---

22 Relating to the Latin for "opening up." [TN]

de-theologized "finitude," and to an Alterity received from a religious tradition that remains profoundly unintelligible and unthought.

What guarantees deconstruction's radical generalization is the substitution of the non-mixed or non-thetic concept of the Other for the philosophical concept of transcendence or for the Greco-Judaic Other. But this concept of the Other must itself be acquired scientifically and described in a rectification-labor on the material supplied either by philosophy or by an other-than-philosophical ethics: for example, Derrida on the one hand, Levinas on the other. It is on the basis of their respective conceptions—they serve as our "support" and "occasion"—that the non-mixed Other will be described insofar as it is still anterior to the disjunction of these two experiences. This operation will be the counter-ordeal of the critique that we have sketched of deconstructions with a "unitary" base.

1. Non-thetic Transcendence is non-thetic like the Other is in Levinas. Experienced "as such" before being inserted into a horizon or a position, it radically suspends Being and the authority of philosophical decision without having to be engaged circularly by them and in them. With Levinas, there is a possibility of breaking the philosophical circle, of freeing the Other from the authority of the Same and of thinking from the former toward the latter, all possibilities which are prohibited in Derrida. But the inconvenience of the Levinas-solution is that the Same is nullified and decision disappears, such that deconstruction lacks an explicit object and is impossible for lack of material to be deconstructed.

2. Non-thetic Transcendence supposes or leaves-be decision as deconstruction's possible material, this time in the manner in which it subsists in Derrida. But Derrida cannot reduce the authority of the PSP which Levinas has suspended in a single stroke. Insofar as he is still Greek, Derrida offers a material to the efficacy of the Other, which Levinas does not do; but he nevertheless cannot free himself from the philosophical authority and sufficiency that he attributes to this material and that he supposes necessary and unavoidable as thought's element, what Levinas manages to deliver himself from.

The interest of non-thetic Transcendence is that it has been acquired by supposing the existence of effective decision but without forming or reforming the circle of a unitary or authoritarian auto-reference with it. Thus it will accumulate the deconstructive capacity of the Derridean Other and the capacity, suspending all philosophical authority, of Levinas' Other. This is why, although it does not represent their *a posteriori* or even, moreover, their *a priori* synthesis but rather their still un-divided Identity and their real content before it is split by philosophical content, non-thetic Transcendence is more universal—henceforth in a non-philosophical sense—than the divided forms of philosophical transcendence.

A generalized deconstruction cannot be acquired by synthesis or reconciliation, by a philosophical operation; it must be acquired *a priori* by a description of its *real Identity* and on the One's real and scientific base. Since the suspension of the PSP is then assured by the One before being assured by the Other, it is understood that this Other can seem more universal in its restrained form. Inversely, since this suspension is not of the order of *effective* destruction, negation, nullification, etc., it can leave-be decision and offer it to the efficacy of the Other.

Non-thetic Transcendence is therefore the "common root," the *a priori* or undivided Identity of the two experiences of the Other that Levinas and Derrida share. This shared root forms a system with the way in which they are given the Other: a) without proceeding to the preliminary elucidation of its essence and of its type of reality but by commandeering it, since they are given it in a transcendent mode in turn toward practical ends of deconstruction supposed "first"; b) by receiving it from the exteriority of a tradition that cannot claim the same human universality as science; c) by supposing it "first" (the *supposed first* Judaic Other) or even co-effective with the logos, a co-efficacy which is once again globally supposed as first. This refusal or this "forgetting" to elucidate the essence of the Other, i.e. the phenomenal givens that make it real or lived by the One, has the most serious consequences. Not only is the Other's grip on the logos or even on the Same never elucidated in its reality, yet simply supposed, imposed upon thought by the violence of the Greek and Judaic traditions, but also its foreign relation to man is even less clarified in its principle. What replaces this scientific description is the liturgical inventory of the *effects* of Alterity, effects as arbitrary and unthought as this Alterity itself.

Thus the Other is either what remains impregnated, despite everything, by a pure and abstract negativity, or it is associated with a philosophical type of decision and position from which it does not manage to free itself and which limits its critical scope. Between Levinas' Other-without-deconstruction and Derrida's Other-to-inhibited-deconstruction (in the metaphysical decision), what reigns supreme is a veritable *dialectic of the Other* that limits the real efficacy of deconstruction and prohibits its generalization. This *antinomy of the Other* emerges when it is supposed first and anterior to the One itself. It condemns thought to oscillate between *an absolute Other but deprived of all foundation*, if not that of a transcendent tradition, and *a founded Other, but not absolute* because it is founded,

206

if not on the logos, at least on its unity-of-mixture or, better yet, of undecidability with it.

If the *dialectic of the Other as first* is critiqued by replacing it in the One from the start and afterwards in the Other's non-thetic *a priori*, then the following alternative will be avoided: either an Other-without-deconstruction or a restrained and not absolute deconstruction. The essence of the Other's non-thetic *a priori* is the phenomenal identity, given before any pseudo-reconciliation, of the Other as absolute and of the Other as founded. Just because the Other is founded, but here in the One, does not detract from its absolute character. And since, due to the fact that it is real, this very foundation by the One is not of the order of a philosophical foundation of negativity exerted upon a material with which it would circle, it alone can give the Other an absolute foundation, the essence of the "non-thetic," and not breach it or transform it in this operation. Deconstruction then stops being first like the Other but becomes absolute in its order, which is the order imposed by science.

In other words, it is contrary to the Greek and Judaic traditions to want to found the Other in this way. It is precisely the Other that has always been, even more than the One, simply invoked and commandeered by these traditions in different ways, but as what was capable of destabilizing every identity and unsettling every foundation; as what opened thought beyond ordinary experience and the immediate given; as the exteriority that could breach the metaphysical will of auto-foundation. This acceptance, which is completely transcendent itself, of transcendence comes naturally for these traditions, but it is fully contestable for a science of thought. Contestable in two ways: by its refusal to found the Other explicitly and to attribute it an essence; by the implicit consequence of this refusal: a *de facto* "foundation," but undetermined and undeclared. In effect, the Other is founded *de facto* by these traditions, for it is transcendentally impossible to do otherwise: but it is then founded in a transcendent way, either in the ultimate but yet unthought authority of a text and its commentator subjects, or in the equally unthought authority of an ontological position, of a supposed unavoidable logos, which the Other is functionally responsible for breaching. In these two ways, the Other requires a prop that is transcendent and external to the reality of thought.

Thus deprived of real foundation in the subject (of) science and left to the avatars of pure historico-religious transcendence (Levinas) or even blended with the ontological (Derrida), the Other is so to speak reflected in itself, and the essence of transcendence is still selected or traced from transcendent things. The grand scientific rule of thought's simplicity—of simplicity rather than economy, Occam's razor so to speak—prohibits this genre from the redoubling or doubling that animates philosophical games, and it requires that one not claim to *reconstitute the essence of transcendence with the transcendent* but that one exhibit its phenomenality of the nothing-but-Other ... One of the effects of this reflexivity imposed on the Other is that, in its Greco-Judaic form, it is itself divided into what remains of its essence: it is the Other-of-the-Other. The motor of every division in turn can only be divided between an experience of the Other that coincides with the empirical, that of a tradition which is here considered as "in itself" (a dogmatic empiricism of the absolute Other or of the Other which *is* not, that of Levinas); and an experience that coincides, but so as to work on it, with the empiricism of an ideal transcendence, that of decision supposed given as necessary.

This lack of the Other's real foundation is identically the genealogy of its philosophical forms and usages, of its dialectic and of deconstruction's dialectic as restrained or unfounded. *It is fitting for philosophical decision to leave real essences obscure, here that of the One and that of the Other, and to manipulate them to function and produce effects through their combination.* Restrained deconstruction accentuates decision's initial defect, which is precisely that of being a de-cision, an undetermined originary operation and a factor of indetermination.

Decision in the PSP regime and restrained deconstruction are founded upon the inversion (one could doubt this) of the real order or of thought's scientific order that goes from the One to the Other irreversibly. More exactly, measured against the criterion of science and of the simplest order that can be thought, philosophical decision:

1) blends or transforms immanence and transcendence into the coordinates of a specific space of thought without asking how they are real for man and thought, for the philosopher who receives them and identifies them with this space;

2) does not blend them without subordinating them to their blending or without considering their unity-of-mixture as an absolute auto-position or a "supposed-given" that dominates its terms and on the basis of which they must be thought from then on;

3) cannot mix them—or does not discover/reflect itself as already existing in the form of this mixture—except by inverting or reversing their irreversible order: by commencing through the Other, Dyad or transcendence. This is why the *inversion* of the *irreversible* means the *reversibility* of two coordinates....

The last possible mutation, what would depose the unitary style absolutely, is the abandonment of ontological structures themselves, of decision and of position, and *before all else* of the blendings to which they have always given rise. That these blendings can be abandoned, that they represent a restrictive and limiting postulate which is not necessary for any thought, has remained until now, since the means were lacking, i.e. due to the excessive pressure of the PSP, a pious vow and a desire. An ethno-religious tradition like the Judaic appears to be freed from this "Greek" constraint, but this is more of an appearance than a reality. The Judaic experience of alterity not only coincides with the Greek, which it requires as soon as it wants to define itself as such, but it is also formulated by an ultra-empirical concept of transcendence, a concept that is itself received from exteriority and whose nonscientific or unfounded character is perceived as soon as one acknowledges that a rigorous foundation of transcendence as non-thetic is possible. As for the other tradition, the Greco-occidental, it has not failed to look here and there for a non-thetic type of experience but without being able to go further to the end, without being given the radical means to do something other than desiring to "depart" from the decisional and the positional, than breaching and unsettling them. Due to this fact alone, it confirms their so-called fated necessity, as always. Such that thought in its essence remains determined, sometimes under the horizon of Being, sometimes in the proximity of the Other person, sometimes ultimately in a combination of these two prejudices; there is no chance of truly escaping this double constraint and accessing the experience of thinking that is every man's. Philosophy's proclaimed sufficiency could very well be nothing but that of two cultural traditions, the one political, the other religious, but both of which are completely transcendent to thought's essence and which put all the more energy into imposing themselves in so far as they are external to man. Science alone gives access to thought's essence and can take every man there: *homo sive scientia*. As soon as it is considered a human and "subjective" *real base*, science—i.e. *the* sciences insofar as they participate in the transcendental structures of vision-in-One that provide the reality of thought—immediately reveals the transcendence of these constraints in which philosophy has always lived without noticing them as such but instead storing its sufficiency in them. Both the Greek and the Judaic dimensions of the unitary postulate fade into unreality and into the contingency that man imposes on them, and the unlimited field of the "non-philosophical" potentialities of thought is deployed for every man. If philosophy does not die ... then it is at this price that every man can ultimately become "philosopher." For it is obviously the characteristic feature of a science to be neither Greek nor Jewish, no more than it would be bourgeois or proletarian. A deconstruction with a scientific base will find its bearing on the hither side of the disjunction of Greek finitude and Jewish alterity. The realest thought, which is that of science, cannot accept the double tradition of Transcendence and cannot allow itself to be dictated by it. Whereas the philosophical type of deconstructions accumulates the arbitrariness of these two traditions, a generalized deconstruction on a scientific base will find its reality on the hither side of this conflict of decisions. By definition, it will be not only founded, but, once again, more *universal* than the two or three experiences that divide up the unique Force (of) human thought.

Chapter VII: The non-philosophical opening

Thought's absolute opening and the "exit" out of philosophy

Is it a question of reactivating the sense of philosophical decision, its possibility? Yes and no. Externally: it is a question of struggling against philosophy's inhibition to which its unitary form leads, a question of struggling against its authority. But the other paradigm, which we have proposed to call "dualitary", cannot simply be substituted for the first in order to fulfill the same functions; it transforms thought's operations, up to and including what can be expected from them (what is, for example, nothing but a philosophical "faith" or "expectation" ...). It is not a question of reactivating a dying possibility, a question of giving breath back to an expiring way of thinking. Instead, it is a question of another, non-philosophical experience of philosophical decision. We have defined the unitary paradigm in a sufficiently broad way, including the contemporary thoughts of the deconstruction of metaphysics, and we have considerably extended enough "bad thinking" in order to no longer be tempted to go back, but also to let the dead bury their dead.

No radical awakening of thought is possible on the terrain of philosophical decision, which imposes a limitation onto it in principle. We are not the ones who will have the absurd idea of "being done" with the unitary paradigm: it is the unitary paradigm that is the one which never stops being done with itself and which mimes its own death in order to be certain of dying well, obviously without really dying because it finds its life in the miming of its death. This is a death that buries itself and that has no life except in this operation. Instead, we are in the right to consider the apportionment of life and death differently than its subject does. It is dead: from the

One's point of view, which must be the measure of philosophy itself, it has been dead the whole time and un-real from the outset. But it is alive—it's true that it lives in its own way, which is to play off life, without any seriousness or productiveness, against death like mirrored masks—in "the-world" or in the sphere of effectivity, to which the One recognizes the right of continuing to put forth their traditional claims for themselves.

In other words, in this order of effectivity the traditional games of opening and of constriction continue to be valid. Unitary systems will be interminably reproduced in this variously balanced mode, where each philosophical decision, crisis or rupture in relation to an old state of thought reestablishes and brings along with itself another way of closing and re-closing the system. In the unitary milieu, decisions are simultaneously open *and* closed ensembles (of determinations), and the unitary paradigm itself is an open/closed ensemble of decisions. It is not static but is instead a tendency, either toward the reversibility of openings and closings (Nietzsche) or toward the primacy of the openings but as simple recommencements, openings that enclose themselves in their own way in their repetition (Heidegger). What is called *inhibition of philosophical decision* is this global phenomenon (thus able to be evaluated only from the dualitary point of view) of a game or of a *fold* that continues more or less immediately, yet very regularly, to associate every opening with a constriction, either new or reworked; to associate every decision with an undecidable in which it will become dull, soften and decline....

Such an inhibition belongs by essence to the unitary paradigm, to the essence of decision, but it no longer essentially belongs to the scientific paradigm. It no longer belongs except as a *support* of non-philosophy, yet not to its real essence. This effective side is necessary for manifesting a decision's *essence*. But if it can have this globally inhibiting game of openings/closings as *signal*, thought's new mode no longer involves this relation of inhibition with the Other and with Being in their non-thetic essence.

This first liberation of thought in relation to its traditional unitary model must be extended by an analysis of the theme of the opening or of the exit. Is it a question of "exiting" from philosophy "into" the real? or into another philosophy? And if that question has no sense, then what sense is there for that which has no sense? First the objection to the claim of an eventual "exit" out of a philosophy into the real will be examined, and then the objection to an "exit" out of one philosophy into another.

Concerning this first point: *the real does not "exit" out of philosophy but determines such an "exit."*

The young Marx posed the problem of an "exit" (*Ausgang*) out of philosophy in order to get back to the real. If the appearance of an exit *out* of unitary philosophy *into* a dualitary thought is what until now has seemed dominant, perhaps even here for philosophers, this is because they have supposed that the One-real was already "outside" philosophy; that the One-real had escaped or leaped out of the unitary circle, out of the difference between the real and the logos; that the One, for example, had to allow the initial exit out of ontico-ontological difference, which is the horizon of metaphysics. Everything would repose on the One's experience, whose philosophically extra-territorial status would echo throughout philosophical decision as Other that would in turn be freed from the unitary paradigm. Thus we will now be asked: how is this exit of the One out of philosophy possible, this detachment of the real from the metaphysical will?

In short, there is no scientific and dualitary answer to this question. This is merely a unitary question and already dictates a response which is overly anticipated: it would be impossible to "exit" radically from the circle of unitary philosophy, because the real, at least half (difference), is comprised by philosophy and because philosophy's decision is the real's co-production. With the unitary paradigm, the games are by definition played out, all of its arguments (the Tradition, the Already-Thought, the Text, History, etc.) remain content with reproducing its own existence and its movement, its perpetual concluding from its effective existence to its essence or its reality, its backwards "ontological argument." It is therefore necessary to simply refuse, if not to speak with, then at least to argue with the Greco-unitary paradigm. *The question of an* "Ausgang" *out of philosophy into the real is a unitary question, i.e. a good philosophical answer and a bad scientific question.* There is no scientific question of an exit out of philosophy into the real. By definition and for whoever knows what the real is, i.e. for every man insofar as he is an unreflected experience of its absolutely undivided essence and insofar as he does not allow himself to be seduced by metaphysics, the real is the Undecided, the One is the Unquestioned.

Indeed, it will not be said that the One is an answer that precedes every question and that the questions are pre-traced by the answers, for the question/answer system, the problematic style in general, perhaps belongs to philosophy but not to the real and to science. It is a philosopher who has said in shame that philosophy until now has interpreted the World and must now transform it: the World is interpretable and thus transformable, but the real is not. One falsifies the real, one conflates it amphibologically with the World when one believes that it is producible, operable, transformable, interpretable with the Greco-unitary paradigm. Thus the problem of an exit out of philosophy into the real, an exit of the latter out of the former, is never posed: it is only posed within the frantic and violent illusion of unitary thought.

The Marxian requirement of an "*Ausgang*" no doubt constitutes a very profound truth, an effect of truth's essence itself, but this is precisely nothing more than an effect. The essence of truth or of the One, by real and not nominal definition, is acting before any possibility of philosophy. The "*Ausgang*" is a requirement that will be fulfilled by the non-thetic Other and non-thetic Being, by the *a prioris*, and this will only happen in relation to effectivity, its mixtures and its circles. But it has no relevance for the One itself. The dualitary and scientific order of unreflected phenomenal givens "commences" through the One, and everything unilaterally en-sues from it. The One precedes, "*a priori*" but really, philosophical decision and has never had to exit—by who knows what kind of miracle that the unitary fantasy projects or extracts from itself in one last trick—from the nets of philosophy. The real does not exit from such nets because it has never entered them, and Greco-occidental philosophers are terrible birdcatchers who capture nothing but their own fantasy.

The One's "thematics" is not a thematics, it is an absolute phenomenal given of which it cannot even be said that it will fracture, overturn or intrigue unitary thought. These would be operations of the Other, and the Other is not the real in its essence. The real's essence has nothing to do with the unitary paradigm and only takes it into consideration as definitively dis-placed when it is emplaced in the secondarized order of the *chôra*. The truth of the "*Ausgang*" is misunderstood and critiqued as impossible because one imagines it to involve the same relation to the real as this metaphysics from which one wants to exit. But the real, because it has never had to exit from metaphysics, is what makes possible that there be an appearance of exiting out of it toward new experiences of thought. *It is not the* "Ausgang" *that determines the real by accessing it, it is the One's undecided real that determines the* "Ausgang" *in the last instance or gives it its phenomenal content—the* "Universe." The veritable exit, truth's exit out of—anterior to—philosophy, has never taken place, for it is not a decision that philosophy can negotiate.

From this point of view, since the means to really determine the "exit" are given with the One, the scientific paradigm ultimately makes it possible to be resolute when shrugging off the objections of some recent unitary thinkers who have superficially and mechanically understood the "exit" out of metaphysics as a re-entry into its essence, a step-back or retrogression that remains shackled or

214

relative (-absolute) to what it surpasses. They are tempted by the exit but estimate that the true "exit" out of metaphysics, if it does not want to be a metaphysical illusion, must be inhibited, suspended, withdrawn, "deferred".... They have substituted "Withdrawal" for the "*Ausgang*" because, as unitary thinkers despite everything, they can only relate the entirety of philosophy to the experience of the Other supposed to be the real or the Undecidable, and they cannot, by definition, commence through the real, which is the One and not the Other but which allows a more veridical experience of the Other, i.e. of philosophical decision. Shackled by their amphibologies, seduced by their circles, fragmented by their aporias, they are condemned to experience the One-real only under the mask of the Other, which is nonetheless merely philosophy's site. At worst, they transcend toward the real; at best, to transcend is the real: in both cases, they lack immanent experience and are condemned to interminably comment on, and sometimes to put back in play, philosophy, its tradition, its texts, its history. And they call that the "real"....

Even interminable, even as an unlimited process of a game of openings and closings, philosophy can no longer satisfy certain long repressed requirements that are now voiced more vigorously. *The thesis of thought's absolute, and not relative, opening as non-philosophy belongs to vision-in-One, which is both scientific and "dualitary."* Not a recommencement of thought, its relaunch or prolonging, but a manner of thinking for which an opening and a possible, without the restriction of a fold and more radical than a simple "game," are phenomenal givens that are absolute in their order. Vision-in-One does not propose to close/open metaphysics, it is not situated within the neighborhood of deconstructions, and it does not think vis-à-vis *neighborhood* and *topology*: from the outset, it is a freedom of the reality of non-philosophical possibles. No doubt, philosophical decision is only relatively closed, but the distinction between the unitary and the dualitary is stronger than that of metaphysical closure and of its deconstruction. In a scientific, i.e. real "milieu", philosophical decision is no longer simply experienced as a totalizing pro-ject, a finite totality or a totalized finitude, etc., but as a multiplicity of openings-without-closings, of transcendences-without-totalities, of ekstases-without-horizons, as well as a multiplicity of positions, but non-decisional, etc.

If the "*Ausgang*" has no validity from the point of view of the One-real or that of unreflected lived experiences, it thus has validity now, but as non-philosophy's "non." *The* "Ausgang" *is the real essence of non-philosophy, for non-philosophy is the operation of "exit"*

215

par excellence, but now in the unreflected sense of this word. Non-philosophy is not *what* exits *from* metaphysics; to make it the *subject* of the exit and to posit the exit as exit out of … metaphysics would be to re-inscribe it in the field of metaphysics in approximation with a displacement. Non-philosophy is through and through an "exit" or *Krisis,* a non-thetic experience (of) a transcending that is not relative to a point of departure and of arrival and is therefore an absolute and unreflected experience. Moreover, this "exit non-thetic (of) self," irreversible or without re-entry, without re-inscription in that from which it would exit, *has its own content that it neither decants from the field of metaphysics nor from the unitary field in general.* The idea of an absolute "exit" is obviously an insupportable claim for the unitary paradigm. But the exit *out of*…metaphysics and more generally out of the unitary paradigm is possible … because it is from the start *real* and thus absolute as "exit." Since the One has never been encircled by unitary thought, philosophical decision finds its condition of the last instance in an "absolute" exit, or an exit without an "out of"—*the non-thetic Universe*—the only exit of which we have "real" experience and which precedes, but merely as one of the *a prioris* (about which we know that, if they precede effectivity insofar as they are immanent *a prioris,* they suppose it as reduced to support), the unitary field from which it precisely does not have to "exit"….

This experience is the only real response to the objection that could have been made: philosophy alone can "exit"—in truth not "exit"—from philosophy. This experience is itself what ensues from the One as non-philosophy, as the very operation (of) exit; consequently, the problem of exiting "out of" philosophy is not posed. There is the "exit" before any "exiting."

This would be an acceptable thesis only if one stops making of the "exit" what the unitary paradigm makes of it: at worst, a catch-phrase or a slogan, at best an auto-supervised, inhibited, reserved critical operation, but always a vicious and aporetic reflection of "absolute transcending" in itself. When the *Ausgang* is recognized as an experience in the rigorous and immanent sense of the term, a phenomenal given *before* metaphysics, denied and falsified by it, it stops being a pro-ject (of "surpassing", of "retrocession" and of "withdrawal" still *in relation* to metaphysics, despite everything) and above all a slogan or a goal: it is manifested as the real content of the last instance of philosophical decision. This is therefore not a transcendent operation left to the arbitrariness of a subject or simply left to the co-operation, to the inter-vention of a deconstructionist. This is to *transcend it, to posit it and totalize it such as they are qua experiences unreflected (of) self.*

The introduction of the slightly paradoxical motif of the exit-without-exiting allows us to specify its phenomenal content. It is obviously this content that we have already attempted to describe in terms of non-thetic Being and the non-thetic Other: including the NTT/NTP correlation, non-philosophy's genetic code deprived of the "out of" or at least deprived of a constitutive reference to an external given. No more than the Other, the Exit is not an empty operation: in a sense, it "makes the void", but it possesses a noematic dimension irreducible to what exits from it afterwards. Deprived of all positionality, this is the exit of the pure possible. What Heidegger calls the "Withdrawal", without being able to think it from the One itself since he is instead and traditionally obligated to think the One from the absolute Withdrawal or absolute Other, therefore has a specific content which supposes that the Withdrawal be definitively purged of all external content or positional reference. Heidegger was not able to notice that the Withdrawal, through which he withdraws, among other things, in relation to Husserl's thetic intentionality, has a completely positive content that is not selected from it or metaphysics. He believed that these latter still would "reflect" themselves irreducibly in the Withdrawal itself and would continue to impregnate it. Since he did not subordinate the Withdrawal to the unreflected One and proceeded to the opposite subordination and denial of the nothing-but-One, he was condemned to think the Withdrawal as more or less still caught up with representation. In reality, the non-thetic Exit is no longer even one last or extenuated formula of Intentionality, a residual transit of the transition from Being toward being. What remains of "transitive causality" in the *difference* of Being *and* being, a difference of the "Super-vening of Being" and the "Arrival of being" (Heidegger), is now definitively evacuated as "*transcendent*" *and falling outside every real experience*. Unreflected immanence is the essence of the last instance of transition or of transitioning, of the exit itself: it prevents them from "folding", from reflecting themselves in themselves, from still being modes of causality through transcendence, from becoming the element and simple transcendent relations for themselves. Here one has stopped taking the Withdrawal and the Exit as empty operations of ... metaphysics or presence and thus still fulfilled by them, or more rigorously, as operations of opening or of ekstasis *in* the positionality of horizonality. This philosophical gesture has stopped being vicious and thus related to itself as though to the real, because it is now determined, only in the last instance, by the real itself which has the force of detaching it from the Greco-unitary state of affairs.

With the One, it has thus become possible to conduct a dualysis of the Marxian "*Ausgang*" and of the Heideggerian "*Entzug*": it has the same sense, in its order which is non-positional (of) self, as the intentional analysis that Husserl conducted on Brentano's *intentio*, which was still caught in the snares of psychologism. With Marx himself and Heidegger, albeit in completely different modes, the hidden *intentio* of the *Ausgang* and of the *Entzug* remains locked into what Husserl could hardly perceive since he opposed a logico-transcendental point of view to psychologism; it was not only locked into "occidental metaphysics," but into what is even deeper than it, the unitary paradigm that defines the "expanded metaphysics" where the attempts of deconstruction are to be replaced. Once the layers of psychologism, of logicism, of ("metaphysical") ontology and of their deconstructive ordeal have been cleared out, what remains is the occident's unitary ground which we will have distanced from *transcendental truth*. It suffices to put ourselves back into it, vision-in-One, in order to perceive the phenomenality proper to Being and the Other and to perceive how they have not really been captive to effectivity, which no doubt announces them and conveys them from its point of view to vision-in-One, but from which we can fully abstract them the moment that it is a question of the essence of these real *a prioris*.

Non-philosophy is not a project (already inhibited as project), a transition that would remain in itself. This would be to return to the unitary amphibology of the One and of Transcendence, for example to the Heideggerian mixture of the One and of the Withdrawal. The real determines transcendence and position only in the last instance, in the sense that they are grasped or lived in the unalterable mode of the One "in itself" and of its phenomenality of immanence.

Consequently, what appears is the *real* signification of the ungraspable *withdrawal of philosophy*, which we propose to radicalize. It is a question of determining in the last instance philosophy's constitutive withdrawal, its own mode of transcendence, by the de-motion, the "real" emplacement or crisis of philosophy by the One, i.e. also by Being non-thetic (of) self and the Other non-thetic (of) self.

Non-philosophy's multiplicity
and the rarity of philosophical possibles

Non-philosophy is multiple like the One itself which gives it its un-reflected or "indivi-dual" essence. By right, there is a multiplicity of modes of the *a prioris*, of versions of the genetic code (*chôra*/TNT/PNT) in which the possibles are programmed as such. Therefore, it is no longer because non-philosophy is also the thought (of) the Other that it is multiple; it is multiple in its essence or, more exactly, by thought in the last instance.

This thesis ensues from the One; it is given with the One's real immanence, which is non-philosophy's unique rule as description of non-thetic experiences and no longer as construction or analysis of concepts. That non-philosophy from the outset be experienced as multiple (and in a way that is neither quantitative nor qualitative, nor the combination of the two: these are "unary multiplicities" that do not arise from a procedure of pure counting) means that it is an absolute experience which collides with the experience of the rarity of effective philosophical systems in "the-world" or "the-history," for example in the "history of philosophy." The rarity of philosophical decisions is both a matter of fact and of principle; it is explained by the game of inhibitions and unitary blendings that constrain philosophy to be incapable of multiplying itself in a relative and not absolute way, by the simple phenomenon of the unlimited variation, extension or intensification of invariants which are rare in principle and indeed unifiable in a single schema, just as the unitary paradigm wishes by definition to believe itself unique and in-divisible. Its modes therefore remain those of a weak or auto-inhibiting multiplicity.

There is yet another form of rarity of philosophical decision. It is also programmed by the unitary paradigm but in a subtler way. This is no longer the factual, i.e. that of individual systems supposed to exist in history, etc.; this is no longer an ideal rarity, i.e. the supposition that there is a unique invariant, a unicity-of-form of philosophy. Neither factual nor ideal, this is the difference of the two, the rarity of the Other insofar as it is the differentiating assemblage of the fact and of the Idea. Contemporary thinkers, those of the destruction or deconstruction of metaphysics, validate this specific rarity of the Other which inhibits, withdraws, delays, defers philosophical deci-sion and specifically every new attempt that would claim to really "exit" from metaphysics, i.e. to show that man has never entered it. Such an attempt is madness in the eyes of metaphysics; in their eyes, it is illusion or fantasy. Nevertheless, we who do not philoso-phize, i.e. who do not commence in decision but through the real, who renounce the illusion of philosophy's omnipotence but do not renounce thought and the unreflected-immanent experience that is its phenomenal content of the last instance, we can no longer allow ourselves to be intimidated by the unitary paradigm—by its lures, nets and traps....

The endless circular argumentation, which would prefer that we demonstrate the impossibility or extravagance of a science of phenomenal givens in general and those of philosophical decision, is immediately returned to the order in which it has validity: the order of effectivity. If in effect we must demonstrate the inhibiting argumentation by which the unitary paradigm continues (through Heidegger and others) to want to paralyze thought and lead it to its closure, to its gathering, to an "exit" which is mitigated and seemingly suspended—then this would no longer be to deny these forms of rarity that have efficacy within the order of effectivity. But, from the One's point of view, effectivity or the *whole* is nothing but an order of reality, it is second and determined in the last instance and is not the whole of reality. Non-philosophy, which has never been under the authority of philosophical decision, is unable to be limited by decision's empirical and ideal rarity.

The attempt to refuse the existence of *phenomenal givens* or of vision-in-One is nothing but one of the modes of the unitary argument, which always concludes from effectivity to reality and, for example, from the possible limited by its effective (empirico-ideal) blendings to every possible in general. There is a fruitfulness of non-philosophy which is neither explained by the possibility of variations on an invariant; nor by an intensification of the latter reduced to the state of continuous variations of variations; nor by the possibility of re-projecting the Other or Difference (of Being *and* being): a multiplicity which is that of the One-real.

The non-positional possibles of the "Universe" are what inspire and nourish the philosophical systems that decant these possibles from the region of the Other and of Being and blend them together, thus creating the illusion of the real. The concept of (*non-*) *philosophical fiction* perhaps has still not been clarified concretely enough. It is at least rigorously founded, i.e. detached from every type of mythological or literary-rhetorical fiction, unleashed from its blending with the latter. There is a specifically non-philosophical fiction which, at least in its origin, owes nothing to the linguistic and more generally to the "blended" means of the unitary paradigm that proceeds sometimes by blending in the restrained sense, sometimes by combination, sometimes by intersection or difference, sometimes by dialectics, always by synthesis and transition from one contrary to another. The One makes this fiction ensue beyond these very blendings, and the ultimate effect of the Undecided is the liberation of philosophical ekstasis "out" of the ontological universals or generalities of "history" and of the institutions that manipulate it. As for philosophy, it does not decline into the real on which it would work and in which it would crystallize; it serves as material for non-philosophy as one of the irreducible orders of reality: philosophy is no longer the "fact" of systems or the metaphysical Greek "factum" but a simple support or occasion for non-philosophy.

If we gather together all the non-philosophical or real dimensions of philosophical decision, then we obtain the following:

1. Within the unitary paradigm and from its own point of view, there are phenomena of closure—whether positional or "metaphysical" or semi-positional and semi-open depending on the case, which is itself very diverse—that would have to be nuanced in the thoughts of Differe(a)nce which do not close metaphysics without re-opening thought.

2. Philosophical decision, insofar as it is transformed as simple support or given by vision-in-One and is no longer auto-posited as metaphysics or unitary thought, is in this way aligned with an opening-without-closure, the "non-thetic Universe," which is thus distinguished from the contemporary unitary experiences of decision that is *half-opened, half-closed.* Dualitary thought does not acknowledge the paralysis or inhibition of decision in its works; it seeks the Undecided of decision, but only in the last instance and without constructing a system of *semi-decision (half-decidable, half-undecidable).*

3. If these two practices of philosophy are put in relation, as is the case from the point of view of the dualitary paradigm, the following situation arises:

a) The unitary closure, whether it be merely metaphysical or instead deconstructive and critical, does not affect unreflected essence, which is decision's last instance. A positional or semi-positional enclosure can empirically or globally serve as occasion, *support and signal* for non-philosophical production, but it cannot affect the latter directly and claim to close or de-limit the non-philosophical paradigm itself;

b) On the other hand, non-philosophical description functions as a veritable universalizing "enclosure" of the unitary paradigm, but it does not proceed to either of the two modes of unitary closure. In effect, this is a non-positional (and not semi-positional) closure of the unitary or (semi-) positional style. In other words, the non-philosophical paradigm is the absolute, unreflected closure of the unitary paradigm in the unilateralizing mode of which the *chôra,* and then the non-thetic Other and Being, are capable. And it is its absolute closure only because it does not transcend *outside* it, does not *exit* it, as its semi-positional or semi-deconstructive closure still partially does. The unitary decision is auto-closing, it is for itself, and even in the case of its deconstruction it is a *relative-absolute* closure. Instead, non-philosophical thought is the absolute closure of unitary decision because it is not at all a self-closure. *A non-decisional and non-positional thought is necessary to absolutely close a positional or semi-positional thought.*

Nevertheless, the nuance of this usage of an "absolute" closure will be noted. Above all, this is not a destruction, a repression or an inhibition of unitary decision. On the contrary, since this closure is non-positional or absolute, non-relative to unitary thought itself, it leaves-be unitary thought and lets it function, for it only needs this thought as a simple support or signal. To critique metaphysics or to deconstruct it? Dualitary thought comprises another experience that allows it to understand the unitary in its own order, whereas the latter can only repress or deny the former ... Above all non-philosophy does not deny that there is a manifold of positions, even of philosophical auto-positions or of systems *in* history, a thesis which is itself, under this form, an auto-position and a philosophical decision. Less still does it deny that it is possible to relate these auto-positions to their Other or their historicity, to a de-limiting outer-closure, like Heidegger and Derrida do in their respective ways. But it reduces all of this activity around metaphysics, all of these effects of vigilance which are one of the last firework displays set off by the unitary paradigm so as to prove that it is real, although it does nothing but exist in the state of occasion and signal for a production of non-thetic *a prioris* or possibles. For example, as was carried out previously, it unleashes the unitary style's genetic code of the last instance and eventually varies it according to the particular sectors of effective experience. It ultimately proposes to establish strictly unilateralizing relations of the *a prioris* to effectivity.

This experience of thought—because it is completed in the Other in particular, instead of commencing through it, since it relegates decision to the state of simple material and guarantees it in non-philosophy a paradoxical opening without limitation and a right to fiction—is therefore distinguished from its Judaic experience. The latter commences through the Other: above all it does not align the Other with the One but grasps the One merely in the derived and conditioned mode of "creature." It is distinguished from the half-Judaic, half-Greek experience of thought: the latter commences through the "différance" (Derrida) of the logos's Greek closure *to* its radical Other and thus cannot avoid any circularity, be it interminably delayed, deferred or extended.

Here a fundamental thesis is that if the Other is not in general aligned with the One, if it does not irreversibly en-sue from it as a simple a priori, it remains a mixture in its own way and must decant its reality from the metaphysical state of affairs that it wants to fracture or deconstruct. It is impossible to escape from this law: differe(a)nce is relative-absolute, it can never be *really absolute*. It is condemned to move within the *reversal* of metaphysical or logocentric hierarchies, and, furthermore, the gesture of this reversal through which it must commence is so irreversible that it is one last guarantee abandoned to *reversibility* that is probably the most elevated, most achieved goal of unitary thought. Thoughts *of* the Other, which are precisely not thoughts (of) the Other because they commence through it and their ("partial") identification with it, instead of commencing through their "identity" of the last instance in the One (here, there is no more of this process of identification of philosophical decision with the One), are condemned to only experience the Other first and foremost in the *relative* (-absolute) mode of a reversal. It has been noted that the non-philosophical experience, since it manifests the Other from the One and from the start does not accede to it in the order of phenomenal givens, does not have to reverse unitary thought and, for example, metaphysics, representation, logocentrism, etc. As philosophy's site, the Other, Being, and the Universe form an autonomous region that is absolute in its order, a phenomenal given to which one does not accede with the assault of violent and destructive operations, but which one remains content with manifesting without constituting it. Contemporary ideology, the pathos of the Other supposed given on the basis of a socio-religious tradition, is presented as experiences of least-violence or of violence's economy. This would be a characteristic illusion of the modern and contemporary forms of the unitary thinker and of his byproduct, the "intellectual": identification with this sort of Other can only be carried out in the midst of universal destruction.

Scientific and dualitary thought instead commences through the One and thus retracts the Other and philosophical decision from their Greco-unitary violence. It no doubt "extracts" the Other and Being from the blendings of effectivity in which they are concealed, but it cannot be said that it *selects* them from it, like a supplementary break selected from the continuum of experience. NTT and NTP are not *neighboring* elements in continuous series; they are not (synthetic, differential) breaks extracted from these series by a process of inversion or reversal of experience. A general characteristic of scientific thought is the following: unreflected experience or the Absolute, whatever its form, rather than being attained by an operation or a necessarily reversible and circular process, is either already given and sufficient or will never be attained, even by an approximation or a so-called "concretization", a becoming concrete which is nothing but an inconsistent overdetermination of generalities or universals. The *a priori* site is absolutely manifest, albeit invisible; this has nothing to do with a "hidden" or "concealed" instance. In general, unreflected essences do not tolerate "primary" or "constitutive" repression, for they are not unconscious structures of experience…. Therefore non-philosophy was not repressed or forgotten *in itself* by the unitary paradigm: it was simply forgotten *for* the latter and from its point of view on it, a forgetting that gave it its violence and the force of illusion. Non-philosophy has been re-conquered, un-veiled, recuperated by an illusion only from the unitary point of view itself. For the remainder, it en-sues from the One rather than being concealed *as* "metaphysics"….

All these effects that belong to the scientific style no doubt form a system of constraints which are received as violent by the dominant thought. On the one hand, they de-rive from the One in an immanent way, and it suffices to be replaced in the One by an "un-reflected posture" in order to see unitary thought reduced to the state of support, without remainder, for the non-thetic *a prioris*. On the other hand, the "dualitary" break introduced here between the One and effectivity, between effectivity and the *a prioris*, can no longer be what founds a new "economy," a new unitary distribution of the forces in play. It consists in putting the One on a unique side and in putting all the phenomena of circularity, difference, aporia, hierarchy, etc., all the *relations* on the other side (their unilateral-ization, which ensues from the One or from its sufficiency). The-world, the-history, the-technology, etc., are globally reduced in this way to the functions of support for non-philosophical possibles.

But this reduction, which has no unitary sense, only has sense in the dualitary order of experiences. It is the result of the real *a prioris,* of the One, no doubt, because they ensue from it. But in a sense the One is too strong for unitary decision or the mixtures of effectivity, which it does not need. It has been seen that the real *a prioris* were a sort of "compromise formation" between the One and effectivity. But on their side, the *a prioris* are detached from unitary effectivity which remains only as occasion. The Other, for example, decants an indifference or a "withdrawal" from its being-immanent that manages to uni-lateralize effectivity and affects it with contingency without being able to render it as contingent as the One does. Both the problem of determination in the last instance and the problem of closure receive new determinations in this way. It is not the One itself that affects unitary decision with contingency or with the closure of "support" or of "occasion," for it is affected by all the *a prioris*. But this contingency must be called "transcendental" because it is an effect of the *a prioris* and, further still, of the One.

All the unitary auto-interpretations of decision are therefore rendered contingent *beyond simple factuality and beyond the facticity proper to the rational fact*. This radical contingency of events that happen in the-world, in the-history, in the-polis, etc. must be elaborated with strictly dualitary means, with a non-thetic conception of transcendence, etc.; it defines *the "minoritarian" or real crisis of unitary thought*, an em-placement of the dominant paradigm by the One no doubt, but above all, in a more attenuated form, by the *a prioris* and ultimately by the "Uni-verse." The absolute *Krisis* is an em-placement without reversal that makes possible a certain usage of unitary procedures and schemata as signal for the experience of non-philosophical possibles.

Their practice should find itself slightly changed. An infinite and positive field of possibles is thus opened to it. It is free for the most radical tasks of creation or fiction, it is freed from the labors of critique, deconstruction, "situation," elucidation, analysis of meaning, un-veiling, etc. in which it inhibits itself.

Perhaps an essential point is this: philosophy stops being merely an instrument in the service of effective experience, simultaneously an instrument and a project, a task that can enjoy itself only by being realized in this experience for which it is unitarily sacrificed. These games of sacrifice, responsibility and domination, which philosophy has knotted between it and what it believes to be the real, ultimately stop. By renouncing these unitary ambitions as mirages, philosophy becomes non-philosophy's instrument qua absolute experience, sufficient in its order, and enjoys itself without wondering if it is useful and responsible.

No philosophy, no more so than a god, could save us. Only the real can save philosophy from its stagnation in effectivity, i.e. in itself. Only a thought without transcendence—at least in "first principle" or in its real foundation—can save us from the philosophies that principally use transcendence without thinking its real essence. It is not a question of "exiting" from the circle or from the mixture of decision-as-difference, it is a question of showing that one has never entered it—*an* a priori *refusal* or *defense* against entering it— *even before the circle and its mitigation in difference is presented. It is a question of thinking "before" the Greeks and more universally than from the Greek commencement or in the Greek opening.*

The scientific *and* dualitary paradigm (*and*: there has been a non-scientific dualism, that of religious gnoses) authorizes us— without fear, without interminably having to account for "unitary" philosophers who wish to prevent us from speaking and thinking, whose first gesture is to inhibit and limit—to dissociate the real essence of philosophical decision from all of its effective conditions, to distinguish three orders without remainder: the real or the One (as "unary" or "minoritarian", rather than as "unitary" or Unity); the possible (the decision-without-project, the open-without-opening, etc.); and the effective. The moment that it is founded in the One in the last instance, decision is no longer conflated with the decisional, the decisive, the voluntary, which all form a system with the institutional and the effective. One cannot conclude from the mixture to the One, from effectivity to reality, from existence to essence. What we have to "oppose" to the Heideggerian style of *withdrawal,* to the backward step and to the "operation" of relative-absolute refuge, is a phenomenality that is absolute from the outset. Philosophical decision decants its reality in the last instance from an unreflected lived experience which, on its side, is not conflated with decision but gives to the possible *this rigor of resistance or* a priori *defense that would precede what it would have to defend itself against.* This is the only way to stop turning thought into a simple reaction of defense *relative* to what it defends itself against—this is still the case of Heidegger and even, albeit to a lesser extent, that of Nietzsche—against Science, against Technics, against Politics. To stop turning thought into a critique or an additional and deferred mode of critique, of vigilance, of the back(ward) step, of retrocession *in relation to* ...—all modes of a defensiveness that makes a vicious circle with effectivity and compromises with it. As possible determined in the last instance by the One, decision is an absolute *a priori* that no longer owes anything—in its essence at least—to the effectivity of the history of philosophy which it therefore no longer even accepts treating in terms of an adversary in a "critical" will.

Non-philosophy cannot resolve the paradox of being an absolute or *a priori defense* prior to even that which contaminates or poisons it unless it is obviously founded in the real-as-One. The determination in the last instance of non-philosophy by the real is the same thing as its absolute withdrawal, not "before" [*devant*] but "before" [*avant*] its history,[23] a *withdrawal founded in a separation specific to the One* and which in turn keeps it separated from its history where it has movement or existence. This absolute separation—which is unilateralizing but not abstract—of the One is the "dual" moment in "dualism" and again makes thought "possible"—real rather—against its philosophical stagnation in its historico-systematic conditions.

---

23 Both "devant" and "avant" can be translated by the English word "before," the former in the spatial sense of "presence before," the latter in the temporal sense. [TN]

We ultimately *know* why we think instead of abandoning ourselves to naive philosophical faith. We perhaps know this in a simply unreflected and in-objective way, but we know it due to a knowledge or a gnosis which is our very life, *our most intimate subjectivity of man, rather than of the philosopher.* Philosophy has never been "human" in the rigorous sense of the absolutely subjective or of the unreflected affect. But it is now a "task" to make philosophy absolutely subjective and to make it "man" in the last instance. Even if from *elsewhere*—henceforth the elsewhere or transcendence also has, "facing" the One, a rigorously founded status—philosophical decision is massively invested by determinations which are political, sexual, religious, juridical, etc., it remains foreign, by its real essence, to these "scenes," to the theatre of society or the family. Non-philosophy, the daughter of man, is foreign to familial scenes. It (is) known in the form of a knowledge (of) self which is never separated *from* self and which is consequently separated *a priori* from everything else. Separated knowledge, yes, but separated from any separation *from* itself, from any alienation. Philosophy must be treated as the daughter of man, unengendered as man.

Non-thetic fiction as an element of universe-languages

Fiction is a marginal and ambitious figure of the philosophical scene. It has suffered under the "real." It has wanted to play a fair game with the real and even to beat it at its own game. Fiction's life is conflated with its struggles to exist and receive a concept; its habits suppose it inseparable from its boundaries and its neighborhoods. This would be the equation: fiction=real, an unstable and polymorphous equation. It has received several interpretations that have unsettled its economy.

1. The fictional is first of all—this is dogmatic rationalism—a least-being, indeed a nothingness that echoes supposed real referents as well as its contraries: science, truth, being, perception, etc. Oscillating between the fictive and the feigned, it is animated by an intimate reference, and as though by an intentionality, to these neighborhoods which surround it and delimit it without tolerating the slightest breathing room; which assign it a place, inferior and sometimes null, alongside madness and unreason. However, this is less a question of determinate neighborhoods than of the style or type of neighborhood.

2. Kant and Fichte found the Copernican Revolution on the imagination in the form of its unconditioned subjectification. The imagination stops being both internalized and excluded by Reason and instead becomes its essence. The imagination receives a transcendental, real and constitutive dimension that detaches it from psychology. On the one hand, it becomes a superior faculty or a constitutive power: it stops simply being opposed to the real so as to assume the synthesis of opposites that is the real—in a new sense of the word—content of Unity. On the other hand, it forms *the objective Appearance*, appearance of ob-jectivity itself, which revolves around the power of the imagination as its ubiquitous reflection. A new menace, a transcendental and non-localizable menace, stretches over the World which is in danger of sinking into the objective unreality of Appearance. A decision becomes necessary, a bifurcation is imposed upon the history of fiction.

3. On the one hand, Nietzsche intensifies fiction by freeing it from the residual identity of the imagination as faculty, namely by freeing synthesis from the constraint of ready-made unity. The fictional and the "false" are henceforth the Other as capacity of synthesis that is co-extensive, without limits, with truth and the real. The real is a fictionalization or a representation, but, furthermore, fiction is as real as it can be: it suffices that it be willed as such. Fiction represents the real for another fiction, the real represents fiction for another real: this is the Nietzschean way of saying that the real is fictional and the fictional real. Such is the first solution to the instability of the transcendental and romantic Imagination: a "headlong flight" into fiction. It is internalized in a radically relational, positive and affirmative mode in an objective Appearance in which objectivity is ultimately delivered from the object and which integrally jeopardizes the old real. This immediate unity of the real and the fictional, of Identity and the Other, is the identity of a big circle of objective appearance (the Same) that envelops the little circle of identity inhibited by the Other. The equation's form has changed, but the equation subsists as thought's form.

4. On the other hand, since this grand identity of the Same proves that the fictional as Other will have merely served to intensify the real to the point of fictionalization and to conserve the metaphysical equation's form, it becomes possible to oppose it to another experience of the Other as more real than any fiction and any ideal reality or reality of the logos: this is the deconstruction of the equation fiction=real. This Other, on the hither side of any fiction, affects the concept or the logos with finitude; it constrains them to abandon their claim to reality and to recognize their fictional nature. Fiction conserves a positive nature but less affirmative

than in Nietzschean simulacra, for it is suspended by the Other as difference of the fictional and of the real. An *Un-fictionalizable* henceforth inhabits fiction endowed with a weakness, which is not its nothingness or its classical annihilation but confines it within the status of the Other's mask or guise. This solution, so to speak, takes the middle path between the rational depreciation of fiction in the name of the real (but which was only ideal, itself still fictive, not the veritable real as Other) and its overvaluation, its Nietzschean over-romanticization.

The history of fiction's philosophical ambitions is without appeal: it is a failure. Not only has fiction ultimately found philosophy *opposing* it once again to the instance of the real and limiting it in its will to power, but it has also not been able to acquire a concept, a reality and an autonomous dignity at last: it remains too close to the artifact. However, the reasons for this failure are clear: fiction has always been thought in philosophy's framework and has combined with the history and crossroads of philosophy. Philosophy tolerates fiction on condition of announcing itself to it and deciding on its essence. Thus, what is being investigated here is not a particular philosophical position of fiction in relation to the real but philosophy's legislation or right over it. To understand what goes on in literature, art, science-fiction, perhaps it is necessary to abandon fiction's submission to the preliminary philosophical operation and to seek the conditions of a rigorous, real and immanent, i.e. quasi-scientific description of the most uncontestable *phenomenal givens* that form fiction's specific *reality* and are accessible to every man, both the artist and the philosopher.

Philosophy's problem in general stems from the fact that it never thinks terms in their specificity but as contraries and in their relations, at best in their boundaries and their neighborhoods. The *concept* of fiction then designates, like any other concept, an amphibological reality, a limitrophy of the real, whether beyond the real, on this side of it or the boundary between the two. From classical rationalism to contemporary deconstructions, fiction has remained caught within this relation of mixture, i.e. unitary. Excluded by the real, internalized in it, in turn internalizing it and completely claiming to co-determine it, fiction has never escaped from these games of inter-inhibition, which are those of philosophy with itself and those in which it was nothing but a pawn among others for a history that claimed to surpass it. What will be opposed to this instability that wants to be and not to be the real—each time according to different proportions—is a rigorous science of fiction. Instead of claiming to trace an always unstable line of demarcation between the fictional and the real, a critical line by which the latter is a degraded form of the former and, at the same time, claims to continue to belong to it and determine it in its becoming, it is a question of modifying the experience and concept of "fiction" and of de-subjecting them from the philosophical yoke. Three complementary operations are necessary for this to happen:

1. Accept the completion of fiction's derealization: radicalize the historical but fruitless attempts to retract every claim to reality or co-production of reality from it. This obviously requires non-classical means (the real no longer as the auto-position of an identity) which are not deconstructive (the real can no longer be the Other first and foremost). If the real is experienced as nothing-but-real, then fiction will no longer be of the order of the false, of the least-real and of non-being.

2. Know how to recognize that this destruction of the equation or of the unitary mixture (fiction=real) is precisely the condition for recognizing a scientific "reality" of fiction and a positivity that it has never had in philosophy: this is the concept of "non-thetic Universe."

3. Stop subordinating fiction to philosophy's authority, but make philosophy re-enter through fiction: conceive philosophy as a mode of this more radical experience, as a "philosophy-fiction."

This threefold operation is possible if the first is realized: how and to what end has been seen. It founds a science of fiction: there is a rigorous science when the circle is not simply broken but eliminated between science and its "object"; when between fiction and the real, for example, there is no longer the reciprocal determination or vicious circle that philosophy puts there. *This unilateral relation of causality, the real determining the fictional without being co-determined by it in return, is the scientific position of the problem of fiction.* This is the condition for its ultimate phenomenal givens or its "immanent" and "ordinary" experience to be able to be exhibited.

Thus, we should first have available an experience of the real which is that of the immanent or absolute givens of this type, a transcendental and not empirical experience, but radically empirical or immediate in its transcendental order. Being absolute or undivided, this experience of the real would by definition be deprived of any fiction or transcendence, and it would be valid, at least by essence, for fiction; it would be that through which fiction participates in the real without then coming to be reflected in its essence and claiming to constitute it. We call *determination in the last instance* this unilateral relation of causality by which the ultimate phenomenal givens determine fiction but without themselves being affected by fictionality. It can "emanate" only from a real deprived of transcendence, of position or of positionality. The phenomenal givens are non-thetic (of) self, non-thetic (of) their "object" (here, fiction) and give to this object, in turn, the essence of the "non-thetic (of) self."

This experience (of the) real, which is not blended with fiction but is valid as its simultaneously immanent and heteronomous essence—thus only in the last instance—is what we are before any philosophy, and we call it the experience, non-positional (of) self, of vision-in-One. Because it excludes fiction outside its own essence, it founds fiction in a rigorous science. *Fiction must no longer be thought as a mode of non-being, of the false, etc. but more positively as a mode of the (non-) One; no longer as a mode of philosophy, but as an effect of the real's unilaterality.* It then stops being *included* and confined in the real interpreted as Being, since the latter already by itself comprises fiction and is devoted to incessantly displacing its boundaries with it. Instead of these conflicting relations that philosophy manages for its own profit as a third instance which extracts a surplus value from this struggle, fiction becomes this radical, not blended, experience that is not accountable to philosophical rationality and is accessible to every man as One: the non-thetic Reflection or Uni-verse.

Fiction has therefore been commandeered and supposed given but not elucidated in its essence by philosophy. Its description is difficult in every way: not being a least-being of objectivity and of positionality, it seems to thwart all comprehension. Nevertheless, a science of it is possible, for a science is not asked to imitate its object, to trace it, to reproduce it and thus contribute to producing it, as philosophy claims to do. So as to mark this passage from philosophy to a transcendental science of fiction, which contents itself with describing immanent givens, we shall no longer speak of the "fictional" [*le fictionnel*] (a mixed or empirico-transcendental concept formed under the "unitary" authority of philosophy), but of the "fictionale,"[24] a non-thetic essence or irreducible kernel of every possible fiction. This is consequently a "non-thetic fiction." Here is a series of "theorems" on it:

1.1. We see all things without ever ob-jectifying or positing them—position is a law of the World, not of the One-real—: this is what we call "vision-in-One." The first quasi-objective, but not objectified, content of this vision is the (non-) One, the weakest charge of negativity that we can "envision" from the One. The fictionale is the (non-) One itself, the dyad of the non-thetic representation (of the) real.

---

24 Laruelle's neologism, "le fictionnal." Since Laruelle is playing off the silent difference of the a/e, the silent difference of orthography has been conserved but by adding an "e", rather than substituting it. [TN]

1.2. This fictionale is still not what is done or feigned: if the real One is a completely passive and frozen lived experience, which can seem to radiate from the One, the (non-) One equally qualifies as such. This would be a lived (un-) reality in an affect of passivity without active or synthetic counterpart.

1.3. Since it is non-thetic or non-positional and never inserted into a position or a horizon, the fictionale is not an object and does not revolve around the One-subject in the manner of objects. A science of fiction or of the "Universe" represents the condition of impossibility of any "Copernican Revolution" in the theory of fiction (and the Universe).

1.4. From the immanence in which we access it, the fictionale is not the real but what depends on it and what cannot return to co-determine it. The fictionale "presupposes" the real in a non-thetic way and also conditions it without ever positing it or inscribing it in Being or the World. The Universe is on the hither side of the World or totally exceeds it.

1.5. The fictionale extended is the unlimited depression of reality that accompanies the excessive embrace (of) the One, the hollowed out mark which it leaves on the World but which depends so little on the World that it already envelops it. This is a mark that is more powerful than its support.

1.6. We no longer posit or dominate this primitive space of fiction, and thus it does not dominate us: it accompanies the One or the individual as the latter's effect "expanded" to the World and as its own causality. This is the place where "All" is possible because it is the possible that overflows the All itself.

2.1. In general, the being-immanent (of) fiction or of the (non-) One is an experience of irreversion, of irreversibility, of distancing and, consequently, of non-consistency; i.e. the diachrony and diatopia of that which no longer has any chance to ever return to itself so as to grasp itself again and re-posit itself in its identity. This is the experience "mission terminated, return impossible" of that which is lost once and for all; of the Other, but insofar as, deprived of aggression, it makes every given distance itself and proceeds further by defending rather than attacking, by distancing rather than defending.

2.2. This is already an expanse, but in the nascent state and gathered in unilateralizing thrusts and without counterpart or reaction; in trails and traces that weave webs, no doubt, in every sense but each time in a unique sense. Rection more primitive than any direction, and which already opens there as the future expanse. Static, non-decisional thrust that puts the World at a distance, an originary expulsion (of the) World by the One and in the form of the *chôra* which emplaces it as far off.

2.3. This is something besides a détente, deconcentration or procession with their complement of return, of concentration and of conversion. The One neither distends itself nor distances itself perpetually. It is a static distant rather than a di-stancing. The One accompanies it instantaneously in an immobile and supra-intelligible fulguration.

2.4. This rection is strictly finite and cannot *be anticipated or surveyed,* no more than it can turn back. The hardest law, the law of fiction, of the production of the possible, is such that it must be passed through diachronically, step by step, but necessarily with a wild speed. In fiction and the possible, thought does not accelerate, it endures a speed and a slowness that are absolute from the outset.

3.1. What statically shines around the One is not an undetermined space but the absolutely determined space of indetermination.

3.2. The static, unilateral rection by which the One distances the World without recourse is the real phenomenal content of *the Universal* and of the *Possible* that philosophy commandeers without elucidating them in their essence. But the essence of the universal is uni-laterality, the side or the turning-toward of that which is unilaterally distanced: a side which is, moreover, unique. This is the bare capacity of the Universal, a cruelly abstract expanse deprived of every worldly given, up to and including the World itself.

3.3. What comes after the individual-without-universal, the One, is the universal-without-mode, poor and deprived of all reflection in itself. This is the possible, the primitive identity, never laid bare by philosophy, of the fictional and of the possible. In some sort, an unlimited eidetic film but without Eidos, without Universe-form or "Reflection."

3.4. The possible, the universal, the fictionale, forms the halo that accompanies the intimate, non-Copernican star of the One. Remaining immobile in itself, it is hardly a gray light that it diffuses: neither a light nor its borderline effect of shadows. This is the sort of obscure and supra-intelligible expanse that can accompany, without betraying it or revealing it indiscreetly, the One's night; for example, the dawn, when it has not yet left the secret of the night, precedes the glory of the World.

4.1. Non-thetic fiction is something other than an "imaginary order" in the manner of Leibnizian space and time: an order, no doubt, and of the most primitive species, capable of affecting the World itself, but not "imaginary" and psycho-metaphysical; an order which is instead transcendental and which is not inscribed in the World. The real utilizes fiction as an order anterior to the World and to philosophy.

233

4.2. The "fictionale" does not reflect the World, is not a double or an image of it, whether or not they are dis-identified to the point of veering toward simulacrum. This is perhaps a reflection, but a reflection non-thetic (of the) real. By its fictionale kernel, fiction has never served to redouble the World but rather to distance it and indifferentiate it.

The "fictionale" is therefore this ultimate essence of all fiction or its phenomenal given. It is what makes fiction real, i.e. accessible to every man before its very usage under the technical conditions of literature, of art, of philosophy. As reflection non-thetic (of the) real, the fictionale is *the primitive element of opening or of possibility of every thought, science and art included: the possible in the originary state.*

In this way what is directly experienced in the One (and without it being necessary to exit from it, without any longer determining it in return) is the Universe as the most general form of the reception of the World and of language. But the fictionale, without ceasing to be in itself or in the One, can become *effective* and be commandeered by art and its technologies. One passes from the fictionale to this fictional by re-taking the World's point of view: the fictional in the aesthetic form is a way not of fleeing the world, but, after having made it flee, of returning there and of legitimizing it. One does not return to the mixed or unitary concept of the fictional (that of philosophy), here one constitutes it as aesthetic object. The fictional now is no longer opposed to the real so as to claim to co-determine it at the same time. Simply, its effectivity or its existence in the World, in art and literature above all, comes to be added to its specific reality.

Then what is it that distinguishes between these two usages? In science, the radical possible is the World's non-thetic reflection, no doubt, but that of the World comprehended under conditions of reality, of stability and of exteriority, scientific conditions which furthermore found a "quasi-objectivity" rather than an objectivity in the classical sense of philosophy, here excluded from the outset. Instead, the properly aesthetic usage of fiction directly relates the fictionale to the World without remaining in this "quasi-objectivity."

Since the fictionale by its essence or its origin is repulsive with regard to the World, this new usage is possible only if the World and what it contains again validate their point of view, a claim which is not excluded by the One. Once the conditions of the problem of fiction in general are posed in this way, conditions which are non-unitary or non-philosophical but scientific, what remains to be described is this "aesthetic" capture of the fictionale by the worldly technologies of art and writing. This capacity of abstract alterity, which furthermore un-realizes the World itself, must then be *schematized* as though under the conditions of the latter. The fictionale must be distinguished from the worldly, intra-literary or intra-philosophical forms of fiction. These forms must not be understood as its continuous modes, it is rather the fictionale that must be thought as a new experience (very "ordinary," but hidden from the eyes of philosophers and of the World) where fiction stops being the simple attribute of another activity and instead becomes a lived experience in-the-One in the last instance. Fiction is in itself a radical subjectivity and must be recognized as an autonomous experience before giving rise to technologically produced effects.

Philosophical experimentation, non-philosophy's simple material

The concept of "philosophical experimentation" does not exhaust the concept of "non-philosophy." Philosophy is already, above all in its contemporary forms, an auto-experimentation under the laws and in the limits prescribed by the PSP or language's usage-of-logos. There is a similar equivocation in the project of "new" philosophical "writings," because philosophy is in every way always exploring such "revolutionary"—merely revolutionary—writings. And the term "writing" can be understood from within the metaphysical logos or even as deconstruction of the logos, but this is no longer what is in question here. Experimental variations, internal to philosophy or which it tolerates in the limits in which it is fixed, are nothing but and nothing other than material of the scientific process and cannot replace it. Inversely, *the Idea of an experimental usage of philosophy in the non-philosophical sense only makes sense for science or vision-in-One*.

It is now a question of knowing if there is a communication—and what kind—between these two types of labor. It seems that science does not unlock the possibility of *internal* modifications or manipulations of philosophical decision, since the latter in effect are supposed to remain in the limits of the PSP or of decision's auto-mastering systematicity. Instead, it adds a completely other dimension to the worldly experimentations (philosophy and literature, philosophy and art, philosophy and technics, etc.) which are basic material for this new treatment. In the same way that the theoretico-technico-experimental complex of the sciences is the primary matter of their *scientific sense* of the transcendental order which is acquired by other means, the experimental labor—whatever it may be—on philosophy here serves merely as basic material and cannot claim to exhaust the non-philosophical or "scientific" sense of decision that it is a question of acquiring. Its sense must pass through all the *a prioris*, which are those of science, and thus it must pass through the ordeal of the (non-) One that prevents the philosophical synthesis from reconstituting itself.

The textual labor on philosophy, like the given diversity of systems, remains the content of the preliminary labor that is still philosophical (the "empirical procedures"). That philosophy itself conflates this labor with its own becoming and its existence, that it gives an absolute or real sense to this life that it leads in the city and in history, is what forms part of its illusory belief in-itself-as-in-the-real. This illusion is the same as what nourishes epistemology. Epistemology, which corresponds with the sciences wrongly called "empirical" by philosophy, and philosophy, which corresponds with transcendental science, both elevate that which for real science is a simple material to the state of the essence of science and therefore falsify the latter. The basic epistemological belief according to which the sciences are reduced to the theoretico-experimental, abstract-concrete coupling, etc. has its correspondent in philosophy, which believes that transcendental science is reduced to the philosophical couplings of contraries, couplings which are its only activity. This material no longer has scientific sense in itself, it has no sense but philosophical. Its scientific sense and truth are brought to it by being put in relation with the transcendental structures of science or of vision-in-One. Instead of leaving it to refer to itself limitlessly and above all to believe that its possible sense ends with this auto-reference—for the latter is not destroyed, what is suspended is its effect of authority and of self-belief—philosophy's auto-reference is at the same time related to the scientific type of objectivity. Philosophical labor does not receive its sense of originary truth, its validity for every man—that which of itself it does not at all have—it only receives its sense of insertion in science. The simply experimental or textual labor on the material does not manage to reach truth, it remains captive to its own resistance.

In order to be the most efficacious, decision's material must pass through two operations, or what one might be tempted to call two reductions:

1) through an experimental labor which remains, as we have come to see, in the limits of the PSP and which can utilize literature or any other procedure of writing or inscription ..., but which remains within the limits of the specific "grammar" or "syntax" of philosophical decision;

2) through a transcendental reduction, that which science exerts and which consists in inscribing the philosophical text produced in this way under the conditions of scientific representation:

236

an elimination or bracketing of philosophical decisionality, positionality and unity. Thus one proceeds within two times, the second of which is absolutely necessary, and the first having already been carried out or already being active in philosophy itself.

The veritable experimentation is the usage that has until now been made of philosophy in view of describing these non-philosophical objects which are: the One, ordinary man, science, etc. *Une biographie de l'homme ordinaire* makes a usage-of-science of language in view of describing a non-philosophical object, but it does so in a spontaneous and not a thematized way. Now, and this would be the true unsettling of philosophical decision, one can describe a philosophical object, and decision itself, with philosophy but utilized scientifically. It is a question of making a description of decision by itself and by utilizing its own language, but by impressing upon it an absolutely universal or "non-philosophical" usage. Deconstruction generalized as such is the strongest when, beyond the usage that is made of philosophy in *Une biographie de l'homme ordinaire* for describing the One, philosophy is utilized in a mode of non-thetic or "non-philosophical" reflection for describing philosophy itself, at least in its reality.

It would be necessary to elaborate the rules of this usage simply, insofar as they express the scientific posture and thereby found a generalized deconstruction whose syntax they constitute. They are more than a "supplement" to intra-philosophical experimentations, they are added to them in a heteronomous way. They imply a re-writing of philosophical texts (whether deconstructed or not) in the non-thetic reflection or Universe, in universe-languages. The rules of these universes-of-language specify operations on philosophical material that cannot be found in the horizon of the latter, but which also leave the material's coherence to it from its point of view. The spirit of originary duality—of the "dual" before dualism—implies respecting philosophy's own rigor, which corresponds with precise invariants, while permitting to treat it, furthermore, as a whatever material for non-philosophical practices. Philosophical rigor is conserved in its order, which is that of Transcendence, effectivity or World, but philosophy becomes a simple first matter for an activity that is "ordinally" anterior to it.

Perhaps we now see it more clearly: it is impossible to free philosophy from within and on its own basis. If the main invariant of decision is the Unity-of-contraries, the co-extensive or simultaneous One and Dyad, it is not by infinitely varying it that it will be made to give thought a qualitative leap. This emergence does not belong to the possibilities included in decision, but to the precedence of vision-in-One, thus of science, over it. This is why the essential idea of "non-philosophy" is not the production of an infinity of philosophical systems unlimited by right but, instead, an infinity of the universe-languages that are inscribed in the dualitary order of the non-philosophical and the philosophical. We have not passed from an equivalence of philosophical decisions existing in history to the thesis of an infinity of decisions still unknown, but rather from this thesis to what grounds it, to a heterogeneous practice exerted on these decisions. No doubt it is useful to experimentally vary what exists, to reveal in historical decisions the cases or specifications of an ensemble of more numerous possibilities that would not have been exploited yet. But this is to remain under the authority of the PSP. The exploitation of the semantic or structural field of decision, the discrimination of its elementary and qualitative types, certain of which tolerate variations and others none or few, is a preliminary task that does no more than prepare the "non-philosophical" labor, the writing of statements which have fictional effects of philosophy or of hyper-speculation but which are unintelligible for philosophy and unacceptable by it, since it will only be able to deploy its self-defense mechanisms against them. Thus one will carefully distinguish between variations or experimentations on such statements or such decisions—variations from which all the attempts of restrained deconstruction arise and which remain under the PSP—and the "non-philosophical" elaboration that radically changes the codes of acceptability of statements.

In this way, one sees what "treating philosophy as a whatever material" means, and one also sees the limits of this formula. It is indeed now a simple material, but without this contradicting or destroying its nature of philosophical decision. It has its own laws of consistency and development as material, and, in a sense, one cannot destroy this syntax but merely vary its invariants. Instead, one can produce on its basis a wholly other discourse that has scientific value and criteria. But one cannot again blend the two planes in a unitary project. For this wholly other usage and only for it, decision is and can be treated as neutral material, and this is done strictly in relations to operations of a wholly other type. This slogan cannot mean—lest it be contradictory—that philosophy becomes a whatever material *for itself* or indifferent to itself…. By definition, it is interested in itself rather than indifferent to itself. Instead, philosophy is indifferent for science, and science can treat it in a "whatever" way. It can treat the logos in a "non-logical" way without falling into a contradiction. There is no contradiction where there is radical duality. There is only contradiction where there is a unitary will…. The catchphrase: "Create your very own philosophy" is a typical unitary slogan, it does not remove the PSP but prohibits that it be thrown on man, who can access philosophy only as barred or divided-as-subject. What has to be announced and spread everywhere is "create your very own non-philosophy." The subject (of) science, ordinary man, is also the subject (of) non-philosophy and of it alone. Democracy and peace cannot enter among the philosophers unless they give up identifying with philosophy and unless they experience themselves as subjects (of) science practicing philosophy under the codes of non-philosophy. If it is accepted that the veritable "common sense" is that of science—"ordinary" sense rather—and if it is no longer founded on the transcendence of historical and political authorities and on the transcendence of philosophical authorities, then one can imagine a "reconciliation" of this communitarian sense of thought through non-philosophy. Without this, philosophers will continue their war, which is what they call "dialoguing," "controverting," "interpreting"....

Non-philosophy as philo-fiction or hyperspeculation

This position of the problem alone can render philosophy contingent, make it become whatever for science and authorize treating it with codes, rules, syntaxes or operations that are no longer drawn from itself. However, what will be produced in this way will be merely, and sometimes—this will be examined further—*non-philosophical effects* without validity within the PSP. They will have been produced by operations which are those of real and rigorous knowledge; but they will still be, if not of essence, then at least and sometimes, not always, of philosophical appearance. On one of their surfaces, they will be *scientific representations of the real* that utilize philosophical elements; but, on the other surface, they will be *philosophical fictions*, fictions "for" philosophy rather than empirical fictions re-interpreted and internalized by it. Measured against philosophical sufficiency, the non-philosophical opening of universe-languages, which is completely "objective" or rigorous, produces a "fictionale" or "hyperspeculative" effect that must be specified. The science of decision is therefore completed in the radicalization of the fictional character—granted to metaphysics by Kant and Fichte, practiced in its own way by one of the forms of deconstruction (Derrida)—and in its extension to philosophy altogether. This extension is possible only because it is "isolated," if not objectified then at least suspended, in the indifference that the One impresses upon it, i.e. science considered in its non-thetic "posture" vis-à-vis the real. The real, "non-philosophical" critique of philosophy includes a usage of philosophy qua fiction. Spontaneous philosophy—it is just as naive as science, but in an auto-denegating mode—is a naive fiction that denies itself as such; its positive critique, beyond its deconstructions which merely attempt to inhibit it rather than to free it, opens it to a new career: "philosophy-fiction" or "hyperspeculation."

"Non-philosophy" is therefore an ensemble of representations that can be read in two ways or can receive two simultaneous usages. Regarded from science, these are true knowledges, albeit rectifiable, produced by the science of philosophy; these are (non-thetic) representations or descriptions of decision. But now regarded from the point of view of philosophy itself, which is still possible as its resistance wants to do, these representations of itself can be nothing but fiction.

Also, the concept of "philo-fiction" or of "hyper-speculation," if it has scientific means or procedures, *has no sense except for philosophy and from its point of view*; a point of view which, furthermore or in the last instance, remains that of transcendental hallucination and of resistance. The signification of this concept is thus complex. On the one hand, for philosophy and its resistance, transcendental science is in turn a fiction, and consequently the scientific usages of philosophy will seem like utopia in its eyes. This is the first, most immediate sense of "philo-fiction"; the latter is then baptized by philosophy: what for science is verified representation, albeit rectifiable, is fiction for philosophy. On the other hand, measured against and related to science, philosophy conversely is reputed hallucination. Such that, for science taken as ultimate or first point of view, the act of baptizing these representations as "fictions" is still a procedure of self-defense or already an effect of the hallucination of the real. In other words, these are the same representations each time, and *the science of decision is philo-fiction*, but there are two heterogeneous ways of evaluating their truth. Here still, it is advisable to "dualyze" this concept.

These non-philosophical representations of philosophy, which are organized by new rules, therefore have specific effects, more exactly: *hyperspeculative* or extra-speculative effects. But they are no longer philosophical knowledges in the sense of the PSP; neither semi-literary, semi-philosophical effects or entanglements nor metaphors or undecidables: all of that remains produced under the authority of the PSP and is inscribed in the space of decision. Here one neither produces a literary effect with philosophy nor a philosophical effect with literature, etc.; all these combinations are possible, but they have no usage here except as simple material of hyperspeculation. The latter is something other than this labor of continual reproduction of mixtures, for it utilizes them under another regime of thought. The products of the scientific and hyperspeculative usage of philosophy have no relevance for philosophy itself, but, since they are obtained on the basis of a material taken from it, they have *a philosophical appearance* that permits arranging them at least in fiction.

Whereas *science-fiction* is a globally literary usage of science (*more so* an index of absolute alterity, which is of the order neither of literary fiction nor of the empirical scientific material utilized but is selected from science's essence), *philo-fiction* is instead a globally scientific usage of philosophy (and of literature, etc.). The index of absolute alterity, supposed given by science-fiction, commandeered and non-founded in the usage that it makes of this alterity, is this time directly contributed by science as point of view on philosophy. Philo-fiction therefore should be more originary than science-fiction and represent its real rigorous form, more exactly *the conditions of its reality*: in particular by the genesis that it can makes of the Other which is its fundamental condition, that from which it draws this affect of radical strangeness. Science-fiction is to philo-fiction what philosophy is to transcendental science considered in the ensemble of their relations.

Non-philosophy's philosophical appearance

Is non-philosophy a simulation of philosophy, and to what, undoubtedly narrow, extent? Is there a philosophical appearance or effect of non-philosophy?

There is a *spontaneous non-philosophical appearance of philosophy* that seems to aim at or to intend a real or an Other outside it, to know it, describe it, constitute it, etc. This is an appearance in every sense of the word, also in the sense of a transcendental illusion, and deconstructions are specifically founded upon it. Instead, if there is a *philosophical appearance of non-philosophy*, it can only be limited, so as not to be a philosophical illusion, and itself reduced to the state of inert material. Non-philosophy describes philosophy only in the last instance, for it only describes in this way the phenomenal states of affairs that are philosophy's real base or last instance. If there is a philosophical appearance of non-philosophy, it can pass only through the narrow channel or the minor path of the material utilized for the redescription of the structures of vision-in-One which are the real conditions of decision. In this way, it could be that, by clearing or trace, the old philosophical sense of material diffuses throughout non-philosophy and creates an equivocation, a philosophical appearance of equivocation. Even if such a phenomenon is normal in a certain way—since decision is conserved with its effectivity at least as "support"—it will also be reduced by its insertion in the *chôra* and will fall into the general case, that of a double possible interpretation of non-philosophy.

Non-philosophy can therefore conserve traces of philosophy in it—traces furthermore reduced—insofar as it does not produce such traces. It does not simulate philosophy; only philosophy can simulate itself. It is by essence a simulation of itself that draws its existence and also the belief in its reality from this activity of auto-simulation by which it is reproduced under the aegis of circles, aporias and battles that are more or less open and indefinitely postponed. What produces non-philosophy in its own mode, that of a radically unreflected phenomenality, has no intelligible sense for philosophers, not because it would have no *sense* or would be absurd, but because it no longer definitively falls under the category of *sense*.

Descriptions of the real produced in this way—apart from what can transmit the philosophical of reduced material—are, in other words, manifest or phenomenal, but they are so in a mode which is no longer that of objectification. They include the form of a certain exteriority or transcendence, but the latter is then in turn no longer itself given in this mode of transcendence, divided with itself and redoubled. They are given in the only mode in which something can be manifested by the One, in the mode of indivision; they are unreflected or non-thetic by their essence, i.e. *neither conscious nor unconscious*, because vision-in-One is a mode of phenomenality distinct even from these two modes that philosophy knows. Unreflected or experienced as undivided each time; ante-rational, perhaps, but not "infra-rational"; ante-differential, but not infra-differential, etc. Fully on the hither side of "effects-of-surface," "effects-of-sense," and "effects-of-philosophy," *de jure* or really preceding "philosophy-in-effect," without experiencing the need for this decision and this technology of "effect," both of which are still too philosophical—non-philosophy is received or is lived as an (auto)-impression, as a lived experience absolutely inherent (to) self in the last instance. The non-philosophical style signifies, among other things, the abandonment of the technological and artifactual pathos of "effect," which is that of simply "open" philosophies. What it produces and describes-as-produced is an absolutely uni-versal human or subjective appearance, not of sense per se, but of effects, of the effects-of-sense.

However, one could suppose the problem of a more complex residual philosophical appearance, which would appear necessary and no longer contingent; the appearance would then seem to concern vision-in-One's essence rather than that of the material.

Vision-in-One's essence can be conquered in effect only by defeating what offers it maximal resistance, i.e. conquered from a particular object whose particularity is universal or is what most strongly denies it —philosophy. If a vision-in-One of philosophy is possible, real rather, just as we have shown it *de facto* by the elaboration and description of its essence, *a fortiori* the vision-in-One of objects other than philosophical is also real and possible. By showing that philosophy, i.e. the objective ideology that grips all objects, is the object of a vision-in-One, one shows that vision-in-One is the posture or the very essence of thought. The vision-in-One of philosophy is identically the essence of other or particular sciences. But then non-philosophy appears directly dependent on philosophy and internalizes an inevitable philosophical appearance. Between them there would be a sort of transcendental affinity. However, the latter cannot be interpreted as a reciprocal conditioning: this would then still be an illusion of philosophy alone, for it would invert the real relation and want to impress a unitary structure onto non-philosophy. In reality, it is necessary to distinguish dually, and not unitarily or by simple scission, between the structures of the real and their description, between non-philosophy's essence in the One and its description with the aid of philosophical material, i.e. its becoming effective as vision (of) philosophy in-One. Furthermore, once again, since the One remains decidedly the unique transcendental guide of thought, these phenomena of affinity between philosophy and non-philosophy arise from the material alone and are limited by the *chôra*: they are therefore transformable in accordance with "vision."

The good news of vision-in-One is this: no longer allowing ourselves to be obsessed with the question that is, however, so obvious, so legitimate: what is it that still ties non-philosophy back to philosophy, and how do we still produce effects-of-philosophy with it? The problem is poorly posed, it is posed in a philosophical or unitary way instead of being posed in a dual or dualitary way. In reality, *non-philosophy no longer has any bond with philosophy-as-fact or as Principle of sufficient philosophy, which is reduced by the* chôra; *instead, it has a bond with another state of philosophy, with philosophy-as-material.* Non-philosophy's essence is *toto caelo* distinct from philosophy, even if by its effective realization it draws on the latter. If there are effects-of-philosophy within non-philosophy: 1) they do not come from it; 2) they come from the material alone and are themselves reduced; 3) they are thus localized in the representational content dispersed onto universal Appearance, but they cannot affect the latter since it maintains a contingent relation with its material. If there is philo-fiction or something like hyperspeculation, then these phenomena do not correspond with any *a priori* decision, any finality external to vision-in-One. Non-philosophy is not a new economy of philosophy but an immanent pragmatics— and therefore heteronomous to philosophy—of philosophical *material*. And if it produces an Appearance, it will be that which is given to vision-in-One and in the mode of being-immanent rather than a new éclat,[25] a new facet of philosophical Appearance.

Non-philosophy produces no effect "in" philosophy

Non-philosophy can be read in two heterogeneous ways. On the one hand, it is what, of the One itself in every way and of philosophy reduced to the state of material, is seen-in-One. It must then no longer be read with the codes, grids, norms of philosophy, lest it be unable to be accepted. It is not irrational and chaotic for all that: this is a rigorous thought in its own way. Simply its mode of presence or of reception is no longer the rational, the logical or the eidetic, the surrational or the metaphysical; it is not manifested as such in a horizon or a transcendence but is only "intelligible," on the one hand, as passively and "obscurely" lived in the immanence of the last instance and, on the other hand, as in turn described in the manner in which it is lived in this way. On the hither side of its eventual illumination by the logos, it is received in the radically unreflected or naive mode of the One: that which is manifested absolutely is not manifested by dividing itself and reflecting itself, but globally as indivisible. It is indeed real, albeit not transcendent, and it is describable in turn as received in this mode. Produced by and for the One, it cannot rigorously have "sense" and above all truth except for the One outside all philosophical horizons and teleologies.

Nevertheless, philosophy remains effective decision and resistance from the moment that it functions spontaneously; it also claims to be an authorized point of view on non-philosophy. But if there is a double reading, it is not divided-unitary: it is instead dualitary. In effect, there are no two readings of non-philosophy that would be foreign to one another: one in accordance with vision-in-One, the other in accordance with philosophy and as the extension of its resistance. More exactly: there are indeed two readings, but their relation is neither that of an unthought juxtaposition nor that of a philosophical dyad, a unique divided reading. The second reading is effective as resistance itself, but it in turn takes place in the

---

25   This word corresponds with the French translation of Hegel's "Schein" and of Kant's usage of "Erscheinung," both of which, in terms of the dialectic, in general relate to and are sometimes translated as "appearance." [TN]

(non-) One, from the start in the *chôra* where it finds its obligated place. Their true relation is therefore that of the dual or of originary duality, a relation which is dualitary, rather than unitary.

This situation permits comprehending the nature of non-philosophical "effects." At first, non-philosophy induces effects of resistance in and "in the home of" [*chez*] philosophy and contributes afterwards to manifesting them *such as they are*. Decision remains what it is spontaneously—auto-factualization and position—but this point of view of spontaneous philosophy is no longer relevant for vision-in-One and is completely suspended, such that resistance is manifested effectively within its suspension as itself reduced to the state of material and as having become inefficacious. This resistance reduced or *manifested-such-as-it-is*, extracted from its hiding place in philosophical faith, is expressed by the refusal, denegation, avoidance and falsification of the One's truth, the accusation of unintelligibility, irrationality and unacceptability, the terrorist argument of terror and of chaos, etc. These would be the two strictly *real effects* on spontaneous philosophy produced by non-philosophy: the self-expression and manifestation of a resistance such as it is. This manifestation in turn is reflected in a transcendent way for whoever observes the whole process from outside; but it is given in an immanent way, as already reduced, for whoever takes the One's immanence as guiding thread.

Apart from this global effect, it is difficult to say that non-philosophy produces effects *in philosophy*, which the One would then suppose to exist as factum and destiny in the same way that deconstructions think their own efficaciousness: for us, for the One, philosophy does not exist in this mode. The formula "in philosophy" is therefore itself ambiguous, according to whether one interprets it from philosophical faith (the effect of suspension of this faith is then local, partial, and re-gives or reactivates it all the more); or from vision-in-One and the suspension that the latter globally inflicts on it. The non-philosophical effect is that of this reduction completed or undivided by its essence, with the labor that follows from the rectification of non-philosophical descriptions or formulations, a labor which is only so unlimited because it has its place within this suspension and because it no longer straddles both the World and the One's immanence.

It is obviously necessary to distinguish this global and undivided effect of immanent origin, this *immanent-effect* on philosophy condemned to the opinion of its resistance, from the effects that arise in the representational content itself—that which is inscribed in Reflection or Appearance—in the material and its transcendent ingredients (vocabulary, syntax, effects which are poetic, literary,

245

scientific, etc.). Nevertheless, this absolute, unilateralizing distinction of the being-immanent of the global manifestation of the philosophical as outside-the-real, and of the transcendent effects or of the detail of the textual events, for example, that take place in the material—does not at all signify that there is between them an abstract and metaphysical distinction and an absence of relation. For these representational, apparently infra-philosophical ingredients, which seem to fall outside non-philosophy's effect on philosophy, can in turn be submitted to an interpretation or a philosophical decision and, *from this angle and not simply from it*, can be affected with suspension and therefore with their manifestation (for vision-in-One) as outside-the-real. Supposing that something in them *a priori* falls—so to speak—outside a virtual philosophical decision, it will also fall outside non-philosophy's labor. In fact, if something *a priori* really falls outside philosophical decision, this is necessarily vision-in-One itself, thus non-philosophy in its essence. All the rest is infinite philosophical auto-interpretation that attempts to appropriate immanent vision for itself.

The non-philosophical or human appearance of thought

There is a global and positive non-philosophical effect "on" philosophy, and it is time to describe it in order to close this treatise. What is the ultimate sense—if there is an ultimate one in a science which by definition excludes all teleology—of this non-philosophical pragmatics of philosophy, but specially "adapted" to it and which does not represent a "pragmatic" auto-degradation of philosophy? This sense is that of a radical "subjectivity," but only of the last instance, of philosophy, of an indivi-dual "propriation" of it. Neither a dialectical "re-appropriation" nor a deconstructive "expropriation" ("*Ent-/Er-eignis*"), nor any "return" to a subject or to a Same, whether this "return" be also and from the start a disappropriation of the subject in view of the Same. It is a question of the becoming-lived, of the becoming-human, but only in the last instance, of philosophical decision, and a question of the suspension, as non-human, of its transcendent, naive or sufficient usage.

This operation gathers together a re-subjectification of philosophical practice, but this would be an appearance, for it cannot be interpreted in this way in a "circular" or philosophical mode. No more than one "exits" from philosophy toward science, or from Being toward the One, one does not make transcendence return from decision toward human subjectivity. As indivi-dual or subject (of) science, "ordinary man" has already preceded decision without having had to precede it "in a single stroke." This subjectification—which in this way goes irreversibly from the absolute proper, ordinary man, toward decision—no longer consists in again grasping the latter such as it is given to a subjectivity which is itself transcendent, but consists in following the thread of causality of the "last instance" and in producing, beyond its auto-philosophical usages, a non-philosophical usage, itself immanent or human, of spontaneous decision. The pragmatic operation is here that of the radical indivi-dual-ization of philosophy detached from its in-human transcendence. It once again comes to replace—to *emplace*—decision in accordance with its *real base* or *base of the last instance*, which is ordinary man or indivi-dual force (of) thought as subject (of) science, and comes to give a rigorous and concrete sense to the slogan which has always been that of radicality: philosophy is made for man, not man for philosophy.

At the end of the non-philosophical *order*, what is it that is seen-in-One? This is what we call by the general term of "reflection" or "universe", but non-thetic, non specular or absolute reflection (of the) real. When this representation, freed on its own account from every function of the real's constitution in which it would be inhibited or paralyzed à la philosophical decision, is specified by its representational content or its material, here explicitly by philosophy, it is called "non-philosophical Appearance"; it is also called "absolute" or "human" because it is the correlate or the content of determination in the last instance which stems from the One, i.e. from what is, moreover, radically human there.

Therefore, this thoroughly "human" but indeed real Appearance is opposed to *the objective philosophical Appearance* which is given to man as a redoubled, and no longer simple, transcendence, a transcendence in transcendence and viciously thought on the basis of itself. It is this auto-posited and auto-fetishized Appearance that is announced to man as philosophy's unavoidable horizon, as its fact, its tradition and its destiny, as a capital that endeavors to exploit the language and thought of man. What belongs to this exploitation, which is technological and capitalist in its own way, of the individual force (of) thought, to this Appearance of philosophical capital which attempts to bar the One (of) man and to require that he identify with it, is to restrain in this way *the full usage of the force (of) thought*. The latter is instead fulfilled in the non-philosophical pragmatics of language and of thought, and of the Appearance which corresponds with it, the most universal Appearance there is, what finite or ordinary man has already accessed as a space freed from philosophical decisions and from the abusive economies that they impose on it.

Non-philosophical pragmatics in this way can then pass for a "program," even though the latter does not escape from philosophical teleology, but is given *before* this very teleology as a future anterior to all finality. This future is the non-Greek opening or universal *for* philosophy. It is founded on the One or science and excludes from this fact the major postulate of philosophical sufficiency: the unitary postulate, concerning which it has been shown that it is completely possible to lift so as to found a non-philosophy. By "dually" distinguishing between the ordinary force (of) thought, the subject (of) vision-in-One or (of) science, and philosophy's subjected subject, the real foundation of a science of philosophy is given along with the necessity of an *a priori* humanity of philosophy against the exploitation of man that philosophy will have directed.

Other books from Univocal
by François Laruelle

Struggle and Utopia at the End Times of Philosophy
trans. Drew S. Burk and Anthony Paul Smith, 2012

Photo-Fiction, a Non-Standard Aesthetics
trans. Drew S. Burk (Bilingual Edition), 2012

Dictionary of Non-Philosophy
trans. Taylor Adkins, 2013

Introduction to Non-Marxism
forthcoming

The Ethics of the Stranger
forthcoming

Univocal Publishing
123 North 3rd Street, #202
Minneapolis, MN 55401
www.univocalpublishing.com

ISBN 9781937561123

Jason Wagner, Drew S. Burk
(Editors)
This work was composed in Garamond and Gill Sans.
All materials were printed and bound
in June 2013 at Univocal's atelier
in Minneapolis, USA.

The paper is Mohawk Via, Pure White Linen.
The letterpress cover was printed
on Lettra Pearl
Both are archival quality and acid-free